The Origins of Nationalism

In this wide-ranging work, Caspar Hirschi offers new perspectives on the origins of nationalism and the formation of European nations. Based on extensive study of written and visual sources dating from the ancient to the early modern period, the author reintegrates the history of pre-modern Europe into the study of nationalism, describing it as an unintended and unavoidable consequence of the legacy of Roman imperialism in the Middle Ages. Hirschi identifies the earliest nationalists among Renaissance humanists, exploring their public roles and ambitions to offer new insight into the history of political scholarship in Europe and arguing that their adoption of ancient role models produced massive contradictions between their self-image and political function. This book demonstrates that only through understanding the development of the politics, scholarship and art of pre-modern Europe can we fully grasp the global power of nationalism in a modern political context.

CASPAR HIRSCHI teaches History at the Swiss Federal Institute of Technology in Zurich. His previous titles include *Wettkampf der Nationen: Konstruktionen einer deutschen Ehrgemeinschaft an der Wende vom Mittelalter zur Neuzeit* (2005).

The Origins of Nationalism

An Alternative History from Ancient Rome to Early Modern Germany

Caspar Hirschi

CAMBRIDGE
UNIVERSITY PRESS

CAMBRIDGE
UNIVERSITY PRESS

University Printing House, Cambridge CB2 8BS, United Kingdom

One Liberty Plaza, 20th Floor, New York, NY 10006, USA

477 Williamstown Road, Port Melbourne, VIC 3207, Australia

314-321, 3rd Floor, Plot 3, Splendor Forum, Jasola District Centre, New Delhi - 110025, India

79 Anson Road, #06-04/06, Singapore 079906

Cambridge University Press is part of the University of Cambridge.

It furthers the University's mission by disseminating knowledge in the pursuit of education, learning and research at the highest international levels of excellence.

www.cambridge.org
Information on this title: www.cambridge.org/9780521747905

© Caspar Hirschi 2012

First published 2012
Reprinted 2 013

A catalogue record for this publication is available from the British Library

Library of Congress Cataloging in Publication data
Hirschi, Caspar.
  The origins of nationalism : an alternative history from ancient
  Rome to early modern Germany / Caspar Hirschi.
      p. cm.
  Includes bibliographical references and index.
  ISBN 978-0-521-76411-7 (hardback) – ISBN 978-0-521-74790-5
  (paperback)
  1. Nationalism–History. 2. Nationalism–Europe–History.
  3. Nationalism–Philosophy. I. Title.
  JC311.H572   2011
  320.5409–dc23
  2011041526

ISBN 978-0-521-76411-7 Hardback
ISBN 978-0-521-74790-5 Paperback

To my parents

Contents

Figures

Figure acknowledgements: cover image and Figure 3 courtesy of
Akademische Druck- und Verlagsanstalt Graz, Austria; Figures 4, 7,
8, 9, 13 courtesy of the department of rare books and manuscripts,
Universitätsbibliothek Basel, Switzerland; Figure 1 courtesy of
Numismatik Lanz, Germany; Figure 2 courtesy of the department
of manuscripts and early printed books, Bayerische Staatsbibliothek
München, Germany; Figure 5 courtesy of Anthony Majanlahti,
Canada; Figures 6, 10, 11, 12, 14 courtesy of Wikipedians and other
anonymous contributors to the public domain.

Preface

In 1963, the political scientist Kalman H. Silvert edited an anthology on nationalism in 'developing countries' with the slightly awkward title *Expectant Peoples*. The book did not receive much attention at the time and has been long forgotten, despite the fact that it made Silvert a pioneer in the field of nationalism studies. In his foreword, Silvert introduced a new question, which would later be raised repeatedly without ever being answered conclusively. The question was: how to justify 'yet another book on nationalism'?

If an author of the early 1960s had to give reasons for a new contribution to the study of nationalism, how severe must the pressure be now, after hundreds, if not thousands more books have been published in the meantime? The answer probably has to be 'very severe indeed'. No author will be able to escape the pressure. However, this is no bad thing. There are still good arguments to justify yet another book on nationalism.

The one given in this work is short and straightforward: I believe that it is time for a fresh start in nationalism studies and that this book can help to encourage it. In the last two decades, research in the field has been dominated by a few works published in the 1980s. Scholars of nationalism benefited greatly from these works, not least by expanding their field enormously, but they also paid a heavy price for building on studies that preferred catchwords to theoretical coherence and broadbrush historical statements to the examination of original sources. I believe that the costs caused by following these studies now outweigh the benefits.

This book will combine a new theoretical argument with a new historical analysis of the origins of nationalism. By doing so, it will try to convince both theory aficionados (most of them sociologists and political scientists) of the merit of source-based historical assertions and staunch positivists (most of them historians) of the worth of theoretical tools. First and foremost, however, it will invite scholars in the field to reintegrate the history of pre-modern Europe into the study of nationalism.

I am aware that publishing this book is an ambitious, maybe even an audacious undertaking. There is a chance that reactions to the work will rebound on the author in the form of a one-way ticket to the no man's land between the boundaries of historiography, sociology and political science. Nevertheless, given the present state of nationalism studies, it seems to me a risk worth taking. If the book can help to overcome the current theoretical and methodical framework of nationalism studies, then its basic purpose will have been achieved. If, in addition, it can motivate some scholars to adopt and extend its approach, then it may be deemed a success.

Compared to my previous book on the topic, published in German under the title *Wettkampf der Nationen* in 2005, this study is larger in scope and smaller in size. It contains a broader theoretical argument, adds further reflections on national honour and gives a more detailed analysis of the political roles aspired to, but not acquired by Renaissance humanists. Finally, it includes three new parts: one on patriotism in Ancient Rome, one on nationalist transformations of language and one on the relationship between nationalism and religious fundamentalism in the early modern period.

Due to the abundance of secondary literature on the subjects covered in this book, I tried to make a virtue of necessity by citing only titles upon which I based an argument, relied on for information or commented on explicitly. I do not suppose that many readers will prefer a heavily referenced tome to a more easily readable book or will want to know about the exact extent of my reading. Those who do are kindly invited to read the footnotes of my German publications.

As to primary sources, I took a different approach because they are the foundation of my method and argument. The book quotes widely from ancient, medieval and early modern documents, ranging from public speeches to legal treatises, royal decrees, political poems, religious pamphlets, humanist histories and correspondences. The majority of these sources are written in Latin, the bulk of the rest are in older forms of German, French and Italian. The English translations given in the book are either my own or taken from English editions (to which I occasionally add slight changes for a more literal rendering). To aid the flow of reading, I cite the original wording only when it adds further value to an argument.

In addition to written documents, I include visual sources which play more than just an illustrative role. Each figure is accompanied by a descriptive caption that clarifies the explanatory function of the image for arguments presented in the main body of the text and is linked with other captions into a narrative of its own.

Writing a book in a foreign language brought all the major excitement and minor horror of a journey through an exotic country. Being equipped with a good map soon proved not enough, and so I felt lucky to find native guides, who were familiar with the territory and climate of the English tongue. Their rescue was especially needed when I made excursions into metaphorical speech. Andrew Liston helped to edit chapters of the first draft, while Katherine Hughes accompanied the whole writing process with an admirably sharp eye for incorrect language and incomplete arguments.

Most of the manuscript was written between 2007 and 2010, when I was a Research Fellow at Clare Hall, Cambridge. In this unique institution, I found a socially and intellectually stimulating environment and, together with my family, an ideal temporary home. Thanks to a generous early career fellowship granted by the Swiss National Foundation, we could afford to rent a beautiful college flat, surrounded by the even more beautiful garden of the Needham Institute.

During the same period, I was able to research and teach at the Cambridge Faculty of History and be part of the Subject Group for Modern European History (owing to a different and ongoing project of mine on eighteenth-century official experts and public critics in France and England). Thanks to the group's weekly research seminar, I received a constant flow of ideas, some of which have found their way into this book. Of particular interest was a seminar series on nationalism and Romanticism organised by Tim Blanning in Michaelmas Term 2007.

Tim contributed to the progress of the book in many other ways. He supported my initial proposal submitted to Cambridge University Press; he later helped me by commenting on the first few chapters, and he eventually read the whole manuscript, thereby providing me with valuable suggestions for the final revision. When visiting him in his Faculty office I usually left with a lot of good advice and a bag of lovely clothes that his children had grown out of and my children were about to grow into.

Another helpful provider of children's clothes and intellectual support at the History Faculty was Ulinka Rublack. Shortly after my arrival, she offered me the opportunity to present my findings on Martin Luther and the German nation to her seminar students. It turned out to be the start of a lively exchange about, among other things, the interrelation of intellectual and material culture in the formation of nations.

When I was interviewed at Clare Hall for the research fellowship competition in early 2007, Alex Watson, as a member of the committee, asked me how I would distinguish between pre-modern and modern nationalism. I do not remember my answer, but however satisfactory it may have been, I was fortunate enough to be given another chance by Alex when he agreed to read the manuscript three years later. His comments and corrections are much appreciated.

Several people helped to complete and publish this book with expert assistance of various kinds: Dominik Hunger of Basle University Library delivered fine reproductions of early modern woodcuts and engravings; Andreas Hauser gave useful advice on how to structure the captions for the figures; an anonymous reviewer of the manuscript enabled me to clarify a few crucial points; and, finally, Elizabeth Friend-Smith at Cambridge University Press showed great patience in discussing the book's subtitle and the length of its captions before overseeing its smooth publication.

The person to whom I owe the most, both for this book and for everything else, is my wife Martina Schlauri. She left a secure job in Switzerland and shouldered the bulk of the burden of parenthood to enable her husband's academic adventure in Britain. While this book was underway, she gave birth to our second daughter, Joséphine, and our third daughter, Mathilda, who have enriched the lives of their parents and their elder sister Charlotte enormously. Thanks to Martina, the shared experience of family life and the solitary pursuit of my studies complemented each other beautifully. Still, the happiest moments during these eventful years came on those rare occasions when I could leave with her for a weekend *à deux*.

1   Introduction

Emperor Frederick III: 'The Empire and the honour of Germany are so dear to me that I would spare no effort or expense. But ... we have to unite the forces of our nation; we have to make of all of us one single body.'

Enea Silvio Piccolomini, Pentalogus, 1443

The English is the enemy of the French, for no other reason than he is French. The Scot is the enemy of the British (*Britannus*), for no other reason than he is Scottish. The German is at enmity with the French, the Spanish with both. ... Are we taking the common word 'fatherland' for such a grave cause that one people seeks to annihilate the other?

Desiderius Erasmus, A Complaint of Peace, 1517

This book offers a new understanding of the historical origins of nationalism, combined with an explanation of the initial formation of European nations. It challenges the currently dominant view among historians and sociologists that nationalism is to be seen as a uniquely modern phenomenon established by industrialisation and mass communication in the nineteenth century. While acknowledging the stimulating effect of this so-called 'modernist' view, I argue that its leading tenets are theoretically unsound and historically untenable. The book also challenges the previous critics of 'modernist' theories, who advocate an integration of pre-modern periods into the study of nationalism. While recognising the validity of many of their objections, I maintain that they have so far not provided a convincing counter-theory, which could successfully challenge the modernist narrative. This book claims to present a more accurate picture of the formation of nations by developing such a counter-theory – and it also claims to offer a historical explanation of why nations and nationalism, despite all prophecies of extinction, happily endure in our seemingly post-national period.

The new model being proposed starts by re-examining the main questions a theory of nationalism is supposed to answer. Today the seemingly self-evident task of a theory of nationalism is to try to identify generic factors and mechanisms that would trigger nationalism in any given setting. If successful, this kind of theory would be able to give a definitive answer to questions such as: why did Estonia become a nation, but not Catalonia? Or, could nations exist prior to industrialisation? I believe that this sort of determinist approach promises much and delivers little, because, to name just one basic problem, it is unhistorical. There is no basis for the assumption that a single law of cause and effect produced nationalism in places as distant and different as England and East Timor.

The theoretical argument in this book is structured by a set of alternative questions: what can be defined as distinctive about nationalism? Where and when can we observe the first appearance of these distinctive features? How are we to understand their emergence historically? And how are we to describe their role in the construction of nations? These questions are based on a different and, I think, more plausible historical assumption, which is that the emergence of nationalism and nations anywhere in the world was only possible (but by no means necessary) because of its original development in one specific place and time. According to my theory, this place and time was Catholic Europe in the Middle Ages. By focusing on the history of Europe, I also suggest reconsidering the role of European political culture within the global history of nationalism. My argument is that while nationalism was able to develop particular characteristics outside of Europe, it was not conceivable outside of the orbit of European culture.

My exploration of theory goes back as far as Roman Antiquity, without regarding Roman political culture itself as nationalist. It relates the origins of nationalism to the legacy of the Roman Empire in the Middle Ages, describing the medieval political culture as secondary Roman imperialism within a fragmented territorial structure. It attributes the emergence of nationalism to the particular tensions created by this contradiction. Nationalism, in a nutshell, is here conceived as a political discourse constructed by chronically failing would-be-empires stuck in a battle to keep each other at bay. It is treated as highly competitive, transforming the monarchical quest for universal dominion into an all-encompassing contest between abstract communities. And it is treated as universalistic, too, forcing each body politic which claimed independence to define itself as a nation. The two key elements are national honour, a precious, but volatile capital shared by all community members, and national freedom, the collective rejection of foreign rule and cultural influence.

While nationalism is treated as the principal producer of nations, scholars are treated as the principal producers of nationalism. In the medieval period, scholars were not only the custodians of Christianity, but also the guardians of Classical Antiquity. From the twelfth century onward, legally and philologically trained clerics tried to adapt the legacy of Rome to contemporary politics; the language of the nation was created in the process. Although the scholarly studies involved in this construction of the nation as an intellectual concept were meant to be of direct political consequence, they did not reshape the political reality immediately. In fact, there was a remarkable time lag between the creation of nationalist language and the implementation of nationalist politics. By the end of the fifteenth century, the concept of the nation was almost fully developed in scholarly literature, whereas in political practice, imperialist, dynastic and religious principles would prevail for another three centuries. To medieval and early modern rulers, nationalism was often attractive as a propagandistic tool, but rarely as an end in itself.

One of this book's main tasks, therefore, is to explain the long-term parallel existence of nationalist scholarship and non-nationalist governance. It does so by analysing the scholarly roles developed by political authors in order to claim public authority and to influence power holders. As these roles systematically failed to provide the desired results, this book will also give an insight into the chronic self-delusions of Western scholars. To understand the origins of nationalism, there is no way around a critical analysis of the same learned culture that today enables us to engage in serious historical research.

The book will start with a general introduction to its subject, method and argument. The subsequent two chapters deal with theory: while the second chapter gives a critical overview of the leading modernist theories of nationalism, the third chapter outlines the new counter-model. From the fourth chapter onwards, this counter-model is unfolded in a historical analysis stretching from the period of the late Roman Republic to the Renaissance and Reformation. The concluding chapter clarifies the historical link between the European origins of nationalism in the Middle Ages and its political triumph in modernity.

1.1   Organism into artefact

The concept of nationhood has always been a dominant theme in modern historiography. The way, however, that it has been perceived and presented by historians has changed dramatically over time. In the nineteenth century, when the past, due to the accelerated change of contemporary life, became increasingly viewed as fragmented and disconnected from the present, nations were still believed to be the leading actors throughout European history. They were described as collective bodies with particular biographies, qualities and characteristics, interacting with each other on the allegedly main stage of history, international politics. While modern historiography introduced change as the fundamental force of history it portrayed the nation as a stable entity, and while change was assumed to be non-linear, the nation was supposed to grow from a seed in ancient times to full blossom in modern times. It was a matter of necessity, standing above the law of historical relativity of all things.

This image of the nation was to a considerable degree shaped by Romantic ideals of an organic community, as opposed to the 'mechanical' structure of modern society. Despite the passing of Romanticism, this idea remained. One reason for its persistence was that it functioned as the agent of continuity within a historiographical narrative that otherwise ran the risk of fragmentation. Another reason was that it divided the huge field of history into manageable chunks that did not need extra explanation because they were simply presented as part of a natural order. And a third reason can be found in the role the nation provided for modern historians themselves: as its chief biographers they were able to monopolise the position of secular priests – teaching citizens and advising rulers about their deeper identities and duties. Never did historians enjoy more public influence and more political weight than in this period and in this particular role.

No wonder, then, that the function of the nation as a dialectical counterweight to the core principles of historiography was so long-lasting. It was even upheld when it threatened historiographical claims to objectivity. At the beginning of the twentieth century, leading European historians, such as the German Nobel Prize winner, Theodor Mommsen (1817–1903), and his younger, hardly less distinguished colleague, Otto Hintze (1861–1940), still saw no point in talking to foreign colleagues because 'national antagonisms' would not allow any common ground for mutual understanding, and so they dismissed 'the idea of an international congress of the historical sciences as preposterous'.[1]

Both scholarship and politics had to undergo major transformations before historians were inclined to treat the nation less as an organism to nourish than as an artefact to deconstruct. There was, to be sure, no complete absence of critical research on the formation of nations during the nineteenth and early twentieth centuries. In fact, a few fine works were written, such as Ernest Renan's (1823–92) lecture *Qu'est-ce qu'une nation?* of 1882 and Carlton Hayes' (1882–1964) *Essays on Nationalism*

---

[1] Erdmann, *Die Ökumene der Historiker*, 66.

of 1926. However, these works were exceptional and only received increasing attention long after their publication.

Politically, reconsidering the place of the nation in history could have hardly been more imperative than after the World Wars. Interestingly enough though, there was only a slow and gradual shift in the historio-graphical description of the nation during the post-war decades. Nations were still portrayed as the pivotal political and cultural force from the early medieval period to the present; the only significant change was that they were now perceived as both very constructive and terribly destructive. Attempts were therefore made to distinguish between two oppositional sorts of national sentiment based on older ideas about dif-ferent types of nations. Some historians separated defensive and mod-erate patriotism from aggressive and extreme nationalism, taking the first as an indispensable element of modern democracy and the lat-ter as a pathological glorification of the nation state. Others followed the broader distinction by the Jewish American historian Hans Kohn (1891–1971) between civic and cultural nationalism, 'civic' meaning Western, territorial, libertarian, rational and integrative and 'cultural' standing for Eastern, ethnic, authoritarian, irrational and exclusive.[2] Having found such a neat and – at least for Anglo-American and French scholars – self-congratulatory solution, it was possible to continue writ-ing national histories almost as before. Furthermore, the dualistic view on national sentiment served equally well in the new situation of the Cold War. Leading historians in many Western countries could main-tain their role as national priests and the public influence and high legitimacy that went with it.

Only when the Cold War turned to a lasting thaw in the 1970s and 80s could the dominant view of nations and nationalism finally start to change. New approaches were facilitated by significant methodo-logical shifts within historiography that had already been underway for a while. Old-style political history was challenged by theoretically more sophisticated social and cultural histories, as was the metaphorical lan-guage concerning the 'organic nature' of the nation.

Still, it needed the initiative of scholars outside the field of history, such as political scientists and social anthropologists, to introduce a fresh and stimulating perspective. Some of these scholars had already formulated their theories of nationalism long before – Karl Deutsch (1912–92) in the 1950s, Ernest Gellner (1925–95) in the 1960s and 1970s – but their studies were only widely read from the 1980s onward. What these men had in common (as had most historians who first joined

[2] Kohn, *The Idea of Nationalism*.

them) was a sceptical, not to say negative attitude towards nations and nationalism, often born of personal experience. Karl Deutsch, Ernest Gellner and Eric Hobsbawm (born 1917) were all of Jewish descent, grew up in Prague between the wars and escaped the Nazis to Britain or to America; Benedict Anderson (born 1936) was the son of a protestant Irish father and an English mother, born in China, brought up in California and educated in England at Cambridge. Their biographical backgrounds not only helped them to question the common assumption of nations' naturalness but also to distance themselves from the scholarly role of national priest.

Although modernist theories differed significantly from the start, they were able to carry a new master narrative that has been dominating the field of nationalism studies ever since. It is based on two main arguments: the 'modernist' turn, according to which nations are an exclusively modern phenomenon emerging only in the late eighteenth or even in the nineteenth century, and the 'constructivist' turn, according to which nations are not formed by 'objective' criteria like common territory, language, habits, ancestry, fate etc. but by the common belief in such criteria; they were, in Anderson's famous formulation, 'imagined communities' and, as Gellner put it, products of nationalism, 'and not the other way round'.[3]

The enormous success of these theories certainly had to do with their originality, intellectual brilliance and, at least in some cases, with the elegant style in which they were presented; all this however would probably not have been enough if they did not serve an ideological purpose, too: for many intellectuals, above all those on the political left, the modernist approach came as a confirmation of the nation's artificial character and as an indication of its elusive appearance in history, being newly invented and soon discarded. Not displaying false modesty, Hobsbawm even considered the modernist achievements as a sign of nationalism's early decline. The Owl of Minerva, he remarked referring to Hegel, only flies out at dusk.[4]

Historians have never shown much talent as prophets and so it is no surprise that nations and nationalism have defied all predictions of their rapid decline and eventual disappearance. On the contrary, a statistical study from 2006 on national pride in thirty-three countries, including most Western states, came to the conclusion, that national pride had risen in a majority of them between 1995 and 2004.[5] Although the

---

[3] Gellner, *Nations and Nationalism*, 55.
[4] Hobsbawm, *Nations and Nationalism*, 183.
[5] Smith and Kim, 'National Pride', 3.

study itself may be of limited significance, its results seem plausible. During the 1990s, the European continent was faced with a multiple clash of nationalities seen in the Yugoslav wars, which made Western Europeans rub their eyes in disbelief, throw up their hands in horror and call the Americans for help. In turn, the terrorist attacks on New York and Washington in September 2001 have boosted American nationalism in an astonishing fashion. And as the culture of the United States is still imitated by friends and foes alike, its reinvigorated nationalism quickly rubbed off on other countries.

Nevertheless, despite these developments, the modernist approach has been the prevalent theoretical framework in nationalism studies for twenty years now, which is all the more remarkable as this field of research has expanded massively in the same period, both in scope and in quantity. Meanwhile, even scholars who favour strong national bonds have largely accepted its narrative and have started to use the constructivist method for their own purpose, which is to demonstrate the creativity of nationalist culture and its identity-fostering functions.

1.2   Fighting the modernist cause – a lost cause?

In the shadow of the modernist paradigm, there has always been a small and constant production of studies on nations and nationalism in premodern societies, pursued and published both in the English-speaking world and on the European continent. In the last ten years or so, this production has noticeably risen and managed to soften some core arguments by modernist scholars, such as the assertion of the inexistence or complete irrelevance of the nation-forming process in Europe before 1800.

The reasons for opposing the modernist representation of history are manifold. Historians specialising in medieval and early modern European history often cannot bring the modernist portrayal of their periods into line with their own perceptions and, in addition, are sometimes unhappy about the exclusion of their field of research from a prosperous scholarly enterprise. Familiar with primary sources that engage in what they understand as a national discourse, they try to reintroduce the pre-modern world into the story of nations and nationalism. Other intellectuals follow different agendas, of which the most influential is probably the so called 'neo-bourgeois' or 'neo-patriotic' movement in France, Germany and other European countries. Alarmed by what they diagnose as a crisis of national identity, primarily caused by the disciples of 1968, these intellectuals, both scholars and journalists, propagate a renewed awareness and pride in the national 'heritage' and therefore seek to reanimate the 'memory' of older storylines in national history. They also declare it their duty to challenge right-wing thinkers for their tenure of national discourse.

A widely noticed and highly lucrative result of these efforts has been the French *Lieux de mémoire*, published in several volumes between 1984 and 1993. Their programmatic concept has since been adapted to quite a few other European countries. The original French work contains 127 essays by leading scholars on a whole range of subjects analysing the 'collective memory' of effective (and rather flattering) facts, fictions, monuments, stereotypes and the like in the French national past from the Middle Ages to the present. And it is about some other 'places', too: not only was the *oeuvre* launched as a campaign to recentralise 'le lieu de la nation' in society but also to reoccupy the classic 'lieu de l'historien' as secular priest with one foot in the lecture hall and the other in the government palace. Pierre Nora, the series' editor and a powerful man of letters with good connections to the French 'classe politique', unambiguously called for himself and his fellow historians to take control of public memory again and to serve the citizens' need for a meaningful national past.[6] Though much of this sounds like a direct revival of the nineteenth century, it is noteworthy that it does not come packaged in botanical or biographical imagery, but in a decidedly constructivist rhetoric labelling the nation a 'political artefact'.[7]

Methodologically, most works on pre-modern nations take a different approach from the leading modernist literature. They tend to be less theoretical and more source-based. The terminology they use varies greatly as do their underlying narratives of nation formation. In terms of content, they generally fall into two categories: there are case studies focusing on a particular region and a short period of time, and there are overviews touching on various periods and places. Each has its advantages, but neither is ideally suited to question the modernist approach fundamentally: while specialised studies have limited explanatory power, general treatises offer little solid proof. These respective handicaps may partly explain why modernist theories have not yet been fundamentally challenged and still remain centre stage in nationalism studies.

This book tries to question the modernist narrative more seriously by proposing a broad theory on the historical origins of nationalism and by applying it to a long period of European history, from Classical Antiquity to Early Modernity. It equally tries to avoid the pitfalls of both specialised and general treatises by focusing on a big region in central

[6] Englund, 'The Ghost of Nation Past'.   [7] Ibid., 311.

Europe – the German-speaking lands of the Holy Roman Empire – and by integrating it into the wider picture of Western European history.

There are two reasons why I concentrate on the Holy Roman Empire. One is practical: its history offers an abundance of written and visual source material, which sheds light on the early making of nations and nationalism from different angles. The other is programmatic: as this book describes nationalism as an unintended product of Roman imperialism, it seems natural to pay special attention to the one European power that officially represented and sustained the continuity of Roman imperialism during the medieval and early modern period. By doing so, however, I will not portray the Holy Roman Empire as the driving force of nationalism; instead, I will attribute the key role to its changing interrelations with other European powers. One result of these interrelations was that the Empire became more and more identified with the 'German nation', which is why this book, through dealing with the Empire, also offers a history of early German nationalism.[8]

With this focus, the book will develop its main line of argument, which is that the origins of nationalism are to be attributed to late medieval Europe, that early forms of nationalism are already to be found in the Renaissance and that modern nationalism could only become such a mobilising force because of its presence in politics, scholarship and art of long ago.

At the same time, the book will describe pre-modern nationalism as a phenomenon in its own right, in many respects distinct from its modern successor, and it will answer the question of how and why the concept of the nation could exist and persist within Old Europe's hierarchical and religious society.

1.3   Turning constructivism downside up

The theory of the origins of nationalism presented in this book is, like the leading modernist theories, based on a constructivist approach; however, it calls into question the understanding of constructivism by Gellner, Hobsbawm and, to some extent, Anderson. Be it in sociology, epistemology, the theory of language or brain research, the rationale of constructivism generally is that all human reality is created and highly variable and therefore leaves no room for the assumption of an original and consistent human nature or a natural way of human life.

---

[8] I hope it will be self-evident why the book tells the history of early German nationalism without any ambitions to add another futile chapter to the German *Sonderweg* debate or to answer the misleading question: 'Which was the first nation in history?'

This basic assumption is not shared by the above-mentioned modernists. As I will show, Gellner's theory is much closer to Romantic thinking than its rhetoric implies because it understands pre-modern society as natural and real, whereas modern society is viewed as artificial and mechanical. The key difference from the Romantic position is that Gellner attributes the nation to the latter and not to the former. Anderson's labelling of the nation as 'imagined community' sounds constructivist, too, but from a constructivist point of view it is, as he concedes himself, meaningless: every community, from family to humanity as a whole, has to be 'imagined' in order to be 'real'. However, Anderson's book title presents the term 'imagined communities' as a label specially designed for the nation. As a result, the term's glorious career in nationalism studies has much to do with its suitability for the denunciation of the nation as an 'illusion' or 'fabrication'. This, indeed, is more an essentialist than a constructivist undertaking and not very helpful for a thorough understanding of the matter.

The constructivist method applied in this book thus differs considerably from most modernist approaches. Its main point of reference is language, primarily in textual and, to a lesser degree, in visual form. Language thereby is understood as an instrument both to construct and represent realities. Political, social, cultural and linguistic realities are assumed to be closely interlinked, though hardly ever consistent, which is here regarded as a source of ongoing tensions and, ultimately, of historical change. For nationalism, this means that the realities it depicted were neither totally at odds nor completely in accordance with social, political and cultural circumstances. I would like to illustrate this fairly complicated issue with three examples, which have been pivotal in European nation formation and which will be detailed in the following chapters.

The first example concerns the identity of the citizen. The language of European nationalism partly builds on the 'political religion' of the Ancient Roman Republic, which can be described as civic patriotism. It commanded that the duty of every citizen was to sacrifice himself, his family and friends for the sake of the fatherland. Furthermore, it was the citizen's responsibility to play an active part in political assemblies and it was his task to fight potential tyrants who might try to grab state power. When these requirements were taken up by late medieval and early modern nationalists, they were attributed to polities which usually bore little similarity to the Roman Republic. Who, for instance, could be addressed as a citizen in a kingdom like France? Authors remained either vague or, more interestingly, awarded the title to contemporary groups who had little in common with its original bearers. In the early modern period, we can find the dignities and duties of Roman citizens attributed to officeholders, members of estates assemblies, academicians or men of letters. Of course, these persons or institutions did not acquire the legal power of Roman citizens by such attributions, but they could be imbued with a symbolic power that made them feel legitimised to consult or criticise their governments. Indeed, the transformation of ancient political language can, to a certain degree, explain why people with no legal right to participate in politics have been firmly convinced of their playing an active part in the political process. And it can explain, too, why pre-modern nationalism was able to appeal to social strata clearly outside the circles of political decision-making.

My second example of inconsistencies between linguistic and social realities is concerned with national stereotypes. To this day, we cannot help defining and comparing 'national characters', especially when abroad, and we still do it even if we know that our generalisations of foreign peoples tend to be beyond any statistical evidence or are at least extremely partial. So where do national stereotypes come from if they are not simple reflections of social realities? A major source is old literature. Many stable 'characteristics' of European nations, for instance, have been derived from ethnographic descriptions by Greek and Roman authors. The image of the sturdy, blunt and outspoken Germans can be traced back to the description of the forest and swamp barbarians in Tacitus' *Germania* (who, incidentally, had never travelled to the Roman province of *Germania* made famous by his account of it), while the image of the arrogant, superficial and effeminate French still echoes Strabo's and Caesar's accounts of the degenerate Gauls. Most of these ancient stereotypes were probably void of empirical value when being reintroduced a thousand and more years after their invention (if they ever had such value). Even so, in order to persist, they needed to appear credible. One source of credibility was, of course, the authority of ancient authors. However, in the long run, this was not enough. If ancient stereotypes were to prevail without reflecting a later reality of collective behaviour, they had to create their own reality. There are, indeed, a few indications that this was what happened. The strongest one is the genre of early modern guides on how to write fiction, the so-called 'poetics'. These texts offered detailed listings of national and regional characteristics, mostly based on old literary conventions and primarily addressed to and used by playwrights, not least by Shakespeare.[9] This is how the same national stereotypes appeared

---

[9] In the sixteenth century, an authoritative guide on the use of national characteristics in literature was Scaliger, *Poetices Libri Septem* (for stereotypes of the French, e.g., see

in different plays time and again and thus could not fail to make an impression on the public. Once the stage was taken for the reality, the reality had to adapt to the stage.

The third example might be the most telling one: national languages. As early as around 1450 and as a provisional result of a complex semantic change, a frequent translation for Latin 'natio' was 'tongue' (or 'tongues'), meaning both a specific language and the people speaking it as their mother tongue. This double signification of 'tongue' can be traced back to at least the twelfth century, but more astonishing is that it amalgamated people who were not even able to understand each other. The term 'German tongue' ('tiutschiu zunge'), for instance, was already used by the minnesinger Walther von der Vogelweide (c. 1170–1230) to designate the people living in the northern part of the Holy Roman Empire, although more than 300 years later the reformer Martin Luther (1483–1546) still came to the conclusion that Germany had so many different dialects that people at a distance of thirty miles could not properly understand each other. How are we to explain this discrepancy? The answer is to be found abroad. To stay with the Germans, it was in Italy where they were first perceived as a people speaking the same language. Hardly anybody in medieval Italy was able to catch a word of what the soldiers, pilgrims and merchants coming from the north of the Alps were saying, and this was exactly how they were able to perceive the strange sounds as a 'common' language. The travellers then picked up this foreign attribution and brought it back home, where they were still incapable of communicating with their new fellow countrymen. However, when the word 'tongue' was fused with the more politicised term 'nation' in the fifteenth century, princely chancelleries in the Reich were about to develop a written High German for diplomatic purposes. And a few decades later Martin Luther translated the Bible into a German version that was supposed to appeal to all German-speaking people and that, in the long run, significantly contributed to the reduction of the Babel of German dialects. Indeed, many nations, just like Germany, paradoxically have their earliest origins abroad, find their first founders among foreigners and owe their existence as a language community to linguistic incompetence on the part of foreigners.

These examples indicate that the understanding of nationalism as a linguistic phenomenon has some major advantages. Firstly, its history can be examined directly from contemporary sources, which, at least for

p. 102); in the seventeenth century, Scaliger was partly replaced by Mesnardière, *La Poëtique* (for the revised list of stereotypes of the French, see p. 122). See also Maurer, 'Nationalcharakter', 63–4.

a historian, is still the most reliable way of gaining knowledge. Secondly, it can be put more precisely into context with the broader realities it was constructed in, addressed at and directed against – such as political systems, social hierarchies, groups of readership etc. Thirdly, contrary to the macro-sociologist approach of most modernist theories, it provides the possibility of viewing the nation as a 'contested terrain' fought for by different groups and their respective discourses – in other words, it brings nationalists and their partisan interests back into the picture instead of treating nationalism as an anonymous mechanism activated by modernity. Fourthly, it helps to abolish the misleading idea of a single national identity that holds together all members of a nation, and it allows insight into the remarkable flexibility of nationalism and the protean nature of the nation. And finally, it enables a distinction between pre-modern and modern forms of nationalism that can surmount the existing standard arguments, whose explanatory power often proves limited on closer inspection.

1.4 The impact of Antiquity, or the power of anachronism

The use of a linguistically based method in this book leads to some new propositions on how to describe the specificity of nations. The initial one will be that definitions of the nation can be more instructive if they do not, as is the usual practice, focus on its *internal* construction as a political and cultural community, but instead highlight its *external* construction that is to say, how the nation is perceived by and interrelates with foreign communities. In Chapter Three, I will introduce an analytical framework that distinguishes nations from tribal, religious and imperialist communities by their construction of the world beyond their own borders. A nation, according to this simple, but fundamental distinction, operates by confronting a multitude of other nations; it interrelates with communities, which are attributed to the same category as one's own, but perceived as significantly different not only from one's own, but also from each other's. A nation's outward relationships can therefore be defined as equal and multipolar. By contrast, imperialist, religious and tribal cultures operate by confronting a single and clearly depreciated collectivity, such as 'barbarians', 'pagans' or 'beasts'; they interrelate with communities of an opposite and inferior category, which are perceived as entirely different from one's own, but not necessarily from each other. Their outward relationships can thus be defined as bipolar and unequal. If we accept this basic distinction, the follow-up question arises, how such a multipolar and equal order of collectivities leading to a 'world of nations' could evolve, as it is no doubt more complex than a system based on bipolar and unequal relationships. I will argue that it could only emerge out of a big cultural entity, which was dominated by imperialist political thinking while being at the same time territorially fragmented without end. Such a contradictory cultural entity was Roman Christianity during the Middle Ages.

In other words, the nation will here be described as the product of an enduring and forceful anachronism: an imperialist political culture, dictated by the ideal of a single universal power inherited from Roman Antiquity, coexisted within a fragmented territorial structure, where each of the major powers was of similar strength (Empire, Papacy, France, England and later Aragon). In the realm of Roman Christianity, this led to an intense and endless competition for supremacy; all major kingdoms aimed for universal dominion, yet prevented each other from achieving it. The language of nationalism in this book is interpreted as a major result of this imperialist competition and as a new stimulus for it, lifting the competition to a more universal level by including the fields of cultural achievements and moral qualities, such as honesty, fairness or chastity.

Describing European nations as a product of heavily contradicting forces is a major departure from the leading modernist theories in itself, as they see cultural and structural processes largely in line with each other and leave the complex impact of tradition on these processes aside.

If nations are conceived as highly competitive communities, the question arises as to what they were actually supposed to compete for. If we are to give credit to nationalist language, then the ultimate aim of the contest was not specific and concrete, such as raising one's own nation's political power and wealth, but highly symbolic: it was about the augmentation of honour and the prevention of shame. Surprisingly, nations have hardly been described and analysed as communities of honour in recent research, maybe because that would be perceived as incompatible with their alleged modernity. In this study, though, national honour is not comprehended as an archaic remnant rattling around in the modern world, but as a highly innovative concept developed in a complex process during the fifteenth century.

In a society of orders, such as medieval Christianity, communities of honour were generally related to each other hierarchically, and the distribution of honour served the purpose of social stratification: noble honour, for instance, elevated aristocracy over the third estate, civic honour set the burghers over the peasants. National honour, on the contrary, integrated all social strata within a defined territory, and the national community of honour confronted other nations on equal terms.

How such a transformation of honour could happen and how a national competition of honour was realised (or simulated) will be a major focus in this book. The initial place of this transformation is located in the Catholic Church or, more precisely, at the Council of Constance from 1414 to 1418.

Another central argument, already implied in this introduction, is that the chief architects of nations throughout European history have been scholars or scholars-cum-politicians. The history of nationalism therefore cannot be separated from the history of European scholarship or, more precisely, from the social roles to which scholars were aspiring and from the roles to which they were assigned (which hardly ever happened to be identical). Thus, nationalism can be, and, indeed, often is part of scholarly self-promotion. The same, of course, applies to anti-nationalism. The material underlying this study shows that among the learned champions of nationalism there was a dominant type of scholar who aimed for a close link to politics and a major influence on political leaders. He portrayed himself as a learned all-rounder, as opposed to purely academic experts, as both a general adviser of the powerful and an advocate for the people.

Contrary to his own self-perception, though, it would be more appropriate to describe this type of scholar as a specialist in rhetoric and literature, acting as the treasurer of the past. His historical 'prototype' is to be found in Renaissance humanism, and already by then, he was subdivided into the roles of poet, orator and philologist. Later, in the eighteenth and nineteenth centuries, these roles were transformed into novelist, journalist and historian, whereby the connecting link remained the claim of authority over the collective past. The construction of national myths and with it the shaping of national 'biographies' and 'characters' was almost exclusively in the hands of historically educated intellectuals.

The impact of scholarly trained elites on the construction of nations has been acknowledged by quite a few historians; however, there still is a strong tendency to underestimate it. One reason for this is that most modernist theories understand nationalism as a mass phenomenon and are principally devoted to the question of how it could have become widespread. As legitimate as this is, I do not think the criterion of nationalism's mass appeal is particularly helpful to understand the historical development of nations. It might be more instructive to use nationalists' proximity to power as a leading benchmark. My point is that nationalists always spoke and acted in the name of the people but often did not need popular support to reach their goals. Even those nationalist movements which led to the foundation of nation states both in Europe and on other continents were predominantly carried out by elite minorities, who sometimes comprised a very small number of people. What they were looking for was access to power, not necessarily popular support. Apart from some long-term unsuccessful separatist movements, nationalism as a mass phenomenon generally came after the main political work had already been done. And with only a few exceptions, such as Britain, the Netherlands and Switzerland, it only reached all social classes in the twentieth century, with World War One as the most energetic nation-builder.

1.5   Nationalism: promoter of historical scholarship?

If scholarly trained elites – in general – and historical writers – in particular – had such an impact on the construction of nations, then the same applies the other way round. Nationalism has been an important impulse for the development of the historical sciences in Europe. Of course, nationalist constructions of the past are to be qualified as mythological (in a functionalist understanding of the term) because they portray history as highly meaningful and tend to blank out events and processes which do not serve their ideological purpose. Still, they can be methodologically sophisticated and, indeed, often are. After all, a solid scholarly appearance has always fostered their credibility.

As key players in the competition for national honour, many historians could not resist the temptation to fabricate a glorious national past, but at the same time they were well advised to corroborate the assertions they were making. Otherwise foreign nationalist historians were all too ready to mock them as fabulists and condemn them as a disgrace to their nation. Therefore mythical and critical thinking often went hand in hand, practised by the same scholars. Both could advance methodological refinement. In national histories from humanism to historicism the same methods were normally used for myth criticism and myth creation. Audacious projects, such as forgeries of source material, proved especially prolific for methodological elaborateness and innovation, simply because the requirements of camouflage were higher.[10] Studying the history of pre-modern nationalism, then, offers the opportunity to consider the history of one's own discipline from a slightly subversive point of view and to engage in some myth hunting, too: namely, the

---

[10] See the exemplary case of Giovanni Nanni of Viterbo (*c.* 1432–1502), whose sophisticated forgeries of 'lost' ancient texts may not have been motivated by nationalist ambitions, but certainly satisfied such ambitions throughout Europe during the early modern period; Hirschi, *Wettkampf der Nationen*, 328–30; Grafton, 'Invention of Traditions'; idem, *What was History?*, 99–105.

idea that the search for truth is the principal motivation in the making of modern historiography is a great myth itself.

If the history of nationalism is so closely intertwined with the history of scholarship and especially with the scholarly species of the historian, it seems presumptuous to make an attempt at writing a history of nationalism from an external and objective point of view. Other scholars, though, seem to have found such a way of proceeding. For Hobsbawm, at least, the task was an easy one: the only thing that mattered to him was that 'the historian leaves his or her convictions behind when entering the library or the study'. Some would, he presumed, have more problems in doing this than others, adding that quite a few 'nationalist historians have been unable to do so'. Fortunately, he saw himself in the happy position of not even needing to leave his 'non-historical convictions' behind when sitting down to write his book on nationalism.[11]

Is it really that easy? I have my doubts. Why should a history of nations and nationalism written by a nationalist be a more partisan enterprise than one by an internationalist? Contrary to other more distant or more 'dead' research topics, one can hardly escape one's own convictions when researching nationalism; the best proof of this is the current literature on the subject, which usually reveals its authors' personal opinions anyway. From this point of view, *denying* the impact of personal conviction is the actual partisan approach.

What distinguishes scholarly research from other forms of intellectual labour is the effort to scrutinise every statement and to make it accessible to critical scrutiny by others. In this respect, clarifying one's own personal interests and constraints before tackling a subject is not a hindrance to serious research but a condition of it. The reason why it is so rarely done, or even ridiculed as a display of personal vanity, is simply that it does not correspond to the scientific rhetoric of objectivity and neutrality and therefore appears as a threat to the actual powerbase of scholarship.

Having made this point, the author of this book owes the reader an explanation of his own position on nations and nationalism and his motivation for engaging in this topic as a historian. Having grown up in Switzerland as a Swiss citizen in the 1980s and 90s, nationalism was most common to me in the form of an allegedly self-evident and rather silent pride in a rich and peaceful country that had not experienced any major turmoil for a long time and that hardly ever felt the need to justify itself to other nations.

[11] Hobsbawm, *Nations and Nationalism*, 12–13.

As a young student, equipped with meagre and unreflecting nationalist attitudes, acquaintance with modernist theories proved stimulating and refreshing. Only when specialising in German Renaissance humanism a few years later did my difficulties with modernism start. In the humanist literature – mostly written in Latin – I was confronted with an obsessive preoccupation with national honour, national character and national politics that I simply could not reconcile with the central propositions of modernist theories. The main reason why I have pursued this problem for the last ten years is that my specialisation in pre-modern history has always been partly motivated by my perception of a widespread short-sightedness in historical explanations of present phenomena. Offering alternative narratives that dig a bit deeper seems to me a central source of legitimacy for the work of medievalists and early modernists, both *vis-à-vis* specialists of different fields and interested lay readers. For this reason, writing a book on nationalism before modernity made much sense to me.

How about my stance on nationalist politics? Under the present conditions of a globalising world, I regard it as counterproductive. I believe that government by nationalist principles is almost impossible today, given its great complexity and its international dimension. If political decisions are taken on nationalist impulses, they sooner or later damage both the state and the politicians in charge. In my view, the prime function of nationalism in today's politics is populist propaganda, stirring strong emotions and lulling the mind. The trouble is that this propaganda can become even more successful as the complexity of politics increases, serving a purely compensatory function. Historians calling for a stronger national identity and trying to act as guardians of national memory are, to my mind, agents of an irretrievable past, who are also cherishing illusions about their own vanished glory.

Nevertheless, I do not think that political nationalism has always been as much at odds with political realities as it is today. What is now an oversimplified ideology was once more complex and more appropriate than rivalling political ideologies. In the late medieval and early modern period, for instance, the old ideal of a single universal empire inevitably clashed with the realities of power relations, while the concept of a plurality of nations reflected them much better. During the eighteenth and nineteenth centuries, nationalism could be an agent of democratisation, especially when used by opposition movements against the ruling classes. A similar conclusion can be made about some African and Asian colonies in the twentieth century.

In sum, my personal statement might explain, to a certain degree, why I consider it worthwhile to look for a middle way in the appraisal of nationalism – somewhere between the negative approach shown by the leading modernists and the positive attitude adopted by many theorists of collective memory and identity.

2   The modernist paradigm: strengths and weaknesses

> Agrarian man can be compared with a natural species which can survive in the natural environment. Industrial man can be compared with an artificially produced or bred species which can no longer breathe effectively in the nature-given atmosphere, but can only function effectively and survive in a new, specially blended and artificially sustained air or medium.
>
> Ernest Gellner, *Nations and Nationalism*, 1983

> In fact, all communities larger than primordial villages of face-to-face contact (and perhaps even these) are imagined.
>
> Benedict Anderson, *Imagined Communities*, 1983

The study of nationalism was profoundly reshaped by three publications that appeared independently of each other in 1983: *Nations and Nationalism* by Ernest Gellner, *Imagined Communities* by Benedict Anderson and *The Invention of Tradition*, a collection of essays edited by Eric Hobsbawm and Terence Ranger. These books did not come out of the blue, of course. Gellner and Hobsbawm had been publishing on the subject since the 1960s, and some of their leading arguments had already been introduced earlier by other scholars – Karl Deutsch[1] in the 1950s and Carlton Hayes[2] as far back as the 1920s. Yet, thanks to their critical and commercial success the books marked a watershed and proved most influential for the boom of nationalism studies and the triumph of the modernist paradigm in the following decades.

---

[1] Deutsch, *Nationalism and Social Communication*.
[2] Hayes anticipated the core idea of Gellner's attribution of nationalism to industrialisation: 'Closer observation of the Industrial Revolution should disclose the fact that its effects, important though they may have been on the world at large, have been much more important within the territorial confines of national states … Only a radical improvement in the means of transportation and communication and a revolutionary change in the social life of the masses could introduce the type of political democracy which would foster nationalism. Nationalism as a world-phenomenon could come, as it were, only by machinery, and actually by the machinery of the Industrial Revolution it has come.' Hayes, *Essays on Nationalism*, 50–2.

Although the theoretical discourse on nations and nationalism has significantly broadened and diversified since then, these three works are still regarded as most representative of the modernist approach, followed by other classical studies, such as John Breuilly's *Nationalism and the State* and Eric Hobsbawm's later lectures *Nations and Nationalism since 1780*. This is why they are to be put at the centre of any critique of the modernist approach. Interestingly enough the books differ strongly both in argument and in content.

Gellner's theory of nationalism is based on a juxtaposition of agrarian and industrial society and argues that nationalism only came into being when it was socially necessary. According to him, this was the case in the mobile society of modern industrialism with its universal and standardised educational system monopolised by the state; the function of nationalism was to identify an old or invented high culture with the state and all its citizens and, with this, to grant the egalitarianism needed for social mobility.[3]

Anderson relates the rise of nationalism to the decline of traditional religion caused by three modernising forces: the replacement of sacred literary languages by secular vernaculars; the disenchantment with monarchy, leading to the separation of state and dynasty; the transformation of the sense of time from a magical unity of past, present and future to a mechanical arrangement set by clock and calendar. Most crucial for the invention of the nation, in his view, were new forms of communication created by print capitalism in the eighteenth and nineteenth centuries. Media, such as newspapers and novels, enabled readers to imagine themselves sharing information and values with other people they did not know. For Anderson, this idea of anonymous simultaneity was crucial for the depiction of the nation as 'a deep, horizontal comradeship'.[4]

In *The Invention of Tradition*, nationalism is but one issue of many, though one which is especially emphasised in Hobsbawm's introduction and in some of the essays. Hobsbawm counts nationalism among those 'ideological movements' that were so unprecedented 'that even historic continuity had to be invented' by creating a distant past through semifiction or pure forgery and by draping the nation with seemingly old but, in fact, 'entirely new symbols and devices', such as national anthems, flags and female personifications of the nation.[5] This is not exactly a full-grown theory of nationalism and neither does Hobsbawm deliver

---

[3] Gellner, *Nations and Nationalism*, 19–38.
[4] Anderson, *Imagined Communities*, 7.
[5] Hobsbawm and Ranger (eds.), *The Invention of Tradition*, 6–7.

one in his own book on nationalism; still, his contribution to nationalism studies proved influential, largely because it helped to portray and analyse the nation as a modern construct disguised as something ancient.

2.1   Nationalism without nationalists

Despite these differences, the three modernist classics from 1983 owe their strong impact on nationalism research to an astonishing amount of accidental conformity between them. First and foremost they postulate that nations and nationalism are exclusively modern and completely incompatible with societies of estates, religious cultures and agrarian economies – in short, with what they regard as principal characteristics of the pre-modern world. Then, no less importantly, they share a common constructivist rhetoric, tagging the nation as 'imagined', 'invented', 'artificial' or 'abstract' and treating nationalism not as patriotism gone bad or another kind of mental pathology (as was a common practice before), but as the chief constructor and sustainer of the nation; if nationalism vanishes, they argue, the nation does, too. Methodologically, they do not tackle nationalism as a set of ideas or a sort of philosophy, but rather as a sociocultural mechanism ensuring a degree of cultural uniformity within a state. What nationalists believe and propagate and why they do so is not of interest to Gellner, Anderson and Hobsbawm because they think that it explains neither nationalism's causes nor its effects. Anderson confronts nationalism's 'political power' with its 'philosophical poverty' and concludes that the former does not depend on the latter,[6] and Gellner even argues that it would be misleading to study nationalist ideology because 'it suffers from pervasive false consciousness'. By this he means that 'its self-image and its true nature are inversely related, with an ironic neatness seldom equalled even by other successful ideologies'.[7] Thus, they described nations as artefacts, but left the artists out of the picture.

In their definitions of the nation they distance themselves from any attempt to find (purportedly) objective criteria, such as common territory, language, customs, history, blood etc. The argument behind this is that such criteria would only produce a normative framework inevitably dictated by nationalist assumptions. Instead they either offer – like Hobsbawm – tautological definitions, calling the nation 'any sufficiently large body of people whose members regard themselves as members of a

---

[6] Anderson, *Imagined Communities*, 5.
[7] Gellner, *Nations and Nationalism*, 124–5.

"nation"',[8] or they refer to subjective criteria, like Anderson, who labels the nation an 'imagined political community – and imagined as both inherently limited and sovereign'.[9] Nationalism, on the other hand, is defined as a simple political principle, demanding that, as Gellner puts it, 'ethnic boundaries should not cut across political ones, and, in particular, that ethnic boundaries within a given state ... should not separate the power-holders from the rest',[10] or, in Hobsbawm's short formula: 'nation = people = state'.[11] According to the modernist view, the only form of state power nationalism accepts, therefore, is the nation state.

Geographically, all three scholars show a preference for exotic examples, measured against the focus of previous nationalism research on Western Europe and North America. Anderson mainly refers to former European colonies in East Asia and Latin America and even makes the case that nationalism originated in the American colonies of Spain. Gellner uses 'Ruritania' within the Empire of 'Megalomania' to exemplify his theory, a fictional country invented by the English novelist Anthony Hope (1863–1933) and modelled on a German-speaking region in the late-nineteenth-century Habsburg Empire, which at that time was regarded as an archaic anomaly in Europe. Hobsbawm's monograph has a vast geographical focus, covering the globe from Brazil to Sri Lanka to the Ottoman Empire to Estonia. Finally, they all present their findings in rather general terms and, with the partial exception of Anderson, do not attempt to corroborate their theories with detailed historical material; their arguments' inherent logic is meant to speak for itself.

2.2   Strengths and shortcomings

The following critical review of the leading modernist theories is subdivided into three sections: it will start by emphasising their lasting accomplishments, which can still benefit today's research (and this book); then it will address their major shortcomings and add some considerations as to how they can be overcome; and finally it will point out their historical misconceptions about European culture and politics

---

[8] Hobsbawm, *Nations and Nationalism*, 8.
[9] Anderson, *Imagined Communities*, 5; Gellner makes a certain exception in this regard offering two different definitions, of which one is deterministic and one voluntaristic: '1. Two men are of the same nation if and only if they share the same culture, where culture in turn means a system of ideas and signs and associations and ways of behaving and communicating. 2. Two men are of the same nation if and only if they *recognize* each other as belonging to the same nation.' Gellner, *Nations and Nationalism*, 7.
[10] Gellner, *Nations and Nationalism*, 1.
[11] Hobsbawm, *Nations and Nationalism*, 19.

before modernity, that is, according to their understanding of the term, before nineteenth-century industrialism and print capitalism. This threefold critical assessment is intended to open the way for a new theory of the origins of nationalism, which can make the claim to be both more accurate historically and more solid theoretically.

Any critical assessment of the modernist paradigm has to underline its achievements – not least because nationalism studies became far more popular thanks to the provocative and inspiring arguments by Gellner, Anderson and, to a lesser degree, Hobsbawm. In this respect, every scholar engaged in nationalism studies today remains in their debt, and even those turning their back on modernist theories cannot help but carry on their intellectual legacy in one way or another. There is no road back to the nationalism studies before 1983, and even the fiercest opponents of the modernists would probably agree that this is for the best.

This book makes no exception in building upon important accomplishments by modernist theorists. It adopts their conviction that nations can only be properly understood from a constructivist point of view, answering the question under what political and cultural conditions it became possible to conceive and create them. Consequently, this study follows in the footsteps of modernists, too, when it comes to offering a definition of nations: applying 'objective' criteria of the sort already mentioned is indeed helpful for nationalist purposes only. Furthermore, it will raise the question of nationalism's social functions, so doggedly asked by Ernest Gellner, and expose the fundamental contradictions that limit its use as a form of social and political guidance. Finally, it regards the works by Anderson and Gellner as great proof that one can write theoretical treatises which remain stylistically elegant while getting to grips with their subject matter; this is not the least of their achievements.

This said, I believe that, apart from literary style, most of these achievements have not been properly exploited by the leading modernists themselves. The main reason is a lack of theoretical accuracy, partly due to a preference for rhetorical effects. A clear example of this is Anderson's catchword 'imagined community'. Anderson's book title introduces the term as a specific characteristic of nations, and it has been overwhelmingly used in the same way ever since. As early as on the first pages, though, Anderson concedes in a somewhat equivocal phrase: 'In fact, all communities larger than primordial villages of face-to-face contact (and perhaps even these) are imagined.'[12] Indeed,

---

[12] Anderson, *Imagined Communities*, 6.

if he plans to make a constructivist argument – and he clearly does in the following chapters of the book – then he has to understand all forms of communities as 'imagined'. To build an assemblage of huts, occupy them with a few dozen people and animals and cultivate the surrounding lands, takes an act of imagination, too, and it even takes a sort of ideology to construct and maintain a 'village' community as such. Therefore, Anderson is right to add that communities are to be distinguished 'by the style in which they are imagined'. One point of reference for this certainly is face-to-face contact because communities without it require a higher degree of abstraction. It is only one criterion of many, however, as Anderson's own definition shows: what denotes the nation, in his view, is the conception of it as 'limited and sovereign'. This is a valid definition, though probably not specific enough. The citizens of the big city states in Greek Antiquity or the Jews in the biblical kingdom of Israel could be listed under the same category, although Anderson would not want to have them there.

Apart from these shortcomings, Anderson's approach to nationalism is more solid and comprehensive than those of Gellner and Hobsbawm. Gellner's theory, as witty as it appears at first sight, proves to be, on closer inspection, a not-so-coherent mixture of functionalist causality, Marxist critique of ideology, constructivist rhetoric and Romantic sociology. Hobsbawm, on the other hand, does not have a worked-through theory of his own, which makes it superfluous to deal with his work at this point.

The inconsistencies of Gellner's theory might have to do with the fact that his book from 1983 is an accumulation of twenty years of research accompanied by several smaller publications. The problems start with the book's claim 'to explain why nationalism has emerged and become pervasive'.[13] What one would expect, then, is a historical explanation of the causes that led to the formation and expansion of nationalism. This is not what Gellner does. His leading argument is functionalist, saying that nationalism is useful or even necessary for industrial societies but useless for agrarian ones. However convincing his point might be, it cannot explain why nationalism emerged. Functions do not have much to say about causes: it does not rain because plants need water.

A second problem with Gellner's functionalism arises when he addresses the ideological pitfalls of nationalism. Here he sounds like a Marxist speaking about religion.[14] All that nationalist ideology purports, as aforementioned, is utterly wrong in Gellner's eyes: 'It claims to

---

[13] Gellner, *Nations and Nationalism*, 139.
[14] O'Leary, 'On the Nature of Nationalism', 219.

defend folk culture while in fact it is forging a high culture; it claims to protect an old folk society while in fact helping to build up an anonymous mass society ... It preaches and defends continuity, but owes everything to a decisive and unutterably profound break in human history.'[15] All of this brings him to the conclusion that nationalist 'doctrines are hardly worth analysing'. The punchline of the Marxist argument about religion was that it was a social ill suitable only for the ruling classes. Gellner, however, argues that nationalism is highly functional for industrial society as a whole. If so, how can an ideology suffering from a complete denial of reality be of general use in a complex system like modern society? On this question Gellner's theory has not much to say.

2.3   Fake communities by 'fake' constructivists

Gellner displays an impressive virtuosity in figurative speech which makes him sound like the most constructivist of modernists. Nationalism, to quote just one example, belongs to a society in which man 'lives in specially bounded and constructed units, a kind of giant aquarium or breathing chamber'.[16] If this is what industrialism looks like, then what construction can agrarian society be compared to? To none, Gellner suggests, it resembles a 'natural environment'. Speaking in metaphors, Gellner might have just evoked an ambiguous association here. A close look at the whole book, though, leads to a contrary conclusion. When it comes to the opposition of agrarian and industrial societies, Gellner systematically speaks in terms of a natural versus an artificial world. Pre-modern man lived in 'communities' attributed as 'genuine', 'rural' and 'sustained by folk cultures reproduced locally and idiosyncratically by the micro-groups themselves'. Modern man by contrast was forced into 'society' labelled as 'anonymous and impersonal' and associated with 'bureaucratic and technological communication' creating 'mutually substitutable atomized individuals'.[17]

This dualism is contrary to the constructivist approach; it belongs to a late nineteenth-century sociological thinking animated by a deeply Romantic spirit. Gellner's (undeclared) model here is Ferdinand Tönnies (1855–1936), a German sociologist whose main work *Gemeinschaft und Gesellschaft* (*Community and Society*) appeared in 1887. In the decade before, Germany had experienced its first economic depression of the modern age, which gave way to broad intellectual pessimism. Tönnies' book presented an attractive theory of modern alienation that offered

---

[15] Gellner, *Nations and Nationalism*, 124–5.
[16] Ibid., 51.   [17] Ibid., 57 / 124.

a conservative answer to Marx. The basic idea was that in the making of the modern world an age of 'society' followed on from an age of 'community' and that for man this transition meant to 'go out into a foreign land'.[18] On this ground, the book took a long look back, tinted with Romantic nostalgia, at the alleged naturalness and healthiness of the pre-modern world. This is where the Gellnerian imagery originates. Tönnies wrote: 'Community means genuine, enduring life together, whereas Society is a transient and superficial thing. Thus *Gemeinschaft* must be understood as a living organism in its own right, while *Gesellschaft* is a mechanical aggregate and artefact.'[19] The only, but decisive difference between the two men is that Tönnies implicitly linked the nation to Gemeinschaft whereas Gellner explicitly ascribed it to Gesellschaft.

Thanks to Gellner, Tönnies' dualism of community and society, long since rejected as both epistemologically unsound and ideologically awkward, experiences a resurrection in nationalism research – now in constructivist disguise. Soon afterwards, Anthony D. Smith, a former student and later critic of Gellner and one of the most influential scholars in nationalism studies of the last decades, referred explicitly to Tönnies' model,[20] and so did Smith's student Oliver Zimmer.[21] On the same essentialist basis, Smith pronounced that 'our investigation of the origins of nations cannot proceed far, until this fundamental question of whether the nation be viewed as construct or real historical process is resolved'.[22] With this, Gellner's missionary fervour to unveil nationalism's falsehood and nationalists' stupidity led to a widespread and long-lasting theoretical confusion, which even affected Gellner's critics.

If many modernists' constructivism is inconsistent or even amounts to an essentialist argument in disguise, what then makes a thorough constructivist theory of nationalism more promising? It is the assumption that *every form* of human reality and social organisation is created, i.e. a consequence of beliefs and social practices, and none can be explained by reference to a stable human nature or to a natural way of life. With this, constructivism does not pretend that human biology is of no importance; on the contrary, it takes it very seriously by assuming that humans are biologically capable of existing in an enormous diversity of social settings and cultural realities. Living in caves does

[18] Tönnies, *Community and Civil Society*, 18.
[19] Ibid., 19.   [20] Smith, *The Ethnic Origins*, 157.
[21] Zimmer, *A Contested Nation*, 108.
[22] Smith, 'The Origins of Nations', 340–1.

not correspond more to human nature than dwelling in skyscrapers. Neither does constructivism lead to a philosophy of 'anything goes': how a given reality is shaped closely depends on social organisation and symbolic representations, such as the meanings a certain language can produce. Constructivism, therefore, offers a particularly suitable methodology for historical research, as it is based on the claim to explain phenomena out of their past – and not out of ours.

The principal question of a constructivist approach to nation formation is a Kantian one: what are the conditions for the possibility of nationalism? By answering it, one can hardly leave, as modernists have suggested, nationalist language out of the picture. If we take Gellner's sentence seriously that 'it is nationalism which engenders nations', then we need to know how nationalists thought and spoke.[23] This book describes nationalist language as a specific, though flexible discourse that is a habitual practice of speaking characterised by a set of leitmotifs and rhetorical patterns. Treating nationalism as a language also helps to replace the 'mechanistic' approach by modernist theories with a more dynamic and flexible model: instead of assuming that nationalism was triggered by an identical mechanism everywhere, we can focus on the historical conditions of its initial construction and then analyse its expansion to and transformation by societies, which adopted it under different circumstances.

Two other conceptual contradictions of modernist theories result from the description of nationalism as a cultural phenomenon similar to religion and from its definition as a political principle demanding a nation state for every nation. Neither of these specifications is very helpful. The first risks being broad to the extent of insignificance and the second reductionist to the point of over-simplicity. Yet, for the modernist cause, at least, the argument that nationalism's actual goal is the establishment of the nation state, has become an almost unquestioned dogma. This is all the more surprising as many leading modernists were (or still are) living and teaching in Britain, where the relationship between nationalisms – British, English, Scottish, Welsh and Irish – and the state is obviously far more complicated than that.

Even in modern times the nation state is only one of several political systems in which nationalists can find their claim for national liberty and self-determination realised. In pre-modern times, nationalists did not dream of nation states at all. However, this is not the only argument suggesting that any reductionist political definition must be dropped. Nationalism is just as much about highly symbolic values, such as honour and purity, as about political self-determination, and it would be rewarding to analyse these different aspects interdependently.

In addition to pseudo-constructivism and political reductionism, a final theoretical problem of Anderson's and Gellner's theories is their predominantly macro-sociological approach. Their explanation of nationalism's emergence and functions is aimed at the whole of society which prevents them from noticing that nationalism can develop different forms and functions according to different social classes, ranks or trades and can indeed remain a sociological micro-phenomenon for a long time without necessarily being politically weak as a result. Consequently, a proponent of a macro-sociological theory cannot grasp that every nation, as soon as constructed, constitutes a contested terrain with opposing groups seeking to enforce their respective understanding of its 'true nature'. Any closer look at this 'internal' competition for the control of national discourse shows nationalism as a socially dividing force, too, and, in addition, shakes the cherished idea of definable national identities.

2.4   Modernist myopia and the 'invention of tradition'

After having outlined the theoretical flaws of modernist theories, I would like to address their historical shortcomings. Here one can differentiate between conceptual problems and simple mistakes. Let us start with the former. The bird's-eye perspective on modern society of Gellner and Anderson brings with it an even more simplified view of pre-modern society. That medieval and early modern Europe was generally more rural and less mobile than modern Europe is a truism. What modernists, due to their conceptual framework, have to block out, however, are Europe's mobile urban minorities before 1800, which happened to be crucial in the process of pre-modern nation-building. These minorities – merchants, scholars, nobles, diplomats etc. – must have experienced their journeys far more intensely than the modern masses on the move generally did. Compared to earlier modes of transport, such as horseback, carriage or boat, a modern trip by car, train or plane almost feels like watching a motion picture; due to speed and physical separation, modern means of travel invariably restrict the engagement with the environment, reduce the perception of distance, and ultimately prevent an intense experience of mobility itself. Today, we can fly around the globe almost without even noticing that we are actually on the move. Thus the step from high mobility to virtual immobility is a small one. In short, pre-modern forms of travel were by no means less well suited for the development of nationalist thinking than modern, let alone contemporary ones.

There are two other conceptual assumptions that make nationalism look too modern in modernist theories. One is Anderson's fascinating argument about a new apprehension of time and space as a precondition for nationalism. His claim that mass media, such as newspapers, enabled people to imagine themselves simultaneously doing the same thing as thousands of others unknown to them, sounds convincing enough, but is hardly a necessary prerequisite for nationalism. If we take nationalist discourse as a benchmark, the favoured time model on which national communities are based is the opposite of Anderson's, looking far more archaic and indeed being close to what he calls, referring to Walter Benjamin, 'Messianic time'. The nation is imagined as a time-transcending community of the living, the dead and the yet-to-be-born, in which all are responsible for each other and for the preservation of the common freedom and honour. Nationalist rhetoric is full of exhortations by national heroes of the past reminding their progeny of their common cause and of their legacy for the countrymen yet to be born. Such conceptions are already to be found many centuries before the first newspaper was printed; they remained just as powerful, when the whole nation read the news at breakfast, and they will probably still be there, when newspapers have long disappeared.

This leads us to the more general conclusion that one cannot, as both Anderson and Gellner do, equate changes in consciousness with changes in technology and social organisation. David Bell puts it as follows: 'Languages do not simply respond, passively, to "deeper" structural changes, like so many loose stones on the slopes of a volcano.'[24]

Probably the most influential historical misconception of modernist theories underscores Hobsbawm's neologism 'invented traditions'. In his introduction to *The Invention of Tradition*, Hobsbawm uses a terminological sleight of hand to portray 'invention of tradition' as specifically, though not exclusively modern. He first asks for a clear distinction between 'tradition' and 'custom', which leads to the paradoxical solution that 'tradition' is atypical of 'traditional societies'. In all pre-industrialised societies, Hobsbawm argues, 'custom' dominated. When he then defines 'custom' in contrast to 'tradition', the precise difference between the two terms is hard to grasp: while invented traditions are to be understood as 'responses to novel situations which take the form of reference to old situations, or which establish their own past by quasi-obligatory repetition', customs 'give any desired change (or

---

[24] Bell, *The Cult of the Nation*, 32.

resistance to innovation) the sanction of precedent, social continuity or natural law as expressed in history'.[25]

This is not the only terminological smokescreen in Hobsbawm's essay – it, too, shares the essentialist dilemma with Gellner and Anderson of being stuck for an answer as to when traditions are to be considered as invented and when not. Still, the alleged contrast between 'custom' and 'tradition' serves an important purpose. It prevents readers from hitting upon the idea that the broad term 'invented tradition' applies just as much to 'traditional' society as to 'modern' society – if not more so!

It would be more appropriate to distinguish modern societies by the term 'invention of innovation', not only because they have introduced a speed of innovation unknown before, but also because they have embraced innovation as an imperative practice. With innovation having such a great legitimating function in modern societies, traditions can hardly be as indispensable and ubiquitous as in pre-modern societies, which tended to sanctify the old and condemn the new.

This is why one could argue that the concept of 'invention of tradition' would be more fitting to the description of medieval and early modern Europe. As pre-modern Western society was both culturally traditional and innovatory, there was a constant need to present the new as a restoration of the old, which could lead, if successful, to the 'invention of tradition'. Thus, pre-modern people tended to be particularly inventive when denying their inventions. There were countless medieval monasteries, towns, universities and dynasties equipped with myths and rituals, which gave account of a heroic origin in ancient or biblical times and which successfully obscured a less old and more profane foundation. These traditions, if proved wrong or unattractive, were either reconstructed or replaced by new ones. And when it came to inventing a cast-iron set of traditions for a radical innovation, such as the Reformation, Europe's traditional culture excelled in virtuosity. The scholars who were engaged in these concerted efforts to portray the newly crafted Protestant faith as the original one used the same methodological tools, which, a few decades earlier, had already proved effective for the construction of national myths: humanist philology.

As to the historical slips by leading modernists, a few hints on themes later raised in this book will suffice to illustrate that at least some 'inventions of traditions' have been invented by modernist historians themselves.

---

[25] Hobsbawm and Ranger (eds.), *The Invention of Tradition*, 2–3.

Hobsbawm counts personifications of the nation, such as the female Germania, Francia etc., among the 'entirely new symbols and devices' of modern nationalism, ignoring the fact that many of them were already widely used long before, both in text and image, and indeed date back to Renaissance humanism or even earlier, being mostly drawn on ancient models such as 'Lady Rome'.[26] To imagine collectives as single bodies of immortal nature, from guilds (and other 'corporations') to kingdoms, is actually typical of pre-modern culture, and so it was the norm to paint the nation as a person as soon as it was forged. As early as 1492, the German humanist Conrad Celtis complained that some Germans 'lived separated from the body of our Germany' (*a corpore Germaniae nostrae separate vivunt*), subjugated and taxed by foreign rulers; to end this 'shame on our nation' (*pudeat nationi nostrae*), Celtis appealed to the 'German men' (*viri Germani*) to 'unite the completely torn borders' of Germany.[27]

Another historical slip, this time by Gellner, is the statement that the governed in pre-modern societies demanded that their rulers should be 'less corrupt and grasping, or more just and merciful' than their predecessors, whereas in modern societies they wanted them to be of their own nationality.[28] This is a widespread cliché, simplistic in many ways and wrong about the absence of pre-modern claims for rulers to belong to the same nation as the ruled. Modernists have not looked at the political systems in which such claims could be raised effectively. While the rights of succession in hereditary monarchies usually did not allow the selection of an heir to the throne based on nationalist criteria, the republican concept of self-government automatically asked for a national identity of governors and governed – if the republic was defined as a nation. More explicitly, however, this issue had to be discussed in a third type of political unit: elective monarchies. During the fifteenth century, legal experts on the Holy Roman Empire were already debating whether a candidate to the throne had to be German, and they were joined by princes and historians in the early sixteenth century with a new election approaching in 1519. The debate then reached, as we will see in Chapter Eight, such public scope that it even forced leading candidates like the Kings of France and Spain to pretend to be true Germans, based on criteria such as ancestry, customs and language. Finally, with Charles of Habsburg, King of Spain, the electoral

[26] Ibid., 7; on the modelling of the 'domina Francia' during the Hundred Years War, see Beaune, *The Birth of an Ideology*, 285–308; on the transformation of the female personification of *Germania* see the figures in Chapter 3.3 and 3.4 of this book.
[27] Celtis, *Oratio in gymnasio*, 47 (translation revised by Hirschi).
[28] Gellner, *Thought and Change*, 153.

princes not only chose the official candidate who paid most, but who was considered the most German, too.

Finally, Gellner is historically mistaken, too, when treating industrialism as a precondition for nationalism (as he understands the term). In Europe, America, Africa and Asia, there are plenty of nation states that were founded before their societies were industrialised, not to speak of the nationalist movements that often predated these foundations by decades. Gellner's blind eye on history is even more evident as his point on industrialism serves as one of the leading arguments of his theory.

3   Foundations of a new nationalism theory

The benefits of a defined territoriality, the politically unifying impact
of ecclesiastical unity, the contribution of two geniuses, Bede and
Alfred, the stabilising of an intellectual and linguistic world through
a thriving vernacular literature, the growth of the economy and of an
effective professional royal bureaucracy, all these are contributive to a
firmly affirmative answer to 'Was England a nation state in 1066?'
Adrian Hastings, *The Construction of Nationhood*, 1997

Some of nationalism's psychological building blocks and fundamental
behavioural qualities, such as collective territoriality, solidarity based
on kinship (real or imagined), and hostility towards outsiders, can be
found among humans at every stage of historical development as well
as among many non-humans such as wolves and chimpanzees.
Aviel Roshwald, *The Endurance of Nationalism*, 2006

It has turned out much easier for specialists on earlier periods of history
to criticise modernists for their historical myopia than to offer an alternative account of equal substance. They are as united in their rejection
of modernist theories as they are divided in their historical location
of nationalism's origins. Some declare early medieval England the
first nation state;[1] others see it all beginning with the Bible and take
the ancient Jews for the fathers of nationalism;[2] some only speak of a
pre-modern 'ethnic' prologue leading up to the modern nation,[3] while
others prefer to speak of pre-modern patriotism turning into modern
nationalism;[4] some, including myself, relate the first forms of nationalism to Renaissance humanism,[5] and others treat it as an anthropological constant in many ways similar to animal behaviour.[6]

---

[1] Hastings, *The Construction*; for an overview on other studies, which discovered an
'Anglo-Saxon nation state' in the early Middle Ages, see Foot, 'The Historiography'.
[2] Goodblatt, *Elements*; Mendels, *The Rise and Fall*; Aberbach, *Jewish Cultural Nationalism*.
[3] This approach is usually based on Smith, *The Ethnic Origins*.
[4] Among the most recent exponents of this old distinction are Wrede, *Das Reich*;
Schmidt, *Vaterlandsliebe*.
[5] Münkler e.a., *Nationenbildung*; Hirschi, *Wettkampf der Nationen*.
[6] See, among others, Roshwald, *The Endurance*.

34

Thus, many anti-modernists today have actually more in common with certain modernists than with other anti-modernists. Still – and this makes things even worse – they tend to be lumped together as 'primordialists' by their modernist opponents, a term reflecting the general confusion about constructivism, as it implies that arguing for pre-modern forms of nation formation is incompatible with a constructivist approach. So the ongoing dominance of modernists in nationalism studies owes a lot to the chronic weakness displayed by anti-modernists.

Furthermore, the criticism of the modernist view on nationalism is constricted by another prevalent pattern. Many anti-modernists confine themselves to producing evidence for an earlier origin of nations and nationalism without trying to explain why and how nations emerged at all. As a result, they are not easily able to develop an alternative theory that can equal the explanatory power of the modernist approach.

Given this situation, the requirements for an effective counter-model to the modernist approach can be outlined as follows: (1) a set of definitions that distances itself from the modernist fixation on state politics and applies to different times and places, clearly defining how to distinguish nations from other communities; (2) a consistent argument about the historical conditions under which nationalism emerged and expanded; (3) broad historical evidence from different times and places taken from contemporary sources; (4) a precise comparison of pre-modern and modern forms of nationalism, stressing both continuities and discontinuities and explaining nationalism's greater power and scope in modern times; (5) a set of methodological tools to link nationalism to its agents and their interests and motivations.

3.1 How to describe the nation?

The starting point of my theory is at one remove from the usual perspective on nations and nationalism. To define the nation as a specific community, generations of scholars have tried to formulate an *internal* design principle. In this regard, modernists are in the same boat as those they criticise for using 'objective' criteria, such as language, customs etc. The results of all these definitions, however, have never been specific enough. Wherever a process of civilisation has developed, complex communities have evolved which believe in a common culture, origin and territory and claim self-determination. All of them are inevitably limited, and many treat political and cultural boundaries as identical, because either they do not distinguish them, like many tribal communities do, or they justify political power by cultural arguments, as many empires did, praising themselves for blessing the conquered with their civilisation.

Instead, it is more promising to separate the nation from other communities by formulating an *external* design principle that is an analytical model about the way the nation constructs the world beyond its borders. Such a definition may draw on a comparison of the nation with other abstract communities of similar size and scope. For this purpose I will choose empires, codified religions and tribal communities. To avoid any misunderstandings, however, I first need to stress that my distinctions do not aim to reveal the 'essence' of nations and nationalism; they simply offer an analytical toolkit to classify the endless varieties of abstract communities, which, in reality, never completely conform to the 'ideal type' of my classification.

What I attribute to empires, codified religions and tribal cultures is a predominantly bipolar and unequal relationship to the world outside. What does this mean? I will start with the example of empires, which is the most important for my argument. Imperialist cultures can be described as expansive entities, based on the ideal of a single universal power, formed by a hierarchical opposition of a civilised self and a barbarian other. As is best known from the Roman Empire, imperialist cultures are able to distinguish between different barbarian collectives, but even if they do so, they classify them together as 'uncivilised' to assert their fundamental otherness and – in most cases – their profound inferiority to the collective self. On the basis of such an unequal bipolarity, a notion of barbarian competitiveness with the civilised world can hardly develop (see Figure 1).

A typical example of imperialist thinking is the ethnographical reasoning by the Roman architect Vitruvius, dating from the first century BC. In the following passage, the term *natio* designates, as was the rule in classical Latin, the barbarian strangers, whereas *populus* is reserved for the civilised Romans:

But although southern nations (*meridianae nationes*) have the keenest wits, and are infinitely clever in forming schemes, the moment it comes to displaying valour they succumb because all manliness of spirit is sucked out of them by the sun. On the other hand, men born in cold countries are indeed readier to meet the shock of arms with great courage and without timidity, but their wits are so slow that they will rush to the charge inconsiderately and inexpertly, thus defeating their own devices. Such being nature's arrangement of the universe, and all these nations (*omnes nationes*) being allotted temperaments which are lacking in due moderation, the truly perfect territory, situated in the middle of the earth, and having on each side the entire extent of the world and its countries, is that which is occupied by the Roman people (*populus Romanus*). In fact,

Figure 1 This Roman coin is the first of four images to illustrate
the cultural transformation from imperialism to nationalism. It was
minted in AD 85 to celebrate Emperor Domitian's (unsuccessful)
campaign against the Germanic *Chatti*. The figure on the right is a
female personification of *Germania*. Her bare breasts, rumpled hair
and tight trousers symbolise barbarism, her mourning gesture and
the broken spear defeat. In contrast, the Emperor on the front side
of the coin embodies victory (laurel wreath) and civilisation (shaved
skin, noble profile). The coin – itself a symbol of civilisation –
was only addressed to the Roman public. It reflects a complete
indifference to the Germanic perception of the military clash. The
two sides can thus be seen as typical of the bipolar and unequal
relationship cultivated by imperialist cultures towards foreigners.

the races (*gentes*) of Italy are the most perfectly constituted in both respects – in
bodily form and in mental activity – to correspond to their valour. Exactly as the
planet Jupiter is itself temperate, its course lying midway between Mars, which
is very hot, and Saturn, which is very cold, so Italy, lying between the north and
the south, is a combination of what is found on each side, and her pre-eminence
is well regulated and indisputable. And so by her wisdom she breaks the cour-
ageous onsets of the barbarians and by her strength of hand thwarts the devices
of the southerners. Hence, it was the divine intelligence that set the city of the
Roman people (*civitas populi Romani*) in a peerless and temperate country, in
order that it might acquire the right to command the whole world.[7]

Drawing upon the Greek geographer Posidonius, Vitruvius explains
the insurmountable gap between barbarians and Romans with climato-
logical and astronomical necessity. His logic goes that there is a direct
link from planets to climate, from climate to bodies, from bodies to wits

[7] Vitruvius, *Ten Books on Architecture* (*De Architectura*), VI, 10–11.

and from wits to achievements. Only the people in the happy medium of temperate regions – those who live 'in the middle of the earth' – are capable of civilisation. It was widespread logic in Ancient Greece and Rome, and indeed well suited to justify cultural exclusiveness on territorial grounds.

As to codified religions, they generally operate with unequal and bipolar oppositions similar to imperialist cultures, and if they happen to be a partial offspring of one, such as Christianity of Greek and Roman civilisation, they share even more than that. Yet, the principal antagonism they are based on is between believers and heathens or heretics. Even the Christian triad of Christians, Jews and pagans can be reduced to a dual *sub specie Dei*, as Jews and pagans ultimately face the same alternative: convert or perish.

Tribal communities, on the other hand, can be associated with an even more radical demarcation pattern; it is more difficult to depict but can be paraphrased as humans vs. non-humans because there is often no term for human beings within tribal languages other than the one denoting their own community; collective names such as *Suomi*, *Inuit*, *Magyar*, *Nanai*, *Nganasan*, *Goths* and *Alemanni* all literally mean 'men' or 'humans'.

The idea of geographical space corresponding to communities built on unequal bipolarity can be called centralist: one's own living space lies, as seen in Vitruvius' treatise, at the centre of the world or even the universe, and the further the distance from the middle, the bigger the anthropological gap; while one's own community is a divine creation and its members are godlike beings, the people on the margins of the world are animal-like creatures or monsters. Such a visualisation of space can be observed from Ancient Persia to Egypt, from Greece to Rome and from China to Japan.[8] Centralist constructions of space are reflected in geographical names, too, such as 'Mediterranean' (*mediterraneus* meaning 'in the middle of the earth') or 'Middle Kingdom' (*chung-kuo*).

3.2   Equality and multipolarity

Compared to empires, tribal communities and codified religions, nations can be described as a marked exception. Their relationships to foreign communities can neither be called bipolar, because they face a multitude of independent communities with unique attributes, nor can they be named unequal, as these communities are assigned to exactly

[8] Smith, *The Cultural Foundations of Nations*, 40–1.

the same category, 'nation'. Nations' 'foreign relations' are instead to be characterised as multipolar and equal and the corresponding conception of space can be described as multicentric. Nations are formed by their relations to other nations.

As a consequence, the creation of nationalism leads to the formation of not only one, but of several nations, and the members of a nation have to engage much more intensely with the world outside than the members of a community based on unequal bipolarity. In a world of nations, one needs to have a certain idea of how other nations see themselves in order to characterise oneself. To draw the same comparison once more, the Romans did not need to take into account the self-image of those humans they viewed as barbarians in order to define themselves as civilised; quite the opposite, they had to ignore it to large degree, because it could not be reconciled with their own image of the 'barbarian' other. The same applies to codified religions and tribal cultures. Concepts of unequal bipolarity are generally not meant to enable an understanding of foreigners' self-perceptions.[9]

By contrast, in a world of nations, the self-image of a nation can only be defined in juxtaposition to the self-images of other nations. This requires a considerable degree of mutual understanding, which in turn requires a considerable degree of cultural common ground.

Erasmus (*c.* 1466–1536) was one of the first to describe the construction of national self-images as a comparative enterprise, not least because he was unhappy with it. Advocating a peaceful political pluralism within Christianity he lamented, in his *Praise of Folly* of 1511, that all nations, instead of being humble, indulged in self-love and tried to acquire recognition for exceptional qualities and accomplishments:

The English think they have a monopoly, amongst other things, on female beauty, musical talent, and fine food. The Scots pride themselves on their nobility and the distinction of their royal connections as much as on their subtlety in dialectic. The French lay claim to polite manners and the Parisians demand special recognition for their theological acumen, which they think exceeds nearly everyone else's. The Italians usurp culture and eloquence, and hence they're all happy congratulating themselves on being the only civilized race of men ... Meanwhile the Greeks, as originators of the arts, imagine they should still share the honours of the illustrious heroes of their past; while the Turks and all the real barbarian riff-raff actually demand recognition for their religion and pour scorn on Christians for their superstition ... The Spaniards admit no rival in the glories of war, while the Germans boast of their height and their knowledge of the magic arts.[10]

---

[9] Koselleck, 'Zur historisch-politischen Semantik asymmetrischer Gegenbegriffe', 213.
[10] Erasmus, *Praise of Folly*, 68–9 (translation revised by Hirschi).

The picture of a multitude of abstract communities comparing themselves with each other at a collective vanity fair is hardly possible outside
a nationalist culture. Erasmus' portrayal of nations may be broad-brush
and disparaging, but it illustrates, too, that the particular quality, territory and history of a nation are always a matter of negotiations and
struggles between members both of different nations and the same
nation. With national discourses being so closely interlinked, nations
are to be seen as outward creations to a considerable extent. In effect,
it is one of the great paradoxes of nationalism that it praises national
self-determination as one of the highest goods while being constantly
transformed by foreign influence.

3.3   The nation: a product of failed imperialisms

Communities that construct their relationship to outsiders on a multipolar and equal basis have serious disadvantages, compared to communities that circumscribe themselves by bipolar and unequal oppositions.
They are more complex and unstable, and the task of proving their
worth and uniqueness is more onerous. So the question arises as to why
and how such a laborious and insecure system could emerge and persist
in the long run alongside bipolar constructions of abstract communities. I will try to answer this both theoretically and historically.

In order to determine the most basic preconditions of nationalism,
I propose to start with a vast space inhabited by a single high culture
and split into several polities; while the overarching culture enables an
intense exchange between the educated elites within the whole space,
the political landscape ensures a multiplicity of powers. Furthermore,
I suggest specifying the overarching high culture as imperialist and the
leading powers as similarly strong. The rest can be deduced: the discrepancy between the imperialist ideal of a single hegemonic power and
the reality of many polities launches a competition for political supremacy. But as the leading powers are of similar strength, they are able to
prevent each other from reaching the goal they all follow. If they are
successful in building temporary coalitions against the strongest power
among them, they all remain would-be empires caught in a multipolar
struggle without end. Over time, their political competition develops
its own dynamics; it expands to a cultural and moral competition, and
finally continues independently of its original imperialist impulse – in
other words, it transforms into nationalism.

To apply the theoretical argument to history, such a space was provided by Roman Christianity in the Middle Ages due to its century-
long simultaneity of an imperialist political culture and a fragmented

territorial structure. In other words, the origins of nationalism can be attributed to an equally persistent and powerful anachronism, caused by the legacy of the Roman Empire.

Although the great migration period in late Antiquity affected all parts of southern Europe, its long-term political effects differed markedly between East and West. While the Eastern Roman Empire survived the foreign invasions largely unscathed, the Western Empire was irreversibly transformed into a plurality of dominions that later underwent profound transformations themselves. However, through all these changes of power structures, the power culture remained shaped by Roman ideals. The Papal Church, claiming the heritage of the Roman Empire, divided its realm along the Roman provincial borders, even if administrative requirements or territorial changes suggested adjustments. Latin preserved a monopoly as the written language and even rose to the status of sacred language, with Hebrew and Greek being lost by theologians of the Roman Church. And with the reign of Charlemagne (768–800), the Papal realm had a Roman Emperor again. Thus, medieval culture, at least on the upper strata, can be described as a secondary Roman civilisation.

Charlemagne's coronation as Emperor by Pope Leo III in 800 was, with hindsight, legitimised by a historico-theological theory, which held that world history proceeded in a series of universal empires, with the Roman Empire as the last, leading to the end of time. The cornerstones of this theory had already been laid down in late Antiquity by church father Jerome (347–420) in his commentary on Daniel. What was later added was the idea that the Roman Empire itself could be transferred both from one place to another – and from one people to another – without coming to an end yet. And so after Charlemagne's coronation, the narrative went that the Roman Empire had first moved from the Romans to the Greeks under Constantine the Great (c. 272–337) and then from the Greeks to the Franks. This theory, later known as *translatio imperii*, became influential throughout the medieval period and some aspects of it (such as the idea of a westward movement of succeeding empires) can still be detected in imperialist thinking in early modern France, Britain and, even later, the United States.[11]

As exotic as the idea of *translatio imperii* might sound to modern ears, it helped to pave the way for nationalism. Soon after Charlemagne's death, his territory was split into three kingdoms with none of them regaining a hegemonic position, but each claiming imperial status. Even when Otto II, Duke of Saxony, was crowned Emperor in 962 and

---

[11] Hirschi, 'Konzepte von Fortschritt und Niedergang'.

Figure 2 This illustration from the Gospels of Otto III (*c.* AD 1000)
indicates the changing position of Germany during the adaptation of
the imperialist culture of Ancient Rome to the medieval Holy Roman
Empire. The relationship between the Emperor and Germany is still
depicted as unequal but no longer as bipolar. Germany now appears
as one of four provincial peoples paying tribute to the Emperor. As
such, she appears as a blonde queen, not as a barbarian woman.
Furthermore, Germany now stands on the same level as Rome, which
would have been unimaginable in Antiquity. Rome only retains the
symbolic precedence to offer her tribute to Otto first. The Emperor
himself is portrayed as a ruler over a plurality of different peoples
(*gentes*), who are of almost equal political weight.

his successors kept hold of the title for centuries, this did not stop other
European kings from regarding themselves worthier of the title and
supporting their views with new reasoning (see Figure 2).

A significant output of such alternative imperialist propaganda was
yet another historical transfer theory called *translatio studii*. It was meant
to buttress the French King's aspirations for imperial status and gained

Figure 2 *cont.*

political weight in the thirteenth century. Its argument was based on the ancient ideal that the centre of political power had to coincide with the centre of civilisation and education. This argument had already motivated Roman authors like Horace (*Epistles* 2,1, vv. 156/57) and Cicero (*Tusculan disputations* 4,1) to indicate a transference of education from the defeated Greeks to the victorious Romans. Now, the University of Paris successfully claimed to be the universal centre of education thanks to the deeds of its supposed founder, Charlemagne. Under his reign, so the story went, there was not only a *translatio imperii* from the Byzantines, but a *translatio studii*, too, and Paris was chosen as the future seat of Christian theology and civilisation. With this, the French were not only portrayed as the true heirs of the Franks, but scholarship was forcefully introduced as a major component of the competition for imperial dignity, and the scholars engaged in these symbolic battles could promote themselves as key players on the stage of 'universal' politics.

3.4   Competing for honour and freedom

Charlemagne's reign transformed the decentralised territorial structure from the early Middle Ages and intensified the competition between the bigger monarchies struggling for 'universal' dominion, while the Papacy tried to maintain a balance of power to its own advantage. Even the inner consolidation of occidental monarchies that evolved in the same period was ideologically based on imperialist arguments derived from Roman law. To make a case for a king's full power within his own territory, jurists declared that he be regarded as 'emperor in his own kingdom' (*rex est imperator in regno suo*) and invoked the duty of all his subjects to serve the common fatherland unconditionally, referring to the language of Roman patriotism as it was reflected in the *Corpus Iuris Civilis*. This legal adaptation of Roman law to the different kingdoms solidified the multipolar territorial structure of Western Europe without mitigating its imperialist political culture; it created a multiplicity of independent mini-empires which were all eager to overcome what was generally seen as an unfortunate interval of political fragmentation. Ironically, this was exactly how the mini-empires prevented each other from becoming the single Christian power (see Figure 3).

With all major medieval powers – the Empire, the Papacy, France, England and, as a late-comer, Aragon – at similar strength, the situation led to a sort of turbulent stability and gave rise to Europe's unique inner dynamic, both politically and culturally. And as time went on, the ongoing anachronism generated even stronger centrifugal forces, which gradually turned the political competition among kingdoms into an all-encompassing competition among territorial collectivities that did not even need an imperialist motivation anymore.

It was here that nationalism came into play. It ensured that the contest between European states was pursued at a more fundamental level, reaching out to a wider audience and including more cultural fields. And in the long run, it weakened the vain dream of a single Christian Empire by the quest to acquire 'national honour' and secure 'national freedom' in competing against other nations (see Figure 4).

During the first stage, this competition was confined to Western Europe, proceeding as a 'domestic' Christian affair. At this point, nationalism was also adopted by lesser European powers without

Figure 3 At the beginning of the early modern period, Germany sits on the throne. This image is part of a miniature triumph drafted and ordered by Maximilian I in 1513. The Emperor dictated that the 'German woman' should wear her hair loose and have a crown on her head. The artist placed the blonde queen on the Imperial throne and invested her with the Imperial insignia. She was thus sitting in the place of the Emperor. The depiction corresponds to Maximilian's self-image as both Emperor and 'King of Germany' as well as to the contemporary formula 'Holy Roman Empire of the German nation'. By omitting other European nations, the miniature painting implicitly acknowledges their independence from the German single-nation Empire.

imperialist ambitions such as Switzerland, which was dragged into the competition by German nationalists around 1500 and later used its standing as a nation to avoid being eaten up by neighbouring monarchies and infighting cantons.[12]

Then, during the second stage of European colonial expansion, the competition quickly reached a global level, but was still monopolised by European nations, combined with a renewed imperialist fervour,

---

[12] Hirschi, 'Eine Kommunikationssituation zum Schweigen', 233.

L'IMPRIMERIE, descendant des Cieux, est accordée par Minerve et Mercure à l'Allemagne, qui la présente à la Hollande, l'Angleterre, l'Italie, & la France, les quatre prémieres Nations chés les quelles ce bel Art fut adopté

Figure 4 This allegorical rendering of the invention and perfection of print, produced in 1740, shows the cultural competition of nations in full swing. It depicts the printing press as a heavenly gift handed over by Minerva and Mercury to Germany, who presents it to Holland, England, Italy and France. All nations hold portraits of famous printers among their own countrymen, thereby forming a group of interacting contestants. The engraving draws on more than two hundred years of nationalist claims to pre-eminence in print. It gives Germany credit for the original invention, but portrays her as one of many nations in the subsequent rivalry for achievements in printing. This illustrates the multipolar and equal relationships between European peoples, out of which the competitive culture of nationalism evolved.

this time mostly projected to other continents. Finally, within the third stage, from the beginning of decolonisation to the present, it spread to a world-spanning, all-inclusive competition, but remained regulated, at least *de jure*, by international organisations and international law.

If nationalism is to be seen as an unwanted product of failed imperialism, it did not, as my historical stage model indicates, replace imperialist aspirations completely. As I will show in the coming chapters, imperialist and nationalist impulses could often go hand in hand or even intertwine. This is still the case today, and my proposition to differentiate abstract communities by external design principles may also be helpful to assess, for instance, in what respects the current political culture of the United States can be described as nationalist and in what respects as imperialist.

3.5   Definitions

At this point, we can attempt an initial definition of nations and nationalism. The nation can be understood as an abstract community formed by a multipolar and equal relationship to other communities of the same category (i.e. other nations), from which it separates itself by claiming singular qualities, a distinct territory, political and cultural independence and an exclusive honour. Nations are thus products and producers of a competitive culture and engage in endless contests about material and symbolic values, from warfare to sports, from the fine arts to gross domestic products, from Nobel Prize winners to beauty queens. At the centre of the competition lies the concept of national honour and national shame, in which all members of the community are supposed to have a share, according to individual status and merit. The 'economy' of national honour works on a highly abstract level, as the nation itself is an abstract community with most of its members not knowing and never seeing each other.

Nationalism can be defined as the discourse that creates and preserves the nation as an autonomous value, 'autonomous' meaning not subordinate (but neither necessarily superior) to any other community. With the criterion of autonomy, I propose to replace another main criterion in many definitions of nationalism during the past decades, which goes back at least to Hayes' Essay 'What is Nationalism?' of 1926.[13] It is the idea that nationalism is a doctrine demanding the highest rank in a 'hierarchy of loyalties' that regulates every individual's thinking and behaviour.

---

[13] Hayes, *Essays on Nationalism*, 6.

I have two reservations here. The first is a general one: I do not think that the concept of a personal 'hierarchy of loyalties' has much analytical value because it implies a far too stable foundation of human behaviour. People tend to reshuffle their values and loyalties in accordance with changing surroundings and circumstances and, instead of following an established list of priorities, negotiate them time and again with families, friends, colleagues, fellow countrymen and fellow believers.

My second reservation is more specific and questions why nationalism needs to repress other loyalties in order to be powerful. Most scholars using this argument do not specify whether nationalism only claims, or indeed enforces, superiority over religion, class or other collective loyalties. The claim itself is undoubted and can easily be traced back, as I will show in the next chapter, to Roman patriotism. However, I believe that one cannot describe the history of nationalism accurately by turning the nationalist claim into an analytical category; on the contrary, I would argue that nationalism became so powerful and widespread because it easily coexisted or even amalgamated with other loyalties and doctrines, using their symbolic resources without necessarily devaluating them. The Irish of the nineteenth and twentieth century did not need to be less Catholic to become nationalists, and the same applies to British Protestants of earlier centuries. Neither did German or Swiss Protestants of the late nineteenth century, who accused their Catholic countrymen of 'Ultramontanism' (loyalty to the Pope), need to clarify if they themselves preferred nationalism to Protestantism; they rather made the point that there was no conflict of loyalties, and thereby revealed that nationalist and confessional issues were inextricably blurred in the *Kulturkampf*.

This is why I use the word 'autonomy'. According to this term, nationalism does not need to clarify its standing *vis-à-vis* other loyalties and doctrines as long as its broad claims are not restrained by them. Neither are these claims to be considered a 'doctrine', as they are not fixed in authoritative scripture and therefore much more malleable and adaptable than the dogmas of codified religions. Indeed, the whole argument of a hierarchy of loyalties may have been deduced from a more comprehensive (mis-)understanding, likewise launched by Hayes,[14] that nationalism was to be seen as a cultural equivalent to and a secular surrogate of codified religion.

Before we can leave the dry business of definition, I have to introduce a third term, 'national discourse', that includes all forms of speaking

---

[14] Ibid., 93–125.

about nations, which are not covered by my definition of nationalism – from, say, Erasmus' anti-nationalism to my own nationalism studies. The reason why it is important to consider these alternative forms, too, is that they can also take part in the construction of nations. An anti-nationalist political propagandist, for instance, is not necessarily less involved in moulding national communities than a nationalist one. From this perspective, it seems appropriate to call these various modes of speaking 'national discourses', and to treat nationalism as a specific form of national discourse, which, as already mentioned, describes the nation as an autonomous value.

In the following chapters, I will specify how the transformation from chronically failing imperialism to slowly prevailing nationalism evolved during the late Middle Ages and the early modern period. In so doing, I will give particular consideration to the social position and role of those who prepared and largely managed this transformation: legally and historically trained scholars. Although, in retrospect, they served as agents of inevitable change, they did so mostly unknowingly, following their own agenda, guided by professional ambitions and social constraints. Thus, their specific places and functions in late medieval and early modern society need to be highlighted too, in order to understand the process of nation formation within Europe.

4 Killing and dying for love: the common fatherland

> The fatherland is so precious to all men that legislators everywhere punish the worst offences with exile as the heaviest penalty at their command. And not only legislators think this way; army generals who want to encourage their troops formed for battle can only tell them: 'Fight for your fatherland!' No one wants to disgrace himself when hearing this; the name of fatherland turns even a coward into a brave man.
>
> Lucian, *An Encomium of Fatherland*, around AD 160

> I see you do not know how sweet the love of the fatherland is: if it was expedient for the fatherland's protection or enlargement, it would seem neither burdensome and difficult nor a crime to thrust the axe into one's father's head, to crush one's brothers or to pull out the unborn child from the womb of one's wife with a sword.
>
> Coluccio Salutati, *Letter to Andrea di ser Conte*, 1366

'All roads lead to Rome' was a phrase unheard of in Antiquity, and neither had it anything to do with the Roman road network initially. 'A thousand roads lead men forever to Rome' (*Mille viae ducunt homines per saecula Romam*) wrote the theologian and poet Alain de Lille in his *Book of Parables* (*Liber Parabolarum*) around 1175. He coined a religious metaphor to describe the wide variety of ways to reach salvation. Most ancient Romans would never have thought in these terms, yet without them, this metaphor would not have been possible. The same can be said about nationalism. There were no nationalists walking the streets of Ancient Rome, but when considering nationalism's origins, all roads lead to Rome.

Of the utmost importance is the language of patriotism. It addressed a basic problem each body politic has to deal with: how can individuals be motivated to become involved in public affairs? The main reason why patriotism has proved so successful to this day is that it establishes a system of strong coercion with subtle force. It subjugates people to the dictates of the body politic by invoking an unconditional love and constant fear for the community, which is aimed at the creation of a collective sense of self-sacrifice for the higher good.

To produce the emotional attachment it needs in order to function, patriotic rhetoric invests much in invoking enemies, but these enemies are not necessarily fashioned as foreigners, and neither is the shaping of the world outside the political community one of patriotism's priorities. Patriotism is a 'domestic' discourse, stipulating the ties between the individual person and the state and between private and public interests. It depends on a complementary discourse with which it is closely interlinked and which defines the relationship between the political community and the foreign world. In ancient Rome, this discourse was generally imperialism, labelling the non-Roman world as barbaric; in modern Europe, it is predominantly, yet not exclusively, nationalism.

Patriotism is a language that uses a set of strong emotions, such as love, fear, pride and hatred, combined with high values, such as liberty, vigilance, selflessness and conscientiousness. They are all vague enough to be helpful for diverse purposes, from fighting a foreign enemy to justifying a literary existence, from expanding to curtailing civil rights; and they are all flexible enough to be attractive to different political systems, from oligarchy to monarchy, from democracy to dictatorship.

To be effective, patriotism requires not much more than a clear sense of territory, understood as an inalienable collective property, and an idea of freedom attached to this territory, designating it as a sphere of complete self-determination.

Besides its chameleon-like adaptability, another reason why patriotism has become a forceful language in many societies all over the world is that it evokes an image of the political community dear to most people in patriarchal cultures: the family. The basic goal of patriotic propaganda is to convince citizens or subjects that there is a bigger family which they belong to and which deserves an even stronger dedication than their own. This is, of course, a simplistic – and in many ways inconsistent – representation of every political power, especially of complex systems, such as the Roman Empire and the modern bureaucratic state. However, it creates a concrete and powerful image of an abstract community, to which it can tie the emotions and values it evokes.

Strong family values of a patriarchal type are thus another requirement for the propaganda success of patriotism. There is, for instance, much to be said for the assumption that patriotic rhetoric sounded more and more ridiculous in the ears of many Westerners from the 1960s onwards because of the simultaneous decline of traditional family values, and it is equally probable that the renewed patriotic fervour in the same countries in recent years is partly due to the parallel revival of conservative, middle-class family ideals.[1]

In ancient Greece and Rome, the principal addressee of patriotic propaganda was the *kyrios* or *pater familias*, the male head of the family, who bore the legal responsibility for the well-being of his dependants and for the defence of his house and land; in Roman law, the patriarch had almost unrestricted power over his children, wife and slaves (*patria potestas*). In most Greek cities, despite considerable constitutional differences, the heads of every household (*oikos*) formed the backbone of the political community (*polis*). When Aristotle described an 'excellent person's' attitude towards his friends and his native country, he gave an implicit portrait of the ideal *kyrios*, who acted according to the same values in his private and in his public commitments:

> It is quite true that, as they say, the excellent person labours for his friends and for his native country, and will die for them if he must; he will sacrifice money, honours and contested goods in general, in achieving the fine for himself. For he will choose intense pleasure for a short time over slight pleasure for a long time; a year of living finely over many years of undistinguished life; and a single fine and great action over many small actions. This is presumably true for anyone who dies for others; he does indeed choose something great and fine for himself.[2]

Aristotle expected sacrifice, but not selflessness, from a great man. His patriotic act would not go unrewarded; on the contrary, an excellent person 'will both help himself and benefit others by doing fine actions'. The understanding of sacrifice in this passage is deeply secular and utilitarian, but the point of reference used to make the argument is opaque. Why is it fine to die for others? Aristotle promised the intensity and honour of a noble existence, driven by the quest to perform extraordinary acts of benevolence for friends and countrymen. His ideal patriot was an aristocratic figure eager to distance himself from the humdrum existence of the many. It was a sign of distinction to prefer risking one's life to one's reputation.

Compared to Aristotle's secular justification of patriotic acts, Roman patriotism had a rather sacred touch. It was an integral part of a complex 'political religion' covering this life and the afterlife of Roman citizens, which was one reason why many patriotic leitmotifs could later be integrated easily into Roman Christianity. Although Rome had developed a strong and distinct cult of the fatherland long before it came under the influence of Hellenic culture, the patriotic language and literature with

---

[1] Smith and Kim, 'National Pride', 3.
[2] Aristotle, *Nicomachean Ethics 9, 8*, 147–8.

Figure 5 Marcus Tullius Cicero (106–43 BC); Augustan marble copy of a bust dating from the late Republic.

which Rome later came to be identified and which exerted the greatest influence on European history, mostly dates from the last century BC, when Roman elites were eagerly imitating their Greek subjects. Indeed, it was one of the most hellenised Roman lawyers, politicians and philosophers who shaped patriotism's outlook more than anyone else. This was Marcus Tullius Cicero (106–43 BC) (see Figure 5).

4.1   Cicero and the construction of the ideal patriot

Why did Cicero's speeches, dialogues and treatises have such an impact on the history of patriotism? Partly because he embodied a long-lasting ideal of a statesman, which he had co-invented and propagated himself; this was the *orator doctus*, a term that stood for much more than its literal translation 'learned speaker'.[3] It represented an ideal combination

---

[3] The term is introduced in Cicero, *On the Ideal Orator* (*De oratore*) *III*, xxxv, 143.

of scholar and politician who excelled in two tasks; he was qualified
to take the right decisions for his political community, thanks to his
deep insights into history, law and human nature, and he was capable
of convincing all participants in the political process of the rightness
of his propositions, thanks to his study of language and his rhetorical
skills.[4] These two skills were combined in the term *humanitas*, which
was largely coined by Cicero, too.[5]

Although Cicero ended as a failed politician, falling victim to the
power struggle between Octavian and Mark Antony after Caesar's
murder in 44 BC, he had accumulated enough political successes during
an extraordinarily long career in the Senate to make his ideal of *orator
doctus* appear credible to both contemporaries and future generations.
The fact that he was from a family of relatively modest origin (his father
was a member of the *equites* class in the small town of Arpinum) made
his rise in Roman politics look even more remarkable.

One of his greatest political triumphs was his discovery and suppres-
sion of Catiline's plot to overthrow the Roman government in 63 BC.
Cicero was consul during that year, and Catiline, offspring of an old
patrician family, had been his competitor for the office, which was the
highest in the Republic; unwilling to accept his defeat, Catiline had
directed his plan of a violent *coup d'état* directly against Cicero and his
followers.

The sense of urgency in Cicero's first Senate speech against the plot-
ter must have seemed genuine to his public, but what might have been
even more important for the outcome of the affair was his ability to
turn the attack on himself into an assault on the Roman fatherland.
The starting point of his argument was the classical reference to family
values; addressing Catiline directly while he was attending the Senate
meeting, he said: 'If your parents feared and hated you, and if you could
by no means pacify them, you would, I think, depart somewhere out of
their sight.'

In the following sentences, Cicero drew the analogy between family
and fatherland by invoking a fearsome but firm lady who was able to
speak for herself; she was the *patria* personified:

Now, your fatherland, which is the common parent of all of us, hates and fears
you, and has no other opinion of you, than that you are contemplating parri-
cide in her case; and will you neither respect her authority, nor defer to her
judgement, nor fear her power? And she, O Catiline, thus pleads with you,

[4] Idem, *On Invention (De inventione)* 5–6; idem, *On the Ideal Orator (De oratore)* I, V–VI, 17–21.
[5] Scholz, 'Der Senat und die Intellektualisierung der Politik', 21–2.

and, though silent, somehow speaks to you: 'For many years now, there has been no crime committed but by you; no atrocity has taken place without you: you alone have murdered the citizens, have harassed and plundered our allies, while escaping punishment and remaining free; you alone have managed not only to neglect the laws and the courts, but to overturn and shatter them. Your previous crimes, intolerable as they were, I bore as well as I could; but now that I should be racked with fear because of you, that at every sound Catiline should be dreaded, that no plot should be formed against me without proceeding from your wickedness, this is no longer endurable. Depart, then, and deliver me from this fear; that, if it be justified, I may not be destroyed, that, if not, I may at least eventually cease to fear.'[6]

The analogy of family and fatherland ended with Cicero's conclusion: 'If your fatherland were to address you just as I have done, ought she not to obtain her request, even if she could not enforce it?' The lady's call was finally heard, but first she had to raise her voice again, this time appealing to Cicero as her chosen protector. After he had stressed that she was dearer to him than his own life, she urged him to action against her enemy.

When Cicero ended his speech, Catiline tried to counter directly by insisting that he was innocent and by making the point that he was a patrician, whereas Cicero was only an immigrant to Rome. Yet it was all to no avail; Catiline was shouted down as a traitor and enemy and had to leave the building hurriedly. In the following night, he slipped out of the city. Sallust, another learned politician who had been in the Senate that day and later wrote a history of Catiline's conspiracy, noted that Cicero's speech had been 'brilliant and beneficial to the state'.[7] The consul's success was all the more remarkable as Cicero had acted on thin legal ground pressing for the conviction and expulsion of a Roman citizen without trial.

On the next day, Cicero addressed the people of Rome in the so-called *contio*, the public assembly where the major magistrates could inform citizens about matters of public relevance, present senatorial policy or submit new proposals for ratification. Cicero repeated his will-ingness to die for the sake of the country, but the rest of his second speech stood in marked contrast to the first. Directing it at an audience who did not know Catiline as well as the Senators did, he attempted a full portrait of him as an enemy of the state. Catiline's political actions appeared as a direct consequence of a lecherous, gluttonous, avaricious and overambitious character, and the whole conflict was pictured as a clash of virtues and vices:

---

[6] Cicero, *First Oration against Catiline* (*In Catilinam I*) VII, 17–18.
[7] Sallust, *The Conspiracy of Catiline* (*Bellum Catilinae*) 31.

On our side fights decency, on theirs depravity; on ours chastity, on theirs perversion; on ours honesty, on theirs deceit; on ours duty, on theirs crime; on ours steadfastness, on theirs hysteria; on ours honour, on theirs disgrace; on ours self-restraint, on theirs self-indulgence; on ours justice, self-control, courage, prudence, and all the virtues, fighting against injustice, extravagance, sloth, recklessness, and all the vices; finally, wealth is fighting against poverty, good principles against bad, reason against madness, and well-grounded confidence against absolute despair.[8]

How could Cicero look credible to the people of Rome giving such a black-and-white account of the affair and painting a Senatorial patrician in the darkest of colours? He argued according to a well-established logic that someone who acted unpatriotically was a creature of a world upside down and could not possibly have any positive character trait at all. As we will see further down, Cicero even had a philosophical foundation on which he could develop this argument.

One month later, after the plot had been thwarted and many of its participants imprisoned, Cicero gave another public speech in the forum. For this event he had, with a sense for stage management, organised the replacement of a damaged statue of Jupiter in order to demonstrate to the people the renewed presence of the 'guardian of this city' who seemed to bless the order restored by Cicero to Rome.[9] Cicero declared that Rome was safe again, thanks to the 'great love of the immortal gods for you and by my labours, counsels and dangers', and he asked from his fellow citizens 'no reward of virtue, no badge of honour, no monument of my glory – except that you will remember this day forever'.[10] While Cicero's second speech had painted a picture of the complete traitor to his country, his third speech aimed at a self-portrait of the consul as a perfect patriot. The task was to claim full responsibility, but no reward, for the happy ending of a terrible constitutional crisis and thus demonstrate that he had accomplished a citizen's highest duty, the *defensio patriae*. His self-promotion proved an instant success, as he was conferred the rare honorific *pater patriae* – a title alluding to the role of *pater familias* – by the Senate shortly after the events.

After stepping down from the consulate, Cicero maintained, despite living in exile for a while, a considerable public influence, partly by editing his successful speeches and by publishing additional treatises and dialogues on political and philosophical issues; they strengthened his reputation as a learned statesman and great patriot and helped him to

---

[8] Cicero, *Second Oration against Catiline* (*In Catilinam II*) XI, 25.
[9] Cicero, *Third Oration against Catiline* (*In Catilinam III*) 29; Fantham, 'The Contexts and Occasions of Roman Public Rhetoric', 114.
[10] Cicero, *Third Oration against Catiline* (*In Catilinam III*) 26.

remain one of the most powerful figures in the Senate up to his death in 43 BC. Shortly before he was killed by pursuers sent from Mark Antony's entourage, Cicero even proclaimed that Mark Antony had not dared to kill him on an earlier occasion because of his patriotic nimbus: 'So great is men's affection for their fatherland, that I was sacred even in the eyes of your legions, because they recollected that the fatherland had been saved by me.'[11]

In his literary works, Cicero expanded his patriotic rhetoric to a rudimentary political philosophy, which was based on a foundation partly adopted from Greek literature. His writings were not only addressed to the citizens of Rome, but to all Roman citizens – that is, the privileged minority of free male inhabitants of both the capital and the provincial towns.

In his dialogue *On the Laws* (*De legibus*), Cicero attributed two different fatherlands to every citizen who was not born and raised in the city of Rome, as was his own case. The first was his *patria naturae* or *patria propria*, the place he came from and grew up in: 'Here is the most ancient origin of our stock,' Cicero said about his own town of origin Arpinum, 'here are our family rituals and our family; here there are many traces of our ancestors.' The second was his *patria civitatis* or *patria communis*, the common fatherland by law, which covered the whole territory of the Roman republic and belonged to 'the entire citizen body'. Both fatherlands deserved strong affections, but while the *patria propria* was related to the love of one's parents and steeped in nostalgic feelings about a blithe childhood in bucolic ambience, the *patria communis* demanded the highest duty and devotion as a body politic 'on behalf of which we have an obligation to die, to which we should give ourselves entirely and in which we should place and almost consecrate everything we have'.[12]

Cicero's distinction of two fatherlands soon became an integral part of Roman political culture and remained pivotal during the rapid expansion of the Empire in the subsequent centuries; it proved an effective instrument for stabilising newly acquired or conquered regions, as it did not deprive local elites of their traditional loyalties and affections, while admitting of no doubt that, as newly minted Roman citizens, they had to accept the supremacy of the common fatherland unconditionally and to change their attitudes accordingly.

As to the influence on modern history, Cicero's associations with the term *patria naturae* served as a model for what came to be called 'local

[11] Cicero, *Second Philippic* (*Philippicae*) 23.
[12] Cicero, *On the Laws* (*De legibus*) II, 3–6.

patriotism' and, perhaps more significantly, his subordination of all common bonds to the *patria communis* provided the central theme of the nationalist (and academic) commonplace of a hierarchy of loyalties – with the nation holding the top spot. In the passage of *De legibus*, Cicero described the two fatherlands as coexisting, but not as conflicting, collectivities; in his treatise *On Duties* (*De officiis*), however, he stressed the potential conflict of obligations that a citizen could face when dealing with their various affiliations. Interestingly, for this argument, which was presented in question and answer form, he replaced the *patria naturae* by the family:

> Does not duty to the fatherland take precedence of all other duties? Yes, indeed; but it is for the welfare of the fatherland to have citizens dutiful toward their parents. What if the father should attempt to usurp supreme authority, or to betray the fatherland? Shall the son keep silence? Yes, but he will implore his father not to do so. If that is of no avail, he will take him earnestly to task; will even threaten him; yet ultimately, if there is danger of great harm to the fatherland, he will prefer the fatherland's safety to his father's safety.[13]

Nothing could highlight the inexorable power of patriotism more than the killing of one's own parent to save the country. For centuries, learned men remained fascinated by this idea and wallowed in study-room daydreams of massacring their whole families out of love for their fatherland. The literary blood frenzy of the Florentine humanist Coluccio Salutati (1331–1406), quoted at the head of this chapter, is not an isolated case, and it is no coincidence either that Salutati was one of the first men in late medieval history to revive the ancient Roman ideal of *orator doctus*, acting as both the Chancellor of the Republic of Florence and as an eminent scholar, discovering, among other things, the lost letters of Cicero.

4.2   Ascetic love

However, the pointless killing spree invoked by Salutati to express his patriotic fervour belied the classical ideal of love of country (*amor patriae*) expressed by Cicero and other Roman authors. For them, although the devotion to the *patria communis* had to be uncompromising and unlimited, it was not supposed to be blinded by passion. It was no *amour fou*, but rather devotedness guided by a sense of duty and rational calculation. If the *patria* was personified as a woman, it hardly ever appeared as a young virgin to fall in love with; the standard

---

[13] Cicero, *On Duties* (*De officiis*) III, 90.

representation was a dignified, though vulnerable old lady, a mother figure, who wanted to be protected, not possessed. Cicero's *patria Roma* of the first *Catilinarian* provided a basic model on which poets of late Antiquity, such as Claudian and Prudentius, could flesh out more detailed personifications.[14] Giving the *patria* a dignified female identity was another subtle means to cement the patriarchal principle of patriotism.

Overall, there was hardly any eroticism resonating in the notion of patriotic love; quite the contrary, it was all about self-control and self-restraint. Love of the fatherland was meant to be a practice of asceticism, as Cicero's writings also point out. His concept of *amor patriae* is flanked by two virtues, which underline its altruistic character, devotion (*pietas*) and benevolence (*caritas*);[15] hence, patriotic love should express itself in acts of service (*officium*) and care (*cultus*).[16] The very same vocabulary was used later, as we will see further down, to compile the Christian catalogue of virtues and to encourage believers to supplant personal interest with religious convictions.

Cicero's ideal citizen was opposed to all sorts of lust and pleasure. In *De officiis* he argued that 'coupling pleasure with moral rectitude' amounted to yoking 'a man with a beast'.[17] These images were inspired by Stoic philosophy and were part of a sharp polemic against the popular doctrine of Epicureanism, which recommended a tranquil life of modest pleasures, avoiding any involvement in politics. For Cicero, such a privatisation of life was close to treason to the *patria*, and his portrait of Catiline, as depicted above, indeed equated to a caricature of a degenerate Epicurean, who had fallen victim to his own desires and, as a last step, tried to enslave the fatherland to his appetites.

The definition of patriotic love as deliberate self-abandonment was crucial in two ways: it distinguished a patriotic man in terms of moral superiority, and it created a mental disposition necessary for self-sacrifice. The categorical denial of physical needs and pleasures paved the way for a virtual disembodiment, from which it seemed only a last small step to suicide for the common good.

Now, while Aristotle presents patriotic willingness to die as an act of noble heroism, Cicero goes further. He develops patriotism into a political religion by declaring, in his famous *Dream of Scipio* (*Somnium Scipionis*) at the end of *On the Commonwealth* (*De re publica*), that 'for all those who have in any way contributed to the preservation, defence,

---

[14] Roberts, 'Rome Personified, Rome Epitomized'.
[15] Cicero, *On Invention* (*De inventione*) II, 66.
[16] Viroli, *For Love of Country*, 19–20.
[17] Cicero, *On Duties* (*De officiis*) III, 119.

and enlargement of their fatherland' death would not only bring an escape 'from the body as if from a prison', but 'a certain place in heaven where they shall enjoy an eternity of happiness'.[18] Thus, by the back door, Cicero holds out the prospect of a post-mortem compensation for foregone pleasures to the austere patriot.

The original stage for the patriot to carry out his duty of defending the fatherland (*defensio patriae*), if necessary to the death (*pro patria mori*), was the battlefield. Owing to the territorial expansion and the reduced military threats during the last two centuries BC, however, the political arena became increasingly relevant. Cicero, a civilian who had renounced a military career at an early age, invested much energy and rhetoric to raise the politician's work to an equal standing with a soldier's service, and received further, though unwanted, support by the constant political turmoil in the late Republic, which made the Senate floor almost as dangerous as a war zone.

Apart from these two platforms for performance of patriotic duty, there was, however, a third one, which was based on another obligation – the praise of the fatherland (*laus patriae*); this was disseminated through oratory and literature and its ideal performer was the learned speaker, poet, philosopher or historian. For Cicero, the greatest learned men were, 'though they have not personally governed the state, worthy of our consideration, because by their investigations and writings, they exercised a kind of political magistracy'.[19] His political rival, Sallust, and later Roman historians did not tire of emphasising that those who commemorated heroic deeds of the past by writing them down ensured that similar deeds would be accomplished in the future.[20] Thus, they presented political writers as masters of patriotic virtues and political writing as an active contribution to the well-being of the country. This was how, as early as in the late Roman Republic, scholars enabled themselves to become key players in the patriotic business.

4.3   Patriotic distortions of politics

Patriotism, as constructed by the late Republican Romans on Greek foundations, was a complex fabric of very different motifs, aimed at mobilising and disciplining all members of the state for almost any political purpose. We do not know how well it worked exactly, but there is a large amount of evidence to suggest that those who used it strongly

---

[18] Cicero, *Dream of Scipio (Somnium Scipionis)*, 13–14.
[19] Cicero, *On the Commonwealth (De re publica)* I, 12.
[20] Sallust, *The Jugurthine War (Bellum Iugurthinum)*, 4.

believed in its immediate effects, and we have even more evidence that its long-term effects exceeded all their expectations.

Yet, both then and later, the power of patriotic rhetoric came courtesy of massive distortions. First, the keynote of patriotic language was (and is) defence, based on the image of a free man's task to shelter his home and family; the patriot is portrayed as a guardian of women and children, a protector of the poor and the weak, a champion of the just cause. The fact that patriotic vocabulary does not propagate aggression and expansion has most significantly contributed to the positive image of patriotism down to the present day, with the confusing consequence that even the most clear-cut nationalists only speak of themselves as patriots.

However, the widely held assumption that patriotism is the good counterpart of evil nationalism stands on shaky ground. What most advocates of patriotism shut their eyes to is that patriotic language has, thanks to its obscuring effect, been helpful in propagating political expansion and aggression throughout history. Fashioning themselves as defending patriots, the Romans conquered the whole Mediterranean area and most of Western Europe, and, to give just the most recent example, the Americans and British have invaded Iraq.

Indeed, patriotic rhetoric is an excellent complement to imperialist policies, as it helps to cover their legal and moral dubiousness. According to its logic, a country's own aggression appears as self-defence and foreign self-defence as aggression, and thus a patriot is always in the right. Such distortions may be helpful to motivate and discipline citizens and subjects for political and military purposes, but they may also be harmful as they cloud perceptions and estimations of the self and others, which generally is a big step on the road to political disaster.

A second and even more prevalent distortion produced by the language of patriotism is the depiction of political power as service and of power holders as servants. To qualify as a patriot, a ruler or officeholder has to present himself as someone who never sought power and influence for his personal advancement, but only for the common good; the execution of his office has to appear as a sacrifice for his people. The cause of this constraint lies in a complete denial that winning personal power and influence can be a morally acceptable motivation for political commitment; its consequence is that politics is perceived as deeply dichotomous, fought over by the forces of good and evil: the selfishly ambitious, à la Catiline, and the selflessly humble, à la Cicero.

Once again, it was Cicero who vividly demonstrated the propagandistic efficiency and practical inconsistency of this attitude. In *De officiis* he stated that a citizen worthy of a chief position in government 'will give himself wholly up to the state, pursuing neither wealth nor power; and he will so watch over the entire state as to consult the well-being of all its citizens', preferring to face death rather than surrender his principles. He concluded his argument by adding that 'a most wretched custom, assuredly, is the electioneering and scrambling for office'. It needed quite a bit of self-denial to make such a point; as a younger man, Cicero himself had spent much time and energy canvassing and jockeying for office, and it was always a source of enormous pride to him to have completed the *cursus honorum*, the sequential order of high public offices, at the youngest possible age. Yet, when fashioning himself as a patriot, he had to obscure both his personal goals and the tactics he applied to achieve them.

The structural dysfunction resulting from the patriotic code of self-lessness is even more serious than the constraint on personal hypocrisy. Political decision-making is severely hampered if disagreement between policymakers carries the risk of mutual accusations of unpatriotic behaviour driven by base motives, and competition for political office is an extremely arduous process if rivals have to paint each other as unpleasant characters. Admittedly, patriotism's moral rigidity, which originally owed a great deal to Stoic philosophy, can be of little harm in a stable oligarchy where the political elite is united by strong common interests and where the competition for office is restricted through limited eligibility; it can be even less damaging in an autocracy where the ruler has no serious internal opponents and can enjoy, as many a Roman emperor did, the unchallenged reputation as the father of the fatherland (*pater patriae*). However, the same moral rigidity aggravates the instability of mobile oligarchies, such as the late Roman republic, and it is even more dysfunctional for the working of pluralist constitutions, such as modern multi-party democracy. Thus, the relationship between patriotic language and the modern democratic state is much more tension-filled than most contemporary politicians and many political scientists and historians of political thought would admit.

4.4   Patriotism's smooth transition from republic to principate

The political order Cicero struggled to uphold vanished with him, but his patriotic rhetoric proved adaptable to the changing circumstances; once the Principate was established, patriotic propaganda could again serve the conservative purpose of defending the political status quo against all attempts at change. Forty years after Cicero's death, in 2 BC, Augustus was given the title *pater patriae* by the Senate, and from then

on the honorific was reserved for emperors who were considered to have
rendered outstanding service to the country.

The transition of patriotism to a new political system was facilitated
by the fact that most political institutions and offices of the republican
era were preserved, albeit void of many of their previous powers and
functions; hence, a Roman citizen could still, at least symbolically, participate in the political process and believe in his civic duty to devote
himself to the country. Under the reign of Emperor Hadrian (76–138), a
Roman jurisprudent repeated that for the sake of the *patria* a son might
kill his father and a father his son, and his statement later became one
of many patriotic principles to be integrated into the corpus of Roman
law established by order of Emperor Justinian (*c.* 482–565).[21]

Even Lucian (*c.* 120–80), the irreverent satirist living at the height of
the Roman Empire, became less mocking when thinking of the fatherland. His *Encomium of Fatherland* (Πατρίδος Ἐγκώμιον) is an earnest,
if not solemn, meditation on the power of patriotism, repeating every
possible commonplace, from the unmatched sweetness of the motherly
status to the moral authority of the fatherland. Throughout his satirical
work, orthodox patriots are only rarely and casually teased, as in his *Life
of Demonax* (Δημώνακτος Βίος), a Cynic contemporary of his, of whom
he reported, 'Once at the bath he hesitated to get in because the water
was boiling hot, and when someone called him a coward, he asked:
"Tell me, is the fatherland expecting me to do my duty?"'[22]

Such remarks were obviously not very useful for compilers of law
books, in marked contrast to Cicero's exhortations to stoic conscientiousness, which, despite their original purpose of upholding the republic, ascended to the official position of codified patriotism during the
Empire. The Roman law of late Antiquity resonated with elements of
patriotic ethics. The *Institutes of Justinian*, for instance, recorded that
'those who fall in battle for the state (*res publica*) are understood to live
forever through their glory,'[23] and the *Digest* took over Cicero's distinction of *communis patria* and *patria propria* – in order to apply it to the law
of exile and deportation.[24] The fact that many patriotic principles dating from the late Republic acquired legal status in the time of Roman
imperial rule, some of them being significantly transformed, is a clear
indicator that the connection between patriotism and republicanism
was much weaker than is often assumed.

---

[21] *Corpus Iuris Civilis, Iustiniani Digesta*, 11.7.35; Kantorowicz, *The King's Two Bodies*, 245.
[22] Lucian, *Life of Demonax*, 42.
[23] *Corpus Iuris Civilis, Iustiniani Institutiones*, I, 25.
[24] *Corpus Iuris Civilis, Iustiniani Digesta*, 48.22.7.15–19.

4.5   From earth to heaven and back: the Middle Ages

Patriotic language underwent a far more profound transformation due to two overlapping processes in late Antiquity: Christianisation and the gradual disintegration of the Western Roman Empire. For centuries, the political order following the collapse of Western Rome remained characterised by a plethora of small-scale territories, many of volatile existence, and most, apart from certain urban societies in Italy, with a feudal structure built on hierarchical allegiances between vassals and lords. The core ideas of Roman patriotism were hardly applicable to this early medieval political landscape. A political sacrifice by a nobleman was expected to come as a personal act of fealty to his lord rather than as a public act of love for his country.[25] The corpus of Roman law, compiled in the Eastern Roman Empire, soon fell into desuetude in the West and was largely forgotten by the seventh century. Cicero's *De officiis*, meanwhile, remained one of the most influential and most copied classical texts throughout the Middle Ages, partly through its reworking and dissemination by the Church Fathers; its stoic message, however, was not directed at rulers and political life, but at clerics and monastic culture.

If elements of Roman patriotism were still applied to the early medieval political landscape, they usually derived from the concept of *patria propria*, the local homeland, which now could refer to both family and feudal bonds, but did not relate to a bigger and more demanding political *patria communis* anymore.[26] Poets and scholars continued to use the word *patria*, too, drawing upon classical models, such as Vergil's *Aeneid* (IV 660ff.) or Horace's famous verse: 'It is beautiful and honourable to die for the fatherland' (*dulce et decorum est pro patria mori*);[27] yet, they hardly ever made reference to the political body in which they lived. On the whole, classical patriotism quickly became obsolete in the early Middle Ages due to profoundly altered political structures, with which it could not be reconciled.

How then could patriotism withstand the political drought for several centuries? Did it just disappear from the surface in order to blossom again under improved conditions? Not quite. The language of the common fatherland, originally attributed to the capital Rome, endured, rhetorically almost unchanged, yet semantically completely altered. The new *patria communis*, resulting from this transformation, was explicitly

---

[25] Kantorowicz, 'Pro patria mori', 477.
[26] Kantorowicz, *The King's Two Bodies*, 233.
[27] Horace, *Odes III*, 2.13.

established against the old one, and this at a time when the Western Roman Empire was still in place.

'What does it matter', the Church Father Augustine (354–430) asked rhetorically, 'under whose government a dying man lives, if they who govern do not force him to impiety and iniquity?' And to abrogate the ancient patriotic culture completely, Augustine argued that the citizens of Rome loved their 'terrestrial fatherland on account of human glory' and even if they killed their own sons to save and worship her, they remained 'lovers of this world', having the wrong, the carnal fatherland in mind.[28] The true one was the *patria aeterna* in the city of God, the heavenly Jerusalem, whose citizens were hostile to all humans engaged in earthly affairs. In book five of his extremely influential *City of God* (*De Civitate Dei*), written in the early fifth century BC, Augustine turned the political meaning of *patria communis* upside down by re-establishing it in the heavens. Thus, 'the community of the blessed and saints was', as Ernst Kantorowicz precisely put it in his classic work on *The King's Two Bodies*, 'the civic assembly of the celestial *patria* which the soul desired to join'.[29]

To mark his disdain for the earthly exile, Augustine emphasised that the heavenly fatherland compelled no one to make Roman-style sacrifices, because it was God's 'remission of sins which collects citizens to the celestial fatherland'.[30] On this point, however, his influence remained limited and medieval political theology took another direction, which, after several momentous turns, led to a renewed approach to classical patriotism, though under markedly different terms. The decisive steps happened from the twelfth century onwards, during the long and often critical consolidation period of Western monarchies. First, the term *patria* regained a distinctively political meaning, designating the whole territory a monarch possessed – or at least claimed to possess by hereditary rights; an early example of this development can be found in Geoffrey of Monmouth's *History of the Kings of Britain* (*Historia Regum Britanniae*), written around 1136, where the *patria* under the reign of King Arthur was defined as 'the monarchy of the whole island'.[31] Similar descriptions of the kingdoms of France and Sicily followed suit.

There was a more far-reaching second development. It started significantly earlier and had been of relevance since the seventh and eighth centuries. It was connected with both the rapid expansion of Islam

[28] Augustine, *The City of God* (*De Civitate Dei*), V, 15–18.
[29] Kantorowicz, *The King's Two Bodies*, 234.
[30] Augustine, *The City of God* (*De Civitate Dei*), V, 17.
[31] Geoffrey of Monmouth, *The History of the Kings of Britain*, IX, 1.

which reached as far as Spain and with the simultaneous Christianising efforts in northern Europe by the Roman church. Pope Nicholas I, in office from 858 to 867, issued a decree that any soldier falling in the defence of faith against pagans died for the eternal fatherland and would be received as a citizen in heaven.[32] This idea echoed the religious promise of classical patriotism as given in Cicero's *Dream of Scipio* and overrode Augustine's clean-cut separation of the Christian and the Roman fatherland. Its full potential was only exploited in the period of the crusades, starting in the second half of the eleventh century, though once again with a significant change. While *patria* still designated the heavenly realm, which crusaders longed to enter through their martyrdom, the remission of sins was now held out for the 'defence' of an earthly territory, albeit one of sacred quality – the Holy Land. Hence, a crusader's calling on earth resembled the classical military duty of *defensio patriae*, whereas his motivation and reward remained religious. From this point, it was only a small step for the heavenly fatherland to come down to earth again, and this time in multiple versions.

4.6   A multitude of New Israels and New Romes

The missing link was provided on the home front of the crusades, where the See of Rome was raising taxes 'for the defence of the Holy Land' (*pro defensione Terrae Sanctae*). During the thirteenth century, many crusades were instigated for conflicts which took place thousands of miles away from Jerusalem and were fought for quite profane reasons. From this point, it was just a small step to the collection of taxes by lay powers 'for the defence of the kingdom' (*pro defensione regni*). If the kingdom was already labelled *patria*, as was the case in England, France and Sicily, paying taxes to the king soon became an act of patriotic defence. The American Vice-President, Joe Biden, probably did not know what an ancient tradition he was drawing on when he justified higher taxes for the rich during Barack Obama's election campaign of 2008 by saying, to the great horror of 'fiscally conservative' Republicans, that it was 'time to be patriotic'.

As mundane as this monetary patriotism might sound, it was, at least in the Middle Ages, loaded with a sacral meaning unknown to Classical Antiquity. In France, where taxes were imposed *pro defensione patriae* as early as the middle of the thirteenth century, attempts were also made to transfer the whole religious weight of the Holy Land to the French kingdom. It appeared as a 'kingdom blessed by God'

---

[32] Kantorowicz, 'Pro patria mori', 481.

(*regnum benedictum a Deo*) or simply as 'France sacred to God' (*Francia Deo sacra*) and it was likened to the mystic body of Christ (and of the Church) by being described as *corpus rei publicae mysticum*. While the French King's position in his *patria* corresponded to God's role in the heavenly fatherland, the French inhabitants were given the identity of the new chosen people.[33] This sacralisation of the earthly fatherland proved not only helpful in imposing new taxes on both laity and clergy within the kingdom, but also in promising soldiers eternal reward for patriotic martyrdom. After 1300, those who died for the king and his kingdom could expect, in the words of a contemporary preacher, to 'be crowned by God as martyrs', while the enemies of the French were said to be waging war against King Jesus, the Holy Land and Catholic doctrine, too.[34]

Such patriotic propaganda may sound radical to modern ears, but we need to keep in mind that it was produced for political systems with hardly any institutional power. Neither the French king nor other European monarchs of the Middle Ages had political apparatuses at their command to assert their claims by administrative enforcement; therefore, it was one thing to impose taxes, but another to collect them, and the same applies to military campaigns. From a practical point of view, medieval political propaganda had to be 'totalitarian' to compensate for the weakness of political administration, and there are signs that it had at least some of the effects it was supposed to achieve. In France, the breakthrough of patriotic propaganda happened during the Hundred Years' War (1337–1453), when French kings repeatedly manoeuvred themselves into emergencies where they had little option but to call for *defensio patriae*. 'Mother France' (*Mère France*) made her debut in French political literature,[35] and in the battles of Agincourt (1415) and Verneuil (1424), both with disastrous outcomes for the French, nobles close to the King of France either willingly died for the French fatherland or invented elements of a patriotic cult of the dead in the aftermath.[36]

Coupling the idea of a sacred fatherland on earth with pretensions to a New Israel was by no means a French speciality in the Middle Ages. The two concepts went hand in hand in Czech-speaking Bohemia before and during the Hussite Wars (1420–34), with the remarkable difference that the collective self-conception as elect people of God

---

[33] Idem, *The King's Two Bodies*, 237.   [34] Ibid., 254–6.
[35] Allmand, *The Hundred Years War*, 141, referring to a poem by Alain Chartier of 1422.
[36] Beaune, *The Birth of an Ideology* (*Naissance de la nation France*), 307–8.

was now theologically grounded in an alternative Christian movement, while Bohemia was linguistically defined as the sole fatherland (*vlast* or *patria*) of all people speaking Czech as their mother tongue.[37]

As to the ritualistic display of patriotic self-sacrifice, combined with religious election, Swiss soldiers proved almost as innovative when butchering enemy troops. Before entering combat, they prayed collectively with their knees on the ground and their arms stretched out 'in the form of a cross' (*in modum crucis*). Such religious conduct was highly unusual and repeatedly placed them under suspicion of heresy, partly because it did not distinguish clerics from laymen and partly because it came with this ostentatious claim to stand as the New Israel, which was equally expressed in popular songs and legends of past battles won. Nonetheless, it received official recognition from the Pope in 1479, and when the town of Basle entered the confederation in 1501, one of its first official acts was to ask the Roman Curia for permission to pray in the same manner and even to be given special indulgence for it, just as other Swiss cantons had been given before.[38]

The medieval journey of patriotic language from earth to heaven and back did not only bring about several New Israels, but a multitude of New Romes, too. Just at the time when the first crusade started to take shape, around 1070, a manuscript of the forgotten *Digest* was found in Italy; a few decades later Roman law was studied and taught at the newly founded university of Bologna, and from there it quickly spread to scholarly institutions, dioceses and princely courts north and west of the Alps. The rediscovery and re-institutionalisation of Roman law in the subsequent centuries became most crucial for the legal foundation of European monarchies as self-determined political bodies, *vis-à-vis* both foreign and domestic powers.

The advancement of European kingdoms to legal independence and equality was facilitated by an unprecedented and enduring weakness of the two traditional universal powers, the Holy Roman Empire and Papacy, in the late medieval period. After 1250, the Empire remained literally (and metaphorically) headless for twenty-three years, followed up by a series of weak rulers for another seventy years; the Papacy, on the other hand, had been moved to Avignon in 1309, where it remained under French control for almost seventy years, only to be torn apart by the Great Western Schism between 1378 and 1417.

---

[37] Hirschi, *Wettkampf der Nationen*, 131; Thomas, *Anne's Bohemia*, 51–3; Šmahel, 'Die nationale Frage im hussitischen Böhmen', 70; Graus, *Die Nationenbildung der Westslawen*, 100–8.

[38] Marchal, 'Bellum justum contra judicium belli', 124–8; Ochsenbein, 'Beten mit zertanen Armen', 148–50.

4.7   Legal scholars: the King's patriotic citizens

Still, it required a considerable amount of rewriting to transfer the
legal applications of Roman law from a single empire to a plurality of
kingdoms. Those who accomplished this transformation soon formed a
new body of learned experts remarkably different from the traditional
scholarly elite: theologians. Although jurists were clerics, too, and often
ascended to high rank within the Church after their university studies, they did not primarily act as a *spiritual elite*, such as theologians,
whose main business was to lead the way to salvation by advocating
higher truths and purifying sinful souls. Instead they took on the role
of a *functional elite* by offering special governmental tools to political
authorities (both secular and ecclesiastical) and by making themselves
irreplaceable in the application of these tools. This new scholarly role
required close study of political processes, ideally combined with direct
involvement in governmental practice as counsellor or chancellor, and
so jurists found their way to the centre of European powers within a
few generations of having invented themselves. Those legal experts who
adapted classical patriotism to the changed circumstances of the late
medieval period were usually writing on behalf of a specific political
authority, to which they were closely related. In the sixteenth century
they even started to compare their role as counsellors and officeholders,
influenced by Renaissance humanism, to the active political life (*vita
activa*) led and championed by Cicero and other Roman authors.[39]

Legal experts of Roman law soon formed a distinct body within medieval jurisdiction and were named legists, in contrast to canonists, the
specialists in ecclesiastical law. To guarantee their kings' independence
from both Pope and Emperor, they multiplied the imperial prerogatives of late Antiquity and assigned them to the different monarchies.
With the two formulae 'the King is Emperor within his kingdom' (*rex
est imperator in regno suo*) and 'the King does not recognise any superior' (*rex superiorem non recognoscet*) they defined the monarchy as a self-
determined territory *vis-à-vis* foreign rulers and the monarch as the
sole holder of power *vis-à-vis* his subjects. However, this arrangement
did not amount to mutual acknowledgement of state sovereignty. The
plurality of territorially limited empires was seen by both jurists and
rulers as a stopgap measure, because, as one jurist declared, 'today the
Empire is in pieces';[40] even after centuries of weak universal powers, the
ideal of a politically unified Christianity remained strong in all parts of

---

[39] Schmidt, *Vaterlandsliebe und Religionskonflikt*, 42–4.
[40] Kantorowicz, *The King's Two Bodies*, 248.

Western Europe, albeit on condition that one's own monarchy would be granted universal power. Hence, many monarchs aspired to advance from political self-determination to universal dominion at the earliest opportunity, and while insisting on the newly established rights of one's own monarchy, the same rights by foreign kings were easily ignored in order to promote imperialist dreams.[41] This accentuated the multipolar blockage by imperialist kingdoms of similar strength, which I pointed out earlier as a key prerequisite for the emergence of nationalism (see Chapter 3.3).

The manipulations of Roman law were often related to patriotic rhetoric, as can be seen in alternative mottoes, such as 'the King is Emperor within his fatherland'.[42] To define the monarchy as *patria communis* with all the legal weight of ancient Rome, jurists had to break through several obstacles. First, the term was still attached to the city of Rome, which was now primarily represented by the Pope (and secondarily by the Emperor), and at least to some jurists, it seemed impossible to separate the two. Jacques de Révigny, a Professor of Law at the University of Orléans between 1260 and 1280 and a supporter of the French King, proposed the solution of leaving the title of common fatherland to Rome, but to reverse the hierarchy of loyalties; answering the question as to which fatherland one had to obey in an event of war with Rome, he said: 'You ought to prefer your own *patria* to the common one.'[43] In the long run, Révigny's suggestion only marked an intermediate step. By 1300, England, France, Spain and Sicily were all labelled *patria communis*, and the kings who claimed imperial status within these fatherlands could now enjoy the full legal status of *pater patriae*.

Another difficulty arose from the fact that the classical common fatherland had constituted a city and not a territory; it was Rome, not the Empire, which held the title *patria communis*. Here, too, legists found their way in a two-step procedure. They first transferred the title to the kingdom's capital, which, for instance, turned Paris into 'France's Rome' and the rest of the realm into different *patriae propriae*, and from there, they enlarged it to the whole kingdom, offering all royal subjects symbolic participation as 'citizens' in the common fatherland.

Of course, this collective integration into the monarchical body politic did not come for free, as it involved the imposition of patriotic duties on all royal subjects. A third obstacle resulted from this. Patriotic language, with its classical emphasis on common commitments, challenged

[41] Post, 'Two Notes on Nationalism', 292.
[42] Kantorowicz, *The King's Two Bodies*, 248.
[43] Post, 'Two Notes on Nationalism', 290–1; Schneidmüller, *Nomen patriae*, 262–3.

the culture of medieval feudalism and the division of medieval society into the three estates of *oratores* (the clergy praying and teaching), *bellatores* (the noblemen protecting and fighting) and *laboratores* (the peasantry farming and feeding and the burghers crafting and trading). Jurists, therefore, had to resolve several problems of conflicting duties, and those advocating the royal cause found the law in favour of patriotic duties to the common fatherland. Johannes Teutonicus (†1245) and Odofredus (†1265), both influential commentators of Roman law, stated that the duty of *defensio patriae* was higher than the feudal obligation of vassal to lord, and Baldus de Ubaldis (1327–1400), the most eminent legal authority of the fourteenth century, argued that a soldier who killed an enemy for the sake of the fatherland accomplished a divine work out of 'public benevolence' (*publica caritas*), a term that overrode a vassal's personal sacrifice out of fidelity (*pro fide*) to his lord.[44] The shift of legal authority from noble intermediary powers to the King, in connection with the rise of royal patriotism, was also mirrored by scholastic theories of just war from the thirteenth century: while the authority to declare and conduct a war was restricted to princes, the defence of the fatherland was explicitly accepted as *casus belli*.[45]

4.8   The downgrading of Empire and Papacy

The second estate of the nobility was not the only target of royal legislation in the name of fatherland. Even more heated, at least in France, were conflicts with the first estate, the clergy. To finance his aggressive military campaigns against England and Flanders in the years before and after 1300, King Philip IV (1268–1314) repeatedly tried to impose taxes on the clergy of his realm on behalf of the necessity and defence of the fatherland, and he urged French bishops, too, to approve of his claims despite fierce resistance from Pope Boniface VIII. The conflict between King and Pope escalated into a long-lasting diplomatic battle, for which Philip and his chief minister and legal adviser Wilhelm of Nogaret (†1313) paid with excommunication, while the Pope ultimately paid with his life. Soon after his death, the Papacy was brought into the 'Babylonian Captivity' under the French King in Avignon. Thus, the Catholic Church was one of the first medieval institutions to realise that patriotic propaganda could produce more than empty words.

The Empire, too, did not emerge unscathed from the rise of royal patriotism and the legal transformation of European monarchies. After

---

[44] Kantorowicz, *The King's Two Bodies*, 246.
[45] Contamine, 'Mourir pour la patrie', 16–17.

the Papacy's move to Avignon, Roman emperors found themselves in the uncomfortable situation of being exposed to coordinated attacks by French kings and French popes on their legal precedence over other temporal powers. Furthermore, their traditional insistence on universal supremacy, based on the concept of *translatio imperii* (see Chapter 3.3), was now challenged by all those European kings who were presented by their lawyers as emperors in their own realms.

To make things worse, the German dynasties taking turns on the Imperial throne in the late medieval period were rapidly falling behind Western monarchies in two crucial areas: they could not seize control of the territories within the fuzzy boundaries of the Empire and their power base therefore remained confined to their family estates, and they failed to surround themselves with learned jurists, who could have helped to sustain their power claims. In the middle of the fourteenth century, the French King and the Pope each had hundreds of jurists at their disposal, the majority of them legists, while the Emperor only had a handful, the majority of them canonists. So if the Emperor did receive legal advice, it often came from high clerics, such as ecclesiastical princes, who were the first to employ legally trained counsellors within the Empire – or had even studied Roman law themselves before climbing up the ecclesiastical career ladder. But while defending the Imperial crown against foreign challenges, they, of course, kept following their own agenda.

What were the holders of the Imperial throne to do in this delicate situation? In order to avoid isolation, they could not just stick to the old theological-historical proof of their rights to universal dominion. Instead, they had to adapt to the new juridical game played by the canonists and legists of their chief adversaries. The most significant efforts to turn the tables on the Pope and kingly would-be emperors by using their own legal devices happened during the reign of Emperor Louis IV (1282–1347); he was elected Roman King (*rex Romanorum*) in 1314 by the German prince electors, but was refused the Imperial crown and later even excommunicated by Pope Innocent XXII, a legally trained Frenchman vindicating Papal supremacy over the Empire under the tutelage of the French King in Avignon. The Pope's legal stance not only disparaged the Emperor himself, but the prince electors, too, which offered a rare occasion for (more or less) concerted action in Germany.

In two simultaneous endeavours from 1338, Louis IV and the prince electors issued decrees to diminish the Pope's right of approval in the election of a new Emperor. While the King declared the candidate elected by the German princes the 'true King and Emperor' (*verus rex et imperator*) downgrading the Papal approval to an act without any legal significance, the princes themselves took a more cautious line, conferring to the elected King all governing rights within the territorial realm of the Empire regardless of the Pope's reaction, but neither the title of Emperor nor the dignities of universal supremacy. Here, the Empire's status was already slightly assimilated to that of a monarchy in order to prevent the Pope from interfering in Imperial elections.

There was a third, unofficial attempt to remove the Emperor from Papal authority, undertaken at around the same time by the legal counsellor of the Bishop of Würzburg, Lupold of Bebenburg (*c.* 1297–1363). His approach was by far the most sophisticated of the three and motivated, according to the author himself, by 'ardent zeal for the German fatherland' (*zelus fervidus patrie Germanie*). Lupold, who had studied law in Bologna, trod the same path as the prince electors, though following it much farther. In his *Treatise on the Rights of the Roman Kingdom and Empire* (*Tractatus de iuribus regni et imperii Romanorum*), completed by 1339, he argued that the German electoral process to select the Roman King had the same legal status as the succession to the throne in hereditary monarchies.[46] As soon as the prince electors had named the new King in the name of 'the German people' (*populus Germanie*), he had full control over his realm, because, as Lupold's slightly manipulated version of the famous legal proposition went: 'the King or King elect does not recognise any superior'.[47] In other words, the Pope's approbation of the election was legally irrelevant and his right to confer the title of Emperor of no further legal consequence. According to Lupold, the realm of the Roman King deserved the title *imperium* as it encompassed three kingdoms being transferred to Charlemagne through the *translatio imperii*: Italy, Burgundy and finally Germany, the true successor of Rome.

Lupold's solution may have been effective to counter the Pope's attacks on the Emperor, but it brought the Emperor down to almost the same level as other Western kings. It acknowledged that the Emperor did not exercise power over other kings, let alone possess universal dominion; his sole distinction was the symbolic weight of his title and the traditional responsibility for the protection of the Christian Church that came with it.

To defend this symbolic distinction against other kings' aspirations towards the Imperial crown, Lupold pursued a further line of

---

[46] For a more detailed interpretation of Lupold's historico-legal line of argument, see Hirschi, *Wettkampf der Nationen*, 94–103.
[47] Lupold of Bebenburg, *Tractatus de iuribus regni et imperii 8*, 312.

argument, which was especially directed against the French, because they, too, asserted that their kingdom was in the direct line of succession from Charlemagne's reign and that their kings descended from the Carolingians. To undermine this claim, Lupold developed a chain of reasoning that was to become popular with German humanists more than 150 years later. On the one hand, he insinuated that the French were not pure descendants of the Franks, Charlemagne's people, but that they had mingled with the native Gauls; he thus labelled them *Francigenae*, that is, liberally translated, 'French bastards', and he called the French King *rex Galliae*, refusing him the title of *rex Franciae*. On the other hand, he advanced a cultural argument, which proved even weightier, answering the anachronistic question as to whether Charlemagne and the Franks were actually Germans or French. Based on literature of previous centuries, he brought forward linguistic, geographical and genealogical proof. Charlemagne, Lupold maintained, had a German father, was born in German Ingelheim near Mainz, gave winds and months German names and enacted laws in the German language. 'From all this follows', he concluded, 'that the Frankish Carl was a German and, consequently, that the Empire was not only transferred to the kings of the Franks in person, but also to the Germans, because it came to his sons and descendants, who were Germans'. Here, political argument is already shaped by cultural means, and we can even find an early appearance of the later belief that both those governing and those governed naturally share the same lineage, laws and language.

Lupold's attempt to liberate the Roman King and Emperor legally from any foreign interference had one serious flaw, though: in order to declare him Emperor within his own realm he had to neglect the extensive autonomy enjoyed by German princes. In other words, as far as his control of the German lands, Italy and Burgundy was concerned, the Roman King did not even qualify for an equal standing to foreign kings; he did not have sufficient authority to raise taxes in most of his realm and neither could he count on military support from most German princes and cities, not to mention French and Italian Imperial territories.

Lupold did not address this dilemma in his *Treatise*, but he offered a sort of counterbalance in another publication, which appealed to the German princes with an urgent call to patriotic duty. It belongs to an intriguing literary genre best described as juridical poem. Entitled a *Lyrical Lamentation about the Present Turns and Defects of the Roman Kingdom and Empire (Ritmaticum querulosum et lamentosum dictamen de modernis cursibus et defectibus regni ac imperii Romani)*, it is composed of 180 rhymed verses accompanied by 31 marginal glosses, amplifying the legal content of the poem. Although it was translated into German by another hand as early as 1341, it soon fell into oblivion and was only rediscovered in 1841.

On a spring stroll, so the story goes, Lupold's poetic persona encounters a lonely, but majestically beautiful, lady wearing three crowns. She reveals herself as the 'Holy Roman Empire' and recounts her biography, starting with the long migration from Rome to Germany and ending with her desperate state among contemporary Germans. The culprits of her misfortune are quickly detected, but contrary to Lupold's *Treatise*, they reside within, not outside the Empire. It is the German nobility which is causing the dignified lady's indignation. Once stalwarts of the Empire and passionate advocates of Imperial rights, they are now, so she complains, treating her with contempt and committing injustices against her: 'Alas! These infidels have become rogues and robbers, and not a few princes are my traitors.'[48] Pursuing their private interests instead of the public good, German nobles weakened the worship of the Empire by the whole people:

> The Germans do not honour me any more, hardly support me and do not even know who I am. You can tell that the Italians despise me by making a mockery of me and by serving their tyrants at will. These insults are a blemish on the German fatherland, but they [the Germans] do not reach for their swords to fight back. While it is the law of the peoples to defend the fatherland, they do not care about me by preserving the rights of the fatherland.[49]

The Roman Empire then directly addresses Lupold's poetic persona, calling on him to remind the German princes and nobles to pay her the respect they owe her and to jointly lead the neighbouring people back into her service.

Contrary to royal patriotic propaganda in France and other Western monarchies, Lupold's bold effort to translate Roman patriotism to late medieval Germany went largely unheard. For once, the discrepancy between political language and political culture was too big; yet, one and a half centuries later, when the Imperial throne was occupied by a strengthened Habsburg dynasty, circumstances were much more favourable for German patriotic propaganda to gain a foothold.

With the Empire legally reduced to a regional power, the competition between European kingdoms for 'universal' dominion was brought to a level of intensity unknown before, both politically and ideologically. Early on, the increased competitiveness transformed patriotic language, too. Legal experts writing in the name of rival kingdoms were

[48] Idem, *Ritmaticum*, vv. 100–4, 519.
[49] Ibid., vv. 125–32, 521–2.

not only praising their own fatherland, but accusing each other of biased scholarship to favour one's country; the common way of doing this was glossing each other's glosses. Responding to a comment by Johannes Teutonicus – nomen est omen – the French canonist Wilhelm of Montlauzun (†1343) drily noted that when championing the superiority of the Emperor over kings, his German colleague had committed 'favour to his fatherland' (*favor patriae*), that is to the region of his 'flesh and blood'.[50] Poor Teutonicus had already been mocked previously by a contemporary of his, the famous commentator Vincentius Hispanus (†1248), whose name, too, reflected his patriotic preference. Speaking to Teutonicus rhetorically, Hispanus let him know 'that the Germans have lost the Empire by their own stupidity'. The Spanish situation was, allegedly, entirely different:

But the Spanish alone have by their valour obtained the Empire ... Do the Spanish not rule in France, in England, in Germany and in Constantinople in virtue of their governance of Blessed Lady Spain ...? The Spanish, therefore, are aided by their merits and their worth. Unlike the Germans, they have no need of a body of prescripts and customs.[51]

Hispanus' portrait of 'noble Spain' (*nobilis Yspania*) might have been a bit irritating to his foreign colleagues, and not only due to the fact that he combined it with unpleasant comments about their countries. In actual fact, there was no Spanish kingdom at the time and there had not been one for most of the medieval period. During Hispanus' lifetime, several kingdoms were scattered across the Spanish peninsula, of which the most significant were Aragon, Castile and Leon, and Portugal; Hispanus himself had been chancellor to the Portuguese King Sancho II before being elected Bishop of Idanha-Guarda in 1229. So why did he pursue juridical studies on behalf of a non-existing body politic and even cross swords in its name with legal commentators supporting other countries? Hispanus must have followed an agenda of political unification, based on the popular model of the early medieval Visigothic kingdom (as famously described by Isidore of Seville) and boosted by the fresh military successes of Aragon and Castile against the Moors in Southern Spain. The evocation of a remote past and the vague promise of the present seem to have been reasons enough for him to let the comparison between Spain and other countries culminate in verses, not forgetting to mention the achievements of his own profession:

[50] Post, 'Blessed Lady Spain', 200.
[51] Idem, 'Two Notes on Nationalism', 307–8.

Who indeed, oh Spain, can reckon thy glories? Wealthy in horses, celebrated for food and shining with gold; steadfast, wise and the envy of all; skilled in law and standing high on sublime pillars.[52]

To compete with other countries on patriotic terms, Hispanus could partly draw on the ancient motive of *patriae laus*, a citizen's duty to praise his fatherland. Yet, the notion of comparison, so distinctive in his discourse, only had a parallel in classical eulogies of *patria propria*, the local fatherland – if at all. In these eulogies, the natural and cultural qualities of the local homeland had occasionally been judged favourably against other regions of the Roman Empire, though with hardly any political undertone. By contrast, the classical concept of *patria communis*, to which Hispanus and his legal colleagues primarily referred in order to construe their patriotic discourse, had not allowed for comparisons with foreign political communities, simply because it had only referred to Rome. The comparative element that Roman patriotism did contain had been related to smaller communities *within* the common fatherland – family, hometown, province – hammering the idea of an indisputable hierarchy of loyalties into citizens' heads.

So, although patriotic language proved its flexibility in the course of the Middle Ages, its political suitability remained restricted to disciplining and mobilising elites in one's own country and to enforcing claims of self-determination against foreign countries. Because patriotism was based on the model of ancient Rome, it was only of limited functionality for the rising competitiveness of late medieval politics between emerging states. In order to adapt to this multipolar dynamic, the patriotic discourse had to merge with a complementary discourse, which would use the mobilising force of patriotism to fuel the competition between European powers. Such a discourse was not to be found in Classical Antiquity, let alone in biblical Israel. It had to be newly crafted, and the way it happened was not so much by invention, but by bricolage: pulling existing bits and pieces out of diverse contexts and putting them together in a form unknown before. The result was the first form of nationalism and its complex emergence will be described in the following chapter.

[52] Ibid.

5 Competing for honour: the making of nations in late medieval Europe

> Would it not be expedient, because of the jealousy between nations about the Papacy, to transfer the Papal seat from nation to nation ...? It would then emerge, against the will of naysayers, which nation has the best candidate, if chronicles are written about them all.
>
> Anonymous, *Avisamentum*, Council of Constance 1415

> Farewell, all Germans, and do not allow our praise, our glory and our honour to be ruined by words and especially by weapons!
>
> Heinrich Bebel, *Apologia contra Iustinianum*, 1509

From Antiquity to the late Middle Ages, the word 'nation' (*natio*) largely lacked positive political or emotional meaning. Compared to *patria*, it had to undergo an even profounder transformation in a much shorter period to become the main term and eponym of nationalism. This transformation started at the beginning of the fifteenth century and was completed by its end.

Natio is derived from *nasci*, which means 'to be born'. Romans used the word to indicate their place or province of birth within the Roman Empire; one could be *natione* – that is 'by birth' – Sicilian, Macedonian or Dalmatian. The phrase was a regular component of the short biographical descriptions on tombstones. It rarely implied belonging to a community of the same name, whose members shared singular histories and habits. It was an individual designation of geographical origin in a mobile society, and it was mostly void of further political or cultural meaning.

In other contexts, however, *natio* could indeed signify a cultural community with unique language, lineage and style of living. In this sense, though, it was usually accompanied by the attributes 'barbarian' (*barbara*), 'external' (*externa*) or 'foreign' (*aliena*). It designated foreign people outside the 'civilised' world and highlighted the cultural gap that separated the Romans from the rest of the human population.[1] While the *populus Romanus* was thought to consist of codified law and

---

[1] For an example, see the long quote of Vitruvius in Chapter 3.1 of this book.

rational politics, *nationes* were allegedly based on blood bonds and blind emotion.

The pejorative implications of *natio* did not disappear with the Christianisation and later disintegration of the Roman Empire. They survived because the term was introduced into a new dichotomy. Jerome's Latin translation of the Bible in the late fourth century led the way by calling all peoples outside the Judaeo-Christian world *nationes*. Soon, the *populus Christianus* was opposed to pagan *nationes*. Together with this semantic realignment, the term 'barbarian' was now applied to heathens and heretics. Thus, the Catholic Church could legitimise its missionary aggression using the same language the Romans had used to justify their conquests. Early medieval letters from the Pope to the King of the Franks included the standard prayer: 'May the Lord grant him to bring all barbarian nations under our eternal peace.'[2]

If *natio* was an old and well-established term to stigmatise strangers as lost creatures, how could it be that fifteenth-century scholars and rulers regularly spoke of their *natio inclita* or, in their respective mother tongues, of their 'renowned' or 'celebrated nation'?[3] And how could it come to pass that by the end of the fifteenth century the Roman Emperor presented himself as a 'lover of the German nation' and appealed to the Imperial estates to unite against 'foreign tongues' for the sake of 'the honour of the German nation'?[4] To answer these questions, we have to return to the meaning of *natio* as engraved in Roman epitaphs. It was the continual usage of the term as a personal indicator of geographical origin that enabled it to become politically and emotionally charged and to be turned into a designation of both a collective self and collective others.

5.1 Corporative honour: 'nationes' at medieval universities

Medieval society is widely believed to have been static, as opposed to what came before or after. Such an assessment may reflect medieval ideals, but hardly medieval realities. For most of the Middle Ages, the inhabitants of Roman Christianity were just as mobile as their ancient ancestors, or even more so. They organised mobility differently, though. People on the move tended to be segregated according to the purpose of their journey; sometimes this happened on the way, sometimes only at

[2] Van Acker, 'Barbarus und seine Ableitungen', 139.
[3] Hirschi, *Wettkampf der Nationen*, 142.
[4] Janssen (ed.), *Frankfurts Reichscorrespondenz*, 478/491–2.

the destination. In much-visited cities, there were different lodgings or even different districts for merchants, pilgrims, knights and students.

From the twelfth century onwards, merchant quarters, universities and other urban institutions that harboured many foreigners started subdividing them into different groups, each of which covered a region of the whole catchment area. These groups were called *nationes*, whereby the term turned from a personal into a collective indicator of geographical origin. However, it was still a far cry from the modern meaning of nation. Membership of a *natio* only lasted for the period of stay at the respective urban institution; in other words, it continued to be a designation for strangers until they headed home.

Furthermore, when naming, defining and implementing the *nationes*, every institution followed its own rules. They could range from pragmatic reasoning to theological number mysticism, with the widest variations evident at the new temples of scholarship, universities. The University of Oxford, for instance, established two *nationes*, dubbed *Borealis* and *Australis*, which were separated by the river Trent and together only covered the British Isles, as there were hardly any students from the Continent; their impact on university life was limited and they did not enjoy any degree of autonomy.[5] In contrast, the then much more prestigious University of Bologna introduced nineteen *nationes*, three attributed to the *citramontani* – the inhabitants of the Italian peninsula – and sixteen to the *ultramontani*; numbers and names could change over time, but the groups themselves developed a solid structure. One of the *nationes'* main functions was to grant legal protection to foreign scholars within the city walls.[6]

While Oxford and Bologna, in terms of numbers, represented the extremes, the University of Paris with its four *nationes* occupied the middle ground. It labelled them *Gallican*, *Picardian*, *Norman* and *Anglican* and circumscribed them pragmatically: while the *natio Gallicorum* was confined to the region of the Île-de-France, the *natio Anglorum* included large parts of Central and Eastern Europe.[7] Although its choice of numbers was followed by many other universities, the Parisian model had its specialities, too. The *nationes* did not consist of students, but of masters, and they were recruited exclusively from the faculty of arts, whereas the higher faculties – medicine, law and theology – had nothing to do with them.

Even if the *nationes* at medieval universities had not much in common with later nations, they marked an important step towards them.

---

[5] Kibre, *The Nations*, 161–3.
[6] Stichweh, 'Universitätsmitglieder', 178–9.
[7] Kibre, *The Nations*, 66.

Like other urban communities, such as guilds and confraternities, most *natiories*, at least on the Continent, were organised as corporations. They had an institutionalised structure with a procurator at its head; they cultivated distinct rituals and chose their own holidays; they worshipped a patron saint and possessed a shrine, in which they stored their seals, flags, gowns and registers.

By taking the form of a corporation, the members of a *natio* claimed a collective honour that was conferred from those leaving to those entering the community. It urged them to behave respectfully, at least in public, and to counter possibly offensive challenges from outsiders. As a consequence, being an honourable community gave much cause for conflict; accordingly, the history of university *natiories* is full of violent struggles against other *natiories* or even against the municipality.[8]

What it meant to preserve the corporative honour can be read out of a resolution, which the *natio Alamanniae* at the University of Orléans passed in 1382. It restricted the public exposure of its community members with measures that were probably not so popular with students: they should not meet in taverns and other public places because they would harm the honour (*decus*) and dignity (*maiestas*) of the *natio* by being dragged into brawls; neither should they meet in town at night 'when darkness and calumny are more apt to prevail against the testimony of truth'; nor immediately after dinner, 'for when the head is swimming with wine and the stomach is distended with food, the discretionary faculty is dulled and one is more easily led into quarrelling'.[9] Finally, the decree even urged members not to use the German language in public any more because it sounded rough and raw. This last measure indicates that vernaculars, too, could become a characteristic of a *natio* – albeit in this case not one to be proud of. Either way, with language entering the discourse, the shadow of a bigger community already loomed large over the little stage of university corporations.

5.2 From concrete to abstract communities: The 'natiories' at the Council of Constance

Yet, it was not at the universities, but at the Great Church councils of the late medieval period, where concrete corporations turned into abstract communities. The decisive events took place at the Council of Constance, which lasted from 1414 to 1418. The Council's *raison d'être* was to resolve the Great Western Schism, which had been ongoing since

---

[8] For the tumultuous events at the University of Prague around 1400, see Hirschi, *Wettkampf der Nationen*, 125–34.

[9] Ibid., 135; for the original text, see Fournier, *Les statuts et privilèges*, I, 145–8, 147.

the return of the papacy to Rome under Gregory XI in 1376. When the Council started, three Popes were simultaneously claiming to be the only one, and all were backed by different secular powers. A permanent solution to the crisis was not to be accomplished without a reform of the Catholic Church from head to toe, and so the Council's business actually concerned the whole body of Christianity. Kings and princes delegated their best counsellors to Constance in order to influence proceedings in their favour, and some of them even made an appearance themselves to weigh in during the debates.

Under these circumstances, the Council of Constance became a focal point for both political conflict and intellectual exchange unprecedented in Western Europe. As to men of learning, everybody who was anybody had to be present. Among the most famous participants were the theologians Jean Gerson (1363–1429) and Pierre d'Ailly (1350–1420), the jurists Francesco Zabarella (1360–1417) and Guillaume Fillastre (1348–1428) and the humanists Poggio Bracciolini (1380–1459) and Manuel Chrysoloras (1355–1415). While Chrysoloras died shortly after arriving at Constance and Poggio went hunting for ancient texts in the libraries of nearby monasteries (with Quintilian's complete *Institutio oratoria* as the most remarkable prey), the experts of canon law and of theology, in a series of heated debates, set up the formal proceedings of deliberation and decision at the Council.

A central element of these proceedings was the division of voting participants into four *nationes*: the *Gallicana*, *Italica*, *Anglicana* and *Germanica*. Their establishment as such did not raise any objections because *nationes* had already played a role in previous Church councils. They had first been introduced at the Second Council of Lyon in 1274, where they were rudimentarily modelled on the example of French universities. At every subsequent council up to the one in Constance they were introduced in one form or another, yet they always lacked an official function and thus were only of minor importance.

This was to change dramatically in 1414. First, the Council decided to recruit the members of the deliberating committees from the *nationes*, and not, as previously done, from the Church provinces. Secondly, because the Italians formed a numerical majority at the outset and supported (Anti-)Pope John XXIII almost *en bloc*, many clerics from the rest of Europe tried to empower the *nationes* with major voting rights in order to circumvent voting by head count in the whole assembly. After a fierce fight they succeeded. Each *natio* could elect its own president, choose its procurators, create its coat of arms, hold its meetings in a proper assembly room, dispatch its delegates to the committees, and, most importantly, pass a single vote for all its members.

However, providing the *nationes* with such unprecedented power proved only a prelude to a new power struggle, staged in the backrooms of the urban convents and fought with talks and treatises. This time it was a multipolar conflict over the control of each *natio*. The greatest stir was caused by the big secular players: the kingdoms of France, England, Castile, Aragon and the Holy Roman Empire. In the process, the meaning of *natio* was fundamentally transformed.

At the beginning of the Council, Emperor Sigismund proclaimed that he would stand above the *nationes* in order to act as a patron of the whole Church assembly, which ultimately gathered in one of his Imperial cities. After realising that he was going to deprive himself of any influence in this superordinate role, he changed tactics and announced that he wanted to play a leading part in three different *nationes* because his dominion stretched over peoples and lands covered by the *Germanica*, *Gallicana* and *Italica*. Yet, when Sigismund attended a meeting of the *Gallicana* on 19 March 1415, the French prelates did not shy away from a scandal; they refused to deliberate in the presence of a stranger and successfully demanded his exclusion from the assembly. As early as one year after the start of the Council, the Emperor was forced to realise that his power base was restricted to only one *natio*, the *Germanica*.[10]

The Council was already two years underway when the prelates and secular envoys from the Iberian Peninsula arrived. They were a small group, but soon made much noise in town. They submitted a request to form a fifth voting body, the *natio Hispanica*. The request was approved, thanks to the active support of the *natio Gallicana*, whose members sensed a chance to challenge the status of the *natio Anglicana*. While the newly minted *natio Hispanica* was quickly absorbed by infighting among the clients of the Castilian, Aragonese and Portuguese kings, the *Gallicana* promoted an incorporation of the *Anglicana* into the *Germanica*. To achieve their goal, the members of the *Gallicana* mainly argued with numbers. The *Anglicana*, they said, lacked a sufficient amount of dioceses, inhabitants, towns and Church provinces to count as an independent voting body, and as Christianity only consisted of four parts, the smallest *natio* had to vanish.[11]

What were the members of the *Gallicana* driven by? To a great extent, they fought a proxy battle of the Hundred Years' War. Just a year before, in 1415, the French crown had suffered a devastating defeat by a smaller English army at Agincourt, from which it had not yet recovered. At the Council, the French King Charles VI was described as the 'worthier and superior part' of the *natio Gallicana*, and, through its prelates, he

[10] Schmidt, *Kirche, Staat, Nation*, 476–7.   [11] Ibid., 479–82.

tried to minimise his enemy's influence on the policy-making process.[12] As the *natio Anglicana* was indeed largely controlled by King Henry V, breaking its power promised a practical solution for this purpose.

It was a hardly a surprise that the English prelates responded resolutely. They published a memorandum that set up leading requirements for a *natio* at the Council: a common descent and way of life, a geographical scope similar to other *nationes* and several language groups.[13] There was no higher logic in these requirements as they mainly served as a disguised self-portrait. The memorandum turned the tables on the *Gallicana* by adopting their quantitative reasoning, while replacing some of their criteria. To counter the French accusations of insufficient size, its authors included the Irish, Welsh and Scottish clerics, although they aspired for nothing of the sort – if they were present in Constance at all.[14] Now, the *Anglicana* could boast a polyglot community, all the more so as it also counted the English possessions in Aquitaine among its side. This was why the number of languages was quickly elevated to a leading criterion of a *natio*.

Despite the improvised nature of the English riposte, the French had nothing much to add to the debate. Once again, events far away from Lake Constance tipped the balance. King Henry, thanks to cleverly forged alliances and further military successes, exercised his influence behind the scenes, thereby making sure that the number of *nationes* remained at five for the rest of the Council.

All the wrangling over definitions, compositions and constitutions of the *nationes* clearly indicates that they were unable to form what the advocates of a strong and independent Church had hoped for: autonomous corporations, which could resist the pressure from secular powers. Even some of those who followed royal directives and fought in the frontline of the war of pens blamed the influence of kings and princes for the animosity between the *nationes*. Pierre d'Ailly, for instance, argued that the dispute over precedence between kings expanded to the convents of Constance because the *nationes* were too dependent on the *regna*. To restore the Council's ecclesiastical autonomy, he proposed to subdivide its participants along the lines of the Church provinces in the future.[15]

---

[12] Mertens, *Reich und Elsass*, 26/34.
[13] Von der Hardt, *Magnum oecumenicum Constantiense concilium*, V, 92.
[14] The Scottish prelates stayed away from the Council for the whole period. Schmidt, *Kirche, Staat, Nation*, 473/481.
[15] D'Ailly, 'De Reformatione Ecclesie', in Miethke, Weinrich (ed.), *Quellen zur Kirchenreform*, 374–5.

Without realising it, d'Ailly had touched the critical point. As soon as the *nationes* had been provided with political power, they came to be regarded as *representative bodies* of parts of Christianity (*nationem, quae habeat vocem seu auctoritatem repraesentativam quartae aut quintae partis Christianitatis*).[16] It was the idea of representation which marked the decisive difference from the *nationes* at universities. And it was this idea, too, that caused the conflicts, since with it came an unresolved question: which part of Christianity was a *natio* supposed to represent? Did it constitute a secular or an ecclesiastical unit? And did it express the will of kings, of clerics or of the whole Christian population? Despite several attempts to clarify the term's meaning, the debates only increased its ambiguity and emotiveness. Introduced as a pragmatic category without any ideological weight, *natio* became a highly politicised and fiercely contested concept within a few years.

When Pope Martin V, in 1418, concluded a concordat with the 'fathers, prelates, doctors etc. who represent and form (*repraesentantes et facientes*) the *natio Germanica* in the General Council of Constance', he even suggested that the *nationes* were both representatives and represented. For the Pope, this formulation, full of inner tension, was an attempt to rescue the *nationes* as parts of the Church both at the Council and beyond. It was a vain endeavour as they were soon to become abstract communities, now represented by secular rulers.

How did this process unfold? It was also initiated at the Council of Constance, and at its outset was another attempt to handle the semantic ambiguity of *natio*. Early on, when the Council fathers noticed that there were far more aspirants to the status of *natio* than the four or five on offer, they made a distinction that later became widely used among them. They spoke of *nationes principales* when referring to the official voting bodies within the Council, and of *nationes particulares* when addressing larger communities outside the Council, defined by common ancestry, territory or language, which were only represented in Constance as parts of a *natio principalis*. The assumed number of *nationes particulares* varied considerably, but could be as high as thirty-six.[17]

What seemed to be a clear-cut distinction at the beginning, soon turned out to complicate matters further. The two terms proved especially confusing for the privileged few who could claim double status as members of a *natio principalis* and *particularis*. In the disputes between French and English prelates, the two categories were repeatedly blurred. And later on, when the Germans, whose *natio principalis*

[16] Von der Hardt, *Magnum oecumenicum Constantiense concilium*, V, 58.
[17] Mertens, *Reich und Elsass*, 33.

included the better part of the Empire plus Scandinavia, Poland, Latvia, Croatia, Hungary and Bohemia, proved incapable of clearly distinguishing between their own different *nationes*, the two terms definitely became obsolete. The way, however, the *natio principalis* and *particularis* blended into each can be seen as groundbreaking for the emergence of nationalism.

Towards the end of the Council, the highly esteemed German jurist Job Vener, a member of the *natio Germanica* and counsellor to Emperor Sigismund, composed an ambitious reform treatise, in which he defined *natio* along the lines of the concept of *natio principalis*: 'I understand *natio* according to the divisions of *nationes* at this Holy General Council of Constance and according to their divisions at future general councils.'[18] However, when he criticised the overrepresentation of French and Italian prelates at the Curia and called for the election of Germans into the College of Cardinals, he switched to a concept of *natio* which included at least all clerics of the German lands:

It is of no importance if somebody says: the Germans have the Empire, ... therefore they must renounce a share in their spiritual father, the Pope, and in their mystical body, the College of Cardinals ... It signifies nothing, either, if somebody says: the Germans do not want to be Cardinals, since the Archbishops of Mainz, Cologne and Trier and others have been offered the cardinalate repeatedly without accepting it. I answer to this: if the cardinalate had been offered to eminent doctors of theology or to provincials, priors, masters or ministers of orders or similar men of the German *natio*, perhaps many would have accepted![19]

As if Vener's insinuation of a deliberate discrimination against the members of the German *natio* had not been enough, he later broadened his accusations against the Italians to an economic and cultural conspiracy theory. Now, all Germans, independent of class and rank, appeared as victims of Italian exploitation and defamation:

Gold and silver are now rare in Germany, so that not even the Emperor of the world, who lives in Germany, has an abundance of it; the mines in Bohemia, Hungary, near Goslar and elsewhere in Germany are exhausted. In Italy, one can find gold and silver. In addition, a few depraved Italians hate and ridicule the Germans. They say: the Italians see with two eyes, the French with one, the Germans with none. Indeed, they even say that the mule of an Italian is still wiser than a German.[20]

It seems that Vener had made acquaintance with some of the early Italian humanists in Constance, who, following the model set by

---

[18] Vener, 'Avisamentum', in Miethke, Weinrich (ed.), *Quellen zur Kirchenreform*, 406–7.
[19] Ibid., 393–6.   [20] Ibid., 414–15.

Petrarch, displayed their sense of cultural superiority with ostentatious disrespect for all scholars north and west of the Alps. It is hard to say whom Vener actually counted among the *Germans* and what he meant by *Germania*; Hungary, for instance, was neither part of the Holy Roman Empire nor dominated by German-speaking people. But what becomes clear is that he perceived the treatment of the German *natio* at Constance as a symptom of a much larger conflict between cultural and political communities. As a consequence, Vener was no longer able to distinguish between the representatives and the represented of the *natio Germanica* and so described both in identical terms. What affected the German clerics at the Council now concerned all Germans – and vice versa.

The cultural logic that enabled the fusion of such disparate communities was the notion of honour. Similar to the *nationes* at universities, the *nationes* at the Council of Constance established themselves as corporations, which claimed a collective honour and dignity for all their members. This understanding was reflected in the official vocabulary used at the Council. The English delegates defended 'the renowned' *natio Anglicana, sive Britannica* against the French in 1416, and Pope Martin V concluded a concordat with the 'renowned' *natio Germanorum* in 1418.[21] The same concordat, presumably to Vener's relief and pleasure, granted the extraordinary admission of candidates to the Cardinalate, and the reason given for this decision was 'the honour of the *nationes*' (*pro honore nacionum*).[22] The Latin word for 'renowned' or 'celebrated' was *inclitus*. Ancient and medieval authors had already used it to emphasise the exclusive honour of a polity or community, but they could not imagine attributing it to the noun *natio*.[23] This match of words only became possible through the medieval labelling of certain corporations as *nationes*. And with the new understanding of *nationes* as representative bodies and the subsequent blend of *nationes principales* and *particulares* at Constance, the collective honour of a corporation was able to flow into an abstract community that transcended the barriers of the medieval society of orders.

At the Council of Constance it became evident that the understanding of *nationes* as communities of honour could have a serious

---

[21] Thomas, 'Die deutsche Nation', 431.
[22] Miethke, Weinrich (ed.), *Quellen zur Kirchenreform*, 516.
[23] See, for instance, Vergil's reference to *illa inclita Roma* in *Aeneid VI*, 781, the highlighting of the *gens Francorum inclita* in the Prologue of the *Lex Salica* dating from the early sixth century, or Baldus de Ubaldis' mention of the *rex Angliae inclytae* in his Commentaries on the *Digests* written in the second half of the fourteenth century (*In primam digesti veteris partem commentaria*, fol. 52ᵛ).

downside. It further intensified the competitive culture in which the negotiations about the reform of the Church were taking place. If all significant decisions by the Council carried the risk of glorifying or shaming a *natio*, it became increasingly difficult to find solutions at all. To reduce the unwanted side-effects of the contest for collective honour, an anonymous author of the *natio Germanica* proposed a provisional rotation of the Papacy from one *natio* to another. He hoped that 'the jealousy between *nationes* about the Papacy' would be reduced in a regulated competition, because 'it would then emerge, which nation has the best candidate, if chronicles are written about them all'.[24] To channel a potentially destructive rivalry by introducing a rotation of office and public evaluation was a sophisticated approach and, in addition, one with a great future in the history of nationalism. Yet, under the heavily politicised circumstances of Constance, it had no chance of realisation.

The effect of the Council's struggle with its *nationes* was immediate and long-lasting: the language of national honour and shame quickly entered the stage of secular politics and reshaped the written propaganda by European kings and the Emperor. Now, *natio* came to mean a political, cultural and linguistic community, inhabiting a territory of its own and sharing an exclusive honour among its members.

5.3   The new dimensions of national honour

The idea that a nation has an honour, which all its members share and cherish, was one of the most powerful ideas of the modern era. Millions have lived for it, and millions have died for it. Although it has lost some of its appeal after the twentieth-century World Wars, it is still familiar today – except to most experts on nationalism. Why nationalists speak so much about honour and shame and what they actually mean by it is rarely asked and still less answered in nationalism studies.

As far as modernist theorists are concerned, one can understand why they avoid the subject. Generations of sociologists and anthropologists have perceived honour as essentially belonging to pre-modern cultures, while being of minor or minimal importance to modern ones. Max Weber, in his influential study on *Economy and Society*, posthumously published in 1922, contrasted the pre-modern 'situation of orders' (*ständische Lage*) with the modern 'situation of classes' (*Klassenlage*), and while treating the latter as 'purely economically determined', he

---

[24] Anonymous, *Avisamentum*, in Miethke, Weinrich (ed.), *Quellen zur Kirchenreform*, 316–17.

regarded the former as 'determined by a specific, positive or negative, social estimation of *honour*, which is connected with any quality shared by a plurality.'[25] More than fifty years later, Pierre Bourdieu, in his equally seminal *Outline of a Theory of Practice*, argued that 'the point of honour only has a meaning and a function in a man for whom there exist things worthy of being defended. A being devoid of the sacred could dispense with the point of honour because he would in a sense be invulnerable.'[26]

Attributing honour to 'orders' and to the 'sacred' is in line with the view of more recent studies; Frank Henderson Stewart, for instance, speaks of 'the collapse of honour' in modern times.[27] To him and to others, the concept of honour looks fundamentally incompatible with modern society; it disturbs social relations, impedes the legal system and hinders economic efficiency – in sum, it is an irrational intruder into a rational world. Some historians only consider one code of honour to be in accordance with the demands of modern society: the idea of an individualised and internalised honour, which allegedly guarantees a certain predictability of human behaviour in a society where people often interact without knowing each other. They describe it as a brainchild of eighteenth- and nineteenth-century Romanticists with no ancestors in pre-modern Europe.

Under these circumstances, the concept of national honour must be irritating to both pre-modernist theorists of honour and modernist theorists of nationalism. The former would probably explain it away as a dysfunctional atavism in modernity, while the latter may count it among the expressions of a 'false consciousness' by the nationalist 'ideology', following Ernest Gellner's assertion that the language of nationalism does not reflect the nature of nationalism at all (see Chapter 2.1).[28]

Both approaches are unsatisfactory because they cannot offer an explanation of why the idea of 'national honour' during the last two centuries was so appealing to people of different class, education and profession, to both winners and losers of modernisation. We need to rethink the history of honour in general to give a better picture of nationalism's role within it. First, instead of arguing for a collapse of honour in modern societies, we should embrace the concept of a transformation, according to which older forms of honour, both

---

[25] Weber, *Wirtschaft und Gesellschaft*, 534; for an English translation, see idem, *Economy and Society*, 932.
[26] Bourdieu, *Outline of a Theory of Practice*, 61 (the English translation was based on a revised and rearranged version of the *Esquisse d'une théorie de la pratique* of 1972).
[27] Stewart, *Honor*, 47.
[28] Gellner, *Nations and Nationalism*, 124–5.

individual and collective, were adapted to the demands of a more mobile and more complex environment. From this perspective, the modern ridicule of the irrationality and destructiveness of traditional honour, as represented by feuds, duels and blood vengeance, did not bring about a new age of rationality, but rather alternative – and no less irrational – forms of honour. Secondly, instead of assuming a rapid change within the economy of honour at the end of the eighteenth century, we should suppose a much slower mutation starting at the end of the Middle Ages and leading to a parallel existence of contrary, but not incompatible, concepts of honour during the early modern period.

As the following chapters will show, the national discourse of the fifteenth century did not only introduce a new concept of collective honour, it also became interlocked with new forms of individual honour, developed by scholars who acted outside traditional institutions of learning. In this chapter, though, we are dealing only with national honour as collective ownership and answering the question as to what this concept signified in relation to older forms of honour in medieval society. For this, we first have to look at the general changes within the economy of honour during the late Middle Ages.

The medieval culture of honour exemplifies the hierarchies within the society of orders and, at the same time, offers an insight into its inner dynamism. It illustrates the tensions between the ideal of a stable social system, in which everybody was supposed to have their predestined place and stick to it, and the reality of an increasingly mobile society, which had to deal with many individuals and even whole groups climbing up and down the social ladder. Medieval honour is to be qualified as a competitive category, albeit one that restricted competitiveness to men of equal rank and order. Being honourable meant to be worthy of a challenge, and being challenged added to the honour of a man. However, any attempted challenge from a man standing lower or higher in the social hierarchy was dishonourable to both challenger and challenged. There could be no competition between a peasant and a nobleman and neither between a Christian and a Jew.

This rule was by no means confined to the Middle Ages. It was still in force at the beginning of the eighteenth century, when the bourgeois Voltaire and the Chevalier de Rohan manoeuvred each other into a lose-lose-situation by exchanging insults; while Voltaire first paid the price with a humiliating beating from the aristocrat's servants and then, after threatening to challenge his opponent to a duel, with a visit to the Bastille, the chevalier suffered the disgrace of having lowered himself to the level of a young would-be aristocrat.

Figure 6 This drawing of a session at the Council of Constance (1414–18) illustrates the reproduction of social hierarchies in space. The Pope has the most elevated seat in the centre of the picture, flanked by two cardinals. The bishops are placed on both sides, but on the same level as the cardinals, whereas the scholars sit at their feet, thereby appearing inferior in honour. The lowest standing is attributed to the lay spectators from the City of Constance, who, together with the open door, also refer to the public nature of the display of honours and hierarchies within the clergy.

Affairs of honour between men of unequal standing did not only diminish their personal honour, but also threatened the collective honour of the order or corporation to which they belonged. In the medieval period and beyond, individual and collective honour were inextricably linked with each other. Competitions for honour, therefore, had a double function: they demonstrated the dignity of an order or a corporation to people outside of it and they distributed 'symbolic capital' among the individuals within it. To fulfil these functions, honour had to be displayed in public, visible ideally to the whole of society and necessarily to inferior orders (see Figure 6). Every community of honour developed a set of rituals, symbols and gestures to parade its collective honour in front of others, and obligated its members to a code of honour, which basically was a set of rules for public conduct. The model to imitate in these respects, from the ninth to the nineteenth century, was the honourable class per se, the nobility.

How complex and sophisticated the culture of honour had become by the end of the Middle Ages can be exemplified by a medieval invention shrouded in myth: the tournament. Contrary to popular belief, the heyday of the tourney came in the late medieval period, when chivalric warfare was already in decline. At the end of the fifteenth century, concerted efforts were made to reserve the right to participate at tournaments to men of immaculately noble pedigree, whose forebears had never soiled their reputation. Fixed rules had already been established for each contest and referees appointed to supervise them. Many of these rules provided for a temporary suspension of the (growing) hierarchies within the nobility; for instance, in a joust – the famous combat between two mounted knights tilting against each other with blunted lances – a knight had the right to challenge a king and vice versa. By contrast, the hierarchical distinctions between the orders of noblemen and commoners were ostentatiously celebrated. Most tournaments were staged in towns – if possible under exclusion of townspeople, who were only allowed to follow the spectacle from outside. In front of these 'walled-in peasants', whose growing economic and political power had already spread to the surrounding countryside, the nobility pretended to have an absolute monopoly on the most honourable of terrains: armed conflict[29] (see Figure 7).

The tournament also offers insight into the challenges the traditional culture of honour faced in the late medieval period. As indicated, its popularity among the noble classes was correlated with the fact that it represented a chivalric ideal of war that was increasingly at odds with the military reality of big infantry units, which were made up of commoners and designed to cause immense casualties. In this respect, the aristocratic investments in the economy of honour at tournaments reflected an attempt to ward off a threat from below rather than a confident display of unquestioned superiority. The conspicuous refusal by noblemen to compete with townsmen actually indicated that they had already been dragged into a wider competition with them. The leading families of many towns and cities were not only much richer than the lower aristocracy, but also more important to kings and princes – as both taxpayers and counsellors.

Indeed, a traditional economy of honour tends to 'overheat' as soon as the balance of power within a society shifts and social mobility begins to break the mould of a single order. It only functions properly when

---

[29] Morsel, 'Die Erfindung des Adels', 355; Graf, 'Der adel dem purger tregt hass', 193.

Figure 7 This woodcut of a joust in a German city, published in
1566, is indicative of the traditional economy of honour. It depicts
a hierarchically organised public observing two tilting knights at
a tournament in a town square. The jousting lists are enclosed
with barriers to separate the noble contestants and spectators from
the common bystanders. The large and crowded stands for the
townspeople on both sides are built behind the barriers, whereas the
two stands for the high-ranking onlookers are placed within them,
one on the portico of the main building and the other on wooden
pillars to the right. In addition, the latter two are more elevated,
enabling the noble audience to look down at the commoners. While
the joust represents an exclusive contest for individual honour
between two noblemen, the tournament as a whole displays the
superior collective honour of the nobility in view of the townspeople,
who, by watching the spectacle, symbolically accept the hierarchy
imposed on them.

people of different orders are in general agreement about the hierarchies between them and therefore able to avoid potentially dishonourable
confrontations. As a rule, the more stable a traditional society is, the
less energy is absorbed by conflicts of honour. Fewer people can clash,
and clashes follow stricter rituals. To look at it the other way round:
when social climbers become too high in numbers to be easily absorbed
by higher orders, the old elites face a contradictory challenge: they have

to enter into a competition with classes rising from below in order to push them back to their previous positions, and at the same time, they must refuse to acknowledge that they are competing at all.

The only solution to this situation is insults in disguise, attacks launched with gestures of indifference. For the rising classes, on the other hand, the goal is to achieve the status of honourable competitors by imitating the old elite's way of distinction and by publicly challenging its members to compete. As a consequence, there is an outbreak of conflicts of honour fought under different terms, and these conflicts more easily escalate, as they are not limited any more by the ritualistic procedure following a mutually accepted protocol. Voltaire's uncontrolled encounter with the Chevalier de Rohan is a late, but typical example of such circumstances.

In many respects, the fifteenth century corresponded to the model of a traditional society of honour shaken up by unprecedented social mobility. Rich patricians and merchants aspired to noble status by abandoning business or by concealing their commercial practices, by buying landed estates and by asking for titles of nobility. The boundaries between orders further blurred due to the secular lifestyle of many clerics, particularly from the upper ranks of the Church, who preferred the prestige and comfort of a courtly environment to the spiritual authority of a deliberately modest existence – even at the cost of higher anticlericalism. And with the new breed of humanist scholars loudly pretending to represent a 'spiritual nobility' (*nobilitas animi*) of higher dignity than the 'inherited nobility' (*nobilitas sanguinis*) of the second order, the aristocracy in general and the lesser nobility in particular saw its traditional claim to superior honour and higher rank challenged from several sides.

One consequence of this situation was an increasingly conflict-laden relationship between urban and landed elites and also between clerics and laymen; another was a growing insecurity of many groups and individuals about their own status and place within society; and a third was a rising disposition for new concepts of collective and individual honour, which promised higher status stability than the traditional ones.

Against this background, the invention of national honour in the fifteenth century can be understood as both a symptom of and an attempted remedy for a traditional culture of honour getting out of control. But before we can see how and why it combined these two opposite functions, we have to clarify the new dimensions of national honour in comparison with the traditional honour culture.

Contrary to older concepts of collective honour, which were primarily aimed at hierarchical relationships (both upwards and downwards) to other communities of honour, national honour classified other nations as coequals. It drew the community boundaries according to a changeable mix of linguistic (*lingua*), behavioural (*mores*), territorial (*regna*) and cosmographical criteria, but not according to order and rank. In other words, it included princes and peasants, soldiers and clergymen, educated and ignorant. This does not mean that it flattened social hierarchies; it complemented hierarchical concepts of honour without putting them into doubt. A craftsman still contributed to the national honour as a craftsman, a nobleman as a nobleman, and a prince as a prince. But when a craftsman made a useful innovation, he shared its prestige with the noblemen and princes of his nation.

An early expression of this idea can be found in the colophon of one of the first prints produced after the invention of the printing press, in 1460. It linked the 'wondrous agreement, proportion and harmony of punches and types' to 'the renowned German nation, which God's grace has deigned to prefer and distinguish above all other nations of the earth with so lofty a genius and liberal gifts'.[30] It is probable that the printer of the book was Johannes Gutenberg, who, a few decades later, was indeed glorified by Renaissance humanists as a German national hero.

The only groups who could not be fully integrated into the nation were those generally regarded as incapable of claiming honour: unfree people. This applied to bondsmen and, to a lesser degree, to women. The legal status of freedom was a prerequisite to both individual and collective honour, because only those who credibly claimed to make independent decisions and to take full responsibility for their actions could be rewarded with honour and punished with shame. Dependants only passively enjoyed or suffered from their master's deeds in the field of honour, if at all. Consequently, the construction of the nation as a community of honour also explains why the idea of freedom was – and still is – so pivotal for nationalism. Just as an individual has to be free in order to share and increase the national honour, the national community as a whole has to be free of external influence in order to act as an honourable body.

5.4   National honour: symptom of an overheating economy of honour

If the concept of national honour was so different from those within the traditional economy of honour, why then can it be seen as a symptom

---

[30] Flood, 'Nationalistic Currents', 131.

of its overheating? There are at least three reasons for this assumption. First, the concept was soon used as a new tool to continue the old fights of precedence between different classes. In the German lands, for instance, clerics, merchants and jurists were accused of dishonouring the German nation – clerics for following foreign commands, merchants for introducing foreign goods and habits, jurists for replacing German law with Roman law. Such accusations had already been brought forward in the fifteenth century,[31] but at the beginning of the sixteenth century they were extended and radicalised by humanist scholars and then popularised in the early years of the Reformation.

To give just a few examples: the Swabian humanist, Heinrich Bebel, published an invective against the disciples of Justinian at German universities in 1509, which he claimed to have written out of 'love of the fatherland' and which he completed with an appeal to 'all Germans' not to allow 'that our praise, our glory and our honour will be ruined'.[32] The Alsatian polemicist Jacob Wimpfeling and his humanist friends in Strasbourg and Augsburg tried to defame German mendicants by calling them 'half-French' (*semigalli*) and 'traitors of the German fatherland'.[33] And the poet laureate Conrad Celtis, in his elegant description of Nuremberg, published in 1502, belittled the merchants of the Imperial city as importers of a degenerate lifestyle, whose impact on citizens he described with the words: 'Consequently ... they do not live on the soil, the sky and the air, but only on money'.[34]

All these texts were written in Latin, but after Luther's initial diatribes against the Roman curia, humanist pamphlets started to appear in German, too. The Imperial knight, political activist and humanist, Ulrich von Hutten, published a series of popular writings between 1520 and his early death in 1523, in which he attacked clerics, lawyers and merchants as robbers of the German nation, both in a literal and metaphorical sense. The order of the priests, for instance, was described as an 'impediment and disgrace to the whole nation' (*ein verstellung vnd vnzyer der gantzen nation*), made up of creatures who 'have nothing German in them' (*haben nichts teütsches an jn*).[35] It was only consistent with this verdict, when Hutten, in another pamphlet, called for a *bellum sacerdotale*, a national war on priests.[36]

---

[31] See Hirschi, *Wettkampf der Nationen*, 147–56.
[32] Bebel, *Apologia contra Iustinianum*, 115, 2.
[33] Mertens, 'Jakob Wimpfeling', 50; Hirschi, *Wettkampf der Nationen*, 345.
[34] Celtis, *Norimberga*, XVI, 74.
[35] Hutten, 'Die Anschawenden', in *Gespräch büchlin*, 178.
[36] Idem, *Praedones*, 402–5.

While humanists tried to disparage certain social or professional groups by portraying them as agents of foreign interests, they fashioned themselves in contrasting colours, claiming to add to the national honour in two ways: on the one hand by publicly commemorating past deeds of national heroes, thereby teaching fellow countrymen how to contribute to the glory of the nation themselves, and, on the other hand, by producing literary masterpieces of lasting value and high prestige. In other words, their discourse of national honour eventually served the self-centred purpose of achieving the status of honourable men and political authorities.

The second reason to regard the concept of national honour as an indicator of an escalating traditional honour culture is the enormous gap between rhetoric and reach of the nationalist discourse. Although all free countrymen were offered a share of the national honour, only few actually had the chance to learn about their newly gained privilege. There is no evidence that the overwhelming majority of the European population – those living in rural areas, moving around very little and having no literary education at all – became acquainted with the national discourse, let alone had any use for its concept of honour. If they lived close to cultural or territorial borders, they could of course harbour xenophobic beliefs, but these were still a far cry from the comparably sophisticated ideas about a competition between nations.

To a large extent, the national discourse remained reserved for the same educated and politicised elites who had dominated the discussions at the Council of Constance, and who later acted as state or church officials. If they brought up the topic of national honour in their mother tongue, they hardly ever addressed the populace, but the princes and patricians, whose literary education did not allow for communication in Latin. In general, the discourse of national honour remained limited to those groups who were considered to have a political, literary or artistic impact. Apart from rulers, scholars, artists and craftsmen, only soldiers were regularly counted among them. Even during the Reformation, nationalistic rhetoric kept, with very few exceptions, an elitist tone, although it was more widespread among urban classes than before. The more populist the religious propaganda was meant to be, the less nationalistic it tended to be.

On the whole, the massive gap between the rhetorical shape and the practical outreach of the pre-modern nation created an 'imagined community' in a much more radical way than Benedict Anderson had ever imagined.

The third and final reason to assume that the concept of national honour was symptomatic of an 'overheated' economy of honour is that a competition between nations, as it was rhetorically invoked, could only work to a limited extent under the circumstances of the time. As mentioned before, conflicts of honour had to be carried out in front of a public which was not directly involved and which shared the roles of witness and judge. In some cases, these roles were clearly divided, as in the tournament, where referees oversaw the competition and the noble public confirmed the outcome. Generally, the traditional economy of honour depended on small-scale competitions, which allowed an eminent place for external observers.

This basic condition was eliminated with the concept of national honour. As all free men were supposed to join the competition, no one could judge it from a detached point of view. As a consequence, apart from the battlefield, where the outcome was generally undisputed, the results of competitions between nations had to remain in limbo. There was no mutually accepted authority to evaluate which nation could justly claim the greatest literary treasures, the most magnificent churches, the highest mountains, the mildest climate, the most fertile lands, the most civilised inhabitants etc.[37] As a consequence, early nationalists often tried to act as both competitors and referees, claiming a superior ranking of their nation and then directly confirming it to their countrymen. With such a shortcut, they created a competitive discourse, which could do without a competition at all.

5.5   How to measure the standing of a nation?

Given this contradiction, one could be tempted to jump to the conclusion that nationalist language was (and is) only good for creating an artificial image of the nation. But that would be missing the point. The main reason why the competition of nations had to run at idle to a considerable degree in the late medieval period can be seen in the massive innovation which the concept of national honour brought about. Measured against the traditional economy of honour, it was far too complex to work properly. With its universalistic principle that every honourable person was part of the competition, it would have had to create supra-national bodies, made up of representatives of all nations acting together as regulators and referees. As we know, it would take several more centuries, plus the uncontrolled clashes of nations in two World Wars, plus enormous financial and political investments before such a supra-national regulatory framework would eventually start to take shape. From this perspective, the establishment and empowerment

---

[37] For examples of such claims, see Hirschi, *Wettkampf der Nationen*, 276–7.

of the UN, the WTO and UNESCO as well as the earlier foundations of international sports organisations, such as the IOC and FIFA, do not mark the end of the age of nationalism, but its culmination.

However, even under the conditions of the fifteenth and sixteenth century, it was possible to establish rudimentary forms of measurement, which allowed, at least in some categories of competition, an unbiased assessment of the standing of one's own nation in comparison to others. One such measurement was enabled by the invention of print. Quite a few Renaissance humanists were already guided by the idea of 'internationally certified' heroes and achievements, when they tried to confirm their claims to national greatness by consulting the writings of foreign authors; the argument was always the same: if a foreigner said something positive about one's own nation, then it had to be true. This was, of course, a broad-brush conclusion, based on an incorrect assumption, but it had logic behind it. As all foreigners were taken for nationalists, they were thought to have no inclination to flatter any nation apart from their own – ergo, when giving a positive comment on a foreign country, they had to be guided by the truth.[38] Nevertheless, in order to offer such proof at all, writers needed the literary production of other countries at their disposal, not least contemporary works, and this was only possible through the printing revolution. German humanists, for instance, could notice proudly around 1500 that in the field of inventions the *Germanum ingenium* had the edge on other nations.[39] Not only the printing press, but also the bombard was universally recognised as a German achievement.

Another way to measure the standing of one's own nation was the communicative behaviour displayed by those challenged. It roughly followed the rules of the traditional economy of honour, according to which the reaction of the challenged honoured or shamed the challenger. When Italian humanists, painters and architects of the *Quattrocento* likened the French and Germans to barbarians, trapped in bad taste, ill manners and creative impotence, they soon had every reason to understand the reception of their insults abroad as a confirmation of their loudly claimed cultural superiority. In both France and Germany, artists and writers reacted by a paradoxical double strategy: they strongly denied the accusations and eagerly imitated the accusers. And when they launched a counter-attack on a different field – preferably moral standards and piety – the Italians saw themselves in the happy position

[38] For examples, see Hirschi, *Wettkampf der Nationen*, 290.
[39] Brant, 'Ad dominum Johannem Bergmann de Olpe', in *Kleine Texte*, vol. I.2, no. 228, 17–30.

of answering with sovereign silence. So what the Germans and French had lost as the challenged ones could not be won back as challengers, whatever insults they uttered. However, the Italian attitude of being comfortably numb to foreign aggressions only worked well as long as the challenges from northern nations were brought forward by ink and pen. It first turned into a liability at the end of the fifteenth century, when most Italian city states overlooked the looming danger of being overrun by the armies of the French King and the Emperor. And it came for a second time with a heavy price after 1517, when the Italian-dominated Curia completely underestimated the danger of Luther's religious reform movement and ridiculed it as a 'monks' squabble' until it was too late.

The clearest possible measurement to assess the standing of nations against each other was also the most political: diplomatic precedence. In the traditional economy of honour, the spatial position of a person or group in a public event was regarded as a direct expression of their honour. Public spots of symbolic value could therefore be fiercely contested, as at the Council of Basle (1431–49), where representatives of the Kings of Castile and England almost ended up sitting on each others' laps in the church, because they went for the same pews. By the end of the fifteenth century, the Papal Court established a protocol for public processions in Rome, which specified the standing of each ruler and their diplomatic representatives in the cortege. According to a scheme drawn up by a master of ceremonies under Pope Julius II in 1504, the Pope came first, then the Emperor, followed by the King of the Romans, the King of France, the King of Spain etc.[40] The Papal order of precedence was presented as an official ranking for the power and status of all monarchs and states within Christendom. While most rulers quickly accepted it as an authoritative public ritual, some aspired to a higher standing for themselves and a lower one for their competitors. As a result, there were many symbolic battles, fought with scholarly propaganda by lawyers and historians, with wrangling among diplomats for the right place in the cortege, and even with blood, when neither party wanted to retreat.

The arguments brought forward in these struggles were to a great extent identical with the literary competition for national honour among Renaissance humanists, and sometimes, the persons involved were identical, too. When Spanish diplomats at the Roman Curia in the late 1550s picked probably the longest and fiercest quarrel for precedence by claiming the spot in front of the French, they made their case with a

---

[40] Anderson, *The Rise of Modern Diplomacy*, 17–18.

whole range of comparative observations. Don Luis de Requeséns, the humanistically educated Spanish ambassador to the Papacy, complained that the current order did not reflect the recent Spanish expansion of power, territory and reputation through the unification of Spain and the conquest of the 'Indies'. He further maintained that the Pope did not consider the seniority of Spain in terms of the antiquity of its realm and the date of its Christianisation.[41] All these points were made in the name of Spanish honour, and so Requeséns and his colleagues were unwilling to concede defeat, even when they realised they were fighting a hopeless cause.

Outside the Roman Curia, Spain's challenge for precedence against France was maintained until the early 1660s, when it came to a sudden end in a telling manner. In September 1661, the Swedish ambassador to England was expected for an official reception at the court of Whitehall. Both the French and the Spanish envoys quickly claimed the first place behind the official guest's carriage. When the host, King Charles II, refused to take a decision, preparations were made for a contest. On the day of the reception, the carriages of the French and Spanish were on site hours before the event, guarded by armed men and surrounded by the populace of London. Thanks to a clever strategy, the Spanish carriage drove off next to the Swedish, leaving behind an urban battle-field with several dead and dozens wounded. Yet, the Spanish victory was short-lived. Louis XIV flexed his military muscles and threatened Spain with war, thereby forcing the weakened Spanish monarchy finally to declare its inferiority. Once again, the order of precedence officially represented the dignity of states and the honour of nations.

5.6   National honour: remedy for an overheating economy of honour

Having demonstrated that the competition for national honour did function to a certain degree, we now have to ascertain whether it actually helped to remedy the effects of an 'overheating' traditional economy of honour. To find clues of such an effect, we need to turn to the use of nationalistic rhetoric in the political propaganda of the fifteenth century. As soon as the language of national honour entered the field of secular politics, it merged with the long-established discourse of patriotism. In 1443, the Italian humanist Enea Silvio Piccolomini, who had just entered the service of Emperor Frederick III while participating at the Council of Basle, published a literary dialogue in which the author's

---

[41] Levin, 'A New World Order', 252/256.

alter ego presented a draft for a speech by the Emperor to the Imperial Diet, where the political dignitaries of the German lands assembled. In his fictitious oration, Frederick declared that he had, after being implored by 'very grave and prudent men of our nation', only accepted the Imperial crown on two grounds: 'care for German honour' (*honori Germanico consulerem*) and the will to 'save the fatherland' (*patrie retinendi*).[42]

As we have seen in Chapter Four, patriotism invoked an image of the political community as an abstract body, whose members willingly sacrificed themselves for the defence of the common freedom. With its stress on the voluntary nature of a citizen's commitment and on collective liberty as the highest good, the patriotic language proved an ideal complement to the discourse of national honour. Through the amalgamation of the two, patriotism became much more competitive, while the concept of national honour multiplied its mobilising force.

During the second half of the fifteenth century, this language was increasingly used to stress the need for political consolidation in order to force back foreign enemies. In the German lands, it was the Emperor and his counsellors who gradually monopolised the rhetoric of collective pride and fear and who spread it in mandates and missives, the official propaganda genres of the time.[43] Interestingly enough, they used it almost exclusively in their communication with German princes and municipalities and hardly ever in their correspondence with foreign rulers.[44] The reason for this separation is to be found in the political function of the national discourse. It was mainly used to compensate for the limited legal means of the Emperor to coerce subsidiary powers within the Empire into supporting his military campaigns outside of the Empire. Appeals to the national honour and patriotic duty were meant to raise the psychological pressure on princes and municipalities to contribute troops or money of their own volition. It would be an exaggeration to say that this strategy was a great success. Both Frederick III and his son Maximilian I received mostly negative answers, but the language of these answers indicates that the pressure was felt. German princes and patricians tried to defend themselves with the same vocabulary the Emperor had used before. With this, they signalled their acceptance of the moral duties which the national discourse laid upon them, while rejecting the specific terms set by the Emperor.

[42] Piccolomini, *Pentalogus 2,2*.
[43] Schröcker, *Die deutsche Nation*, II/93.
[44] Hirschi, *Wettkampf der Nationen*, 161.

When German humanists joined the political propaganda at the end of the fifteenth century, they predominantly acted as staunch supporters of the Emperor. Bebel, Wimpfeling, Celtis and others called for a halt to all strife between German estates for the greater good of the national honour and the freedom of the fatherland. Any wasting of political energy for power and precedence within the German lands was condemned as selfish and self-destructive behaviour. In this sense, the concept of national honour now served the purpose of cooling down the traditional economy of honour in order to increase the competition between national communities. It can be understood as an early attempt to collect and redirect rising social aggression to the borders of the political community. Although this attempt was thwarted by the Reformation, the nationalistic ideal of inner peace and outer aggression eventually prevailed.

I would like to close this chapter with an anecdote from one of Maximilian's many military adventures abroad, which ended with empty pockets and deserting troops. In the autumn of 1516, the old Emperor faced a rebellion by his German soldiers, after having in vain tried to oust the French King from Lombardy. Running out of cash and provisions, with the winter looming, he desperately tried to keep his army together. According to the *Memorabilia* of the Austrian nobleman Georg Kirchmair (1481–1554), written after the Emperor's death in 1519, Maximilian was lampooned by his men as 'Apple King' (*apfelkunig*) and 'Straw King' (*strokunig*) and then addressed them with the following words:

Listen to me, my beloved Germans! My beloved, famous and familiar Landsknechts! ... If you do not want to reprieve me, so remember the honour of the German nation! After all, you are German, unless the air here [in Italy] during the last five years, since you have been here, has transplanted Italian hearts and dispositions into you. Remember that you are Landsknechts and not Swiss![45]

The comparison at the end alluded to the reputation of Swiss mercenaries to render their services to the highest bidder and to turn their back on them as soon as another prince offered more. We do not have to believe that Maximilian addressed his soldiers in exactly these words, but it is telling enough that he could have done it.

---

[45] Kirchmair, 'Denkwürdigkeiten seiner Zeit', in Wiesflecker-Friedhuber (ed.), *Quellen*, 249.

6 The nationalist transformation of borders and languages

Nature speaks our German language in all things which make a sound. Thus, quite a few wished to think that the first man, Adam, had only been able to name the birds and all other animals with our words, because he expressed every innate sound according to its nature; it is no surprise, therefore, that most of our root words conform to the sacred language.

Georg Philipp Harsdörffer, *Treatise to Protect the Work on the German Language*, 1644

The bond of language, customs and even of the common name unites humans in such a strong, yet invisible way and creates, as it were, a kind of kinship. A letter or a journal concerning our nation can offend or delight us.

Gottfried Wilhelm Leibniz, *Exhortation to the Germans*, 1679

When the members of the English and French *natio* were about to cross swords at the Council of Constance, a clergyman in the little town of Bielefeld, a few hundred miles further north, completed a world chronicle with the title *Cosmidromius*. His name was Gobelinus Person, and in his introduction he made the following observation:

While the ancients considered a division of provinces following the border-lines and the ends of rivers, mountains, forests and seas, the modern populace makes such distinctions according to the differences of vernaculars.[1]

As a consequence, Gobelinus continued, it was now possible that a local community, depending on the means of measurement, belonged to two different provinces. By calling his contemporaries, who defined boundaries based on linguistic criteria, *vulgares*, Gobelinus indicated that he did not approve of this change. He perceived the replacement of natural with cultural demarcations as a bottom-up process, which was generally considered the wrong direction in late medieval society.

If we compare Gobelinus' clear-cut distinction with other writings of the fifteenth century which deal with the political significance of

---

[1] Gobelinus Person, *Cosmidromius*, 3.

vernaculars, we come to a contrary conclusion. The identification of political and linguistic boundaries seems to have been introduced top-down, from royal courts to princely estates to city councils to villages etc. In the following paragraphs, I will present the case of the German lands as an example of a more general process in Western Europe.

Identifying political borders with language boundaries seems to be obvious from a present-day perspective. However, this is the result of a long and largely violent process of demarcation; populations were linguistically unified through education and migration, and territorial borders were shifted to separate people who belonged to different language groups.

This process had barely started at the beginning of the fifteenth century, when Gobelinus noticed a changed perception of political borders. In most medieval territories, different language groups lived alongside each other, often within the same local communities. The term 'language group' is itself problematic because most vernaculars lacked a standard language that enabled people from different regions to understand each other. Martin Luther, whose translation of the Bible had an enormous impact on the standardisation of German, discussed this issue repeatedly with his learned friends in his *Table Talks*. On one occasion, they proudly pronounced that the 'German language is the most perfect of all', but conceded that 'there are many dialects and manners of speaking in the German language so that often one man does not properly understand the other, such as the Bavarians the Saxons etc., especially those who have not been on the move'.[2]

As to political borders, they rarely had the shape of a clear and officially accepted demarcation line; rather, they formed a frontier region marked by overlapping territorial claims as the local authorities had allegiances to rulers on both sides. On the whole, Gobelinus' account did not reflect the political reality of his time, but it anticipated a development which would completely transform the political landscape in the centuries to come – and which would start well before the age of nation-states! As early as 1552, for instance, senior German princes decided to hand over permanently the Imperial cities of Cambray, Toul, Metz and Verdun to the King of France, only on the ground that their citizens did not speak 'the German language'.[3]

---

[2] Luther, *Tischreden*, fol. 606.
[3] Pariset (ed.), *La France*, 259.

6.1   'Tongue' as political space

How were scholars of the late medieval period, such as Gobelinus Person, able to anticipate a process that was barely visible during their lifetime? If the speakers of German languages were hardly capable of understanding each other, let alone claim a common allegiance to a political community, they needed incentives from abroad to define themselves as both a linguistic and political unit. This was exactly what happened. The Germans, one could say, are an Italian invention. During the Middle Ages, German-speaking princes, knights, merchants and monks had a regular presence on the Italian peninsula, not least because it was part of the common Holy Roman Empire. Even in the late tenth and eleventh century the local population started to label the visitors from the north as one single language group by calling them *Teutonici*. They were able to do so because they could not understand their language. Instead, they perceived it as one single noise. Over time, the German-speaking visitors to Italy adopted the foreign attribution and imported it to their homelands when going back over the Alps.

As early as around 1200, the word 'German tongue' (*tiutschiu zunge*) was used in the vernacular. 'Zunge' could mean both the language and the people speaking it as their mother tongue. In his political lyrics, the minnesinger Walther von der Vogelweide (*c.* 1170–1230) even used 'tiutschiu zunge' to address the people in charge of the Holy Empire.[4] However, it took another two hundred years for the term to become a standard element of the political vocabulary. For a few decades during the fifteenth century, 'Zunge' or 'Gezung' was used as the vernacular equivalent to Latin 'natio', before it was replaced by the German neologism 'Nation' at the end of the century.

By then, 'Zunge' or 'Gezung' often carried the double meaning of the language group and the land allegedly possessed by it. In other words, the term precisely conveyed the idea that linguistic and political spaces were identical. German princes and the Emperor discussed how the 'German tongue' could be defended against 'the vileness and undue infractions and invasions by other tongues'.[5] Between 1450 and 1490, the term 'foreign tongues' (*fremde gezung*) could, depending on the political situation, refer to the Hungarians, the French and the Turks. Significantly, it made no distinctions between Christian and non-Christian powers.

---

[4] Walther von der Vogelweide, *Reichston*, in *Spruchlyrik*, 74.
[5] Johannes von Lysura, 'Ratslagung', in Weinrich (ed.), *Quellen zur Reichsreform*, 313.

During the same period, the chancelleries of the cities and principal-ities of southern Germany assimilated the written vernaculars for official correspondence, legal matters and public statements. 'Upper Germany' (*Oberdeutschland*) and Alsace were not only the economic and cultural engine of the Holy Roman Empire, driven by Imperial cities such as Augsburg, Nuremberg and Strasbourg, but also its political centre. The Habsburg dynasty, which had been in possession of the Imperial crown since 1440, had many allies and hereditary lands in southern Germany, while it was hardly present in the north. Accordingly, the Imperial chan-celleries played a major role in the assimilation of official vernaculars.[6] Another important factor was the institutionalisation of supra-regional politics through the convocation of regular diets, the construction of diplomatic networks and the extension of written communication.[7] It is unclear if the process of language assimilation was deliberately pushed by political authorities or simply brought about by these struc-tural changes. Anyhow, it helped the people involved to imagine 'the German tongue' as a political space well before the printing revolution had any significant impact on late medieval government.

The 'German tongue' was also characterised as a community of honour, reflecting the meaning of 'natio' according to the Council of Constance. At the Diet of Ratisbon in 1454, Johannes Lysura, a legal scholar acting as an envoy of the electoral princes, argued vis-à-vis the Emperor's representatives that the German electors, when declining Frederick's request to help him fight the Turks, were pursuing 'in par-ticular the honour, benefit, improvement and welfare of the laudable German tongue' (*des loblichen Deutschen gezunges ere, nutz, frummen und wolfarn*). In the same speech, Lysura called the German tongue 'such a genteel and noble country' (*solich fürnemig und edel land, als Teutsch gezunge ist*).[8] About forty years later, Maximilian promoted an extra tax to finance a war against the Hungarians and the Turks in order to prevent these 'two outlandish, un-Christian and foreign tongues' from diminishing the 'honour and dignity' of the 'German nation'. His terminology excluded a minor Christian power from the commu-nity of believers, while treating the most threatening non-Christian power as one 'tongue' among many. Using the words 'Dewtsch nation', the Emperor's writing also reflected the declining appeal of the word 'Gezung'.[9] Semantically, 'nation' was less precise and, thus, politically

---

[6] Tennant, *The Habsburg Chancery Language*.
[7] Polenz, *Deutsche Sprachgeschichte*, I, 161–2.
[8] Johannes von Lysura, 'Ratslagung', in Weinrich (ed.), *Quellen zur Reichsreform*, 309–14.
[9] Janssen (ed.), *Frankfurts Reichscorrespondenz*, 571.

more suitable. Those using the term, could, according to political expediency, stress the criterion of language, lineage, custom or territory, while seemingly speaking of the same thing.

Treating a language group as a community of honour did not mean, though, that the language itself was regarded as a source of collective honour. There are only rare indications of such a positive attitude towards vernaculars in the late medieval period, most of them from Tuscany. German men of learning found it particularly hard to esteem their mother tongue because it had the reputation of being raw and unpolished – in short, a *lingua barbara*.

One of the few who tried to reassess the general perception of German dialects was the Zurich-born Dominican Felix Fabri (1438/39–1502). He undertook various pilgrimages, which brought him as far as Jerusalem and Alexandria. In his Latin reports from his journeys, he interposed an anecdote here and there to highlight his veneration of German, which he considered 'the noblest, clearest and most refined language' (*lingua nobilissima, clarissima et humanissima*).[10] According to him, even animals shared this view. When waiting in Venice for the boat to the Holy Land – one anecdote goes – Fabri stayed in a place with the telling name 'The German House'. This hostelry, lying close to the *Fondaco dei Tedeschi*, where the German merchants took quarters, had traditionally accommodated pilgrims from north of the Alps and now counted among its personnel a famous watchdog, which made sure things remained that way. When German-speaking foreigners – from whatever part of their country – entered the place, he welcomed them happily, wagging his tail; when Italians, French, Slavs, Greeks and other Non-Germans stepped in, he rejected them with hostile barking.[11]

6.2   'Adam was a German'

The German-loving Venetian watchdog of Fabri's account was still a harmless creature compared to an anonymous chauvinist who wrote a *Book of a Hundred Chapters* around 1500. It was only discovered in the late nineteenth century and its author was then given the misleading name 'Upper Rhine Revolutionary'. Far from calling for a violent renewal of the political and social order, the German writer braced himself against the idea that things were allowed to change at all. What he was particularly unhappy about, was the dominance of Latin over German, which he regarded as very recent and, consequently, utterly wrong. According

---

[10] Fabri, *Evagatorium in Terrae Sanctae*, III, 349.   [11] Ibid., I, 84.

to him, the 'holy German language' (*heilige dudesche sproch*) was the oldest in the world: 'Adam was a German', he claimed, which was why the Germans were called 'Almans' – all men. When God confused the languages at Babel, so the author said, Noah's son Japheth, the first German, had already moved to Germany with his people, where they stayed ever after.[12]

The 'harmful Latin language' (*schedlich sproch Latin*), on the contrary, was invented by a slave called Latinus at a time when the Germans were still ruling the world. According to the anonymous writer, Latin united the slaves against their masters and established an unlawful law, whose principle was 'this is mine, that is yours' (*das ist min, das ist din*), and finally helped a people, whose progenitor – Romulus – was the son of a whore, usurp universal power.[13] Before the end of time, all traces of this perverse order created by the Romans had to be removed, starting with the present organisation of the Church. At last, the world would return to what it had been at the start: a place where German was spoken and Germans had the say.

The so-called Upper Rhine Revolutionary must have been a legally trained scholar, but his complete inability to cope intellectually with the changing realities of his time separated him from most other nationalist authors of his generation. The unpopularity of his ideas is all the more remarkable, as some were not completely new; the German-speaking Adam, for instance, had already appeared in a Latin text from the thirteenth century.[14] Yet, no other author around 1500 felt inclined to use this idea as a source of national pride, let alone as a linguistic proof that the Germans were God's chosen people. It is therefore not a complete coincidence that the *Book of a Hundred Chapters* was only discovered four hundred years after it had been written.

Most authors who praised the German language before the Reformation preferred to do so in Latin, thereby indicating that they saw no point in challenging the status of the official language of learning and literature. They had other reasons to stick to Latin, too. It was the only tool to inform foreign readers about the greatness of the German language, and it thereby upheld the idea of a competition between nations.

Among the German Renaissance humanists, there were only a few who brought up the vernacular to boost the reputation of their nation.[15]

---

[12] Franke (ed.), *Das Buch der hundert Kapitel*, fol. 14ª/33ᵇ–34ª.

[13] Ibid., fol. 51ᵃ⁻ᵇ/73ᵇ.

[14] Schnell, 'Deutsche Literatur und deutsches Nationsbewusstsein', 306.

[15] Günzburg, *Ein zamengelesen bouchlin von der Teutschen Nation*, 39.

Those who did, however, introduced elements of an argument which would be exploited by later nationalists for centuries to come. They had two sources of inspiration for this. One was the linguistic purism of humanist philologists trying to restore the alleged original beauty of classical Latin. The other one was a little ethnographic text that had been rediscovered in a German monastery after 1450; it was soon attributed to Cornelius Tacitus and given the title *Germania*. We will look at its impact on humanist nationalism in the following chapter, but what we need to know at this point is that it described the ancient *Germani* as an indigenous people free of foreign influence.

The young Swabian humanist Franciscus Irenicus (1494–1553) expanded on this myth of genealogical purity in his *Explanation of Germany* (*Germaniae exegesis*) of 1518. While the Italian vernacular, he argued, had been contaminated by the idioms of the invading Dacians, Lombards and Goths, the German language had only adopted from Latin and Greek those words which the unconquered Germans deemed appropriate; it thus preserved its original richness. Furthermore, German was older than Latin, Irenicus declared, which had originally been regarded as a barbarian language, too.[16]

A more purist stance was taken by the Bavarian humanist Johannes Aventinus (1477–1534) in the German reworking of his Latin *Annals of the Bavarians* (*Annales Boiorum*). In his introduction, he made the case for translating Latin texts only into 'the old, natural, generally intelligible German' (*das alte, natürliche, iederman verstendige teutsch*), condemning any use of 'kitchen-Latin' (*kuchenlatein*) – a German riddled with Latin vocabulary.[17] A few pages further down, he added the story that 'our forefathers, the old Germans, were a bit more audacious and superstitious in this respect; they refused alien, foreign, incomprehensible words as an ill-fated thing, which neither meant nor brought anything good, and so they only used the words of their own language'.[18] Here, the purity of the language is already linked to the health of the nation.

6.3   Purifying the German language (and the German people)

Several generations later, in the seventeenth century, the German literati took the next big step in charging the vernacular with nationalist meaning. For this, they needed some inspiration from the French, who

---

[16] Irenicus, *Germaniae exegesis* II, 30, fol. 38ʳ.
[17] Aventinus, *Bayerische Chronik*, vol. IV/1, 5–6.   [18] Ibid., 15–16.

in turn had been inspired by the Italians. Starting with Dante's *On the Eloquence of the Vernacular* (*De vulgari eloquentia*) around 1300, Italian philologists had been slowly but successfully transforming the 'volgare' into a standard literary language of equal value to Latin. When the French tried the same with their vernacular in the decades after 1530, they added a significant element: Latin was now turned into a foreign language, which had to be expelled, and the revaluation of French was declared a matter of national honour.

Joachim du Bellay (1525–60), Pierre de Ronsard (1524–85) and others gave authors writing in French the title of 'good Frenchmen' (*bons François*) while attacking French Latinists as 'enemies of the French name' (*enemys du nom Françoys*).[19] Some of the *bons François* then reversed the standard chronology concerning the origins of languages. In this way, Latin became a bastardised version of French. A few overly ambitious scholars even argued that the French deserved the credit for achievements traditionally attributed to the Greeks. For Pierre de la Ramée (1515–72), there was no doubt that the ancestors of the French, the Gauls, 'were the first authors of philosophy' (*les Gaulloys fussent premiers autheurs de la Philosophie*), and Étienne Pasquier (1529–1615) reinforced the conviction held by fellow countrymen that the Greek alphabet, too, was a Gallic invention.[20]

Ironically, most of the French authors engaged in the nationalist re-evaluation of their mother tongue were trained humanists and drew on their mastery of Latin when transforming the French vernacular into a standardised literary language. Some even continued to write and publish in Latin as well, which shows that purist rhetoric and pragmatist practice did not necessarily exclude each other in the early modern period.

When German authors of the seventeenth century undertook a coordinated attempt to turn their own vernacular into a literary language, which would increase the national honour, the French served both as a model to imitate and as an adversary to attack.[21] By then, French had already become the dominant courtly and diplomatic language in many parts of Europe, especially in the Holy Roman Empire. Presenting the cultivation of German as a question of national honour, patriotic duty and moral purification was a suitable means of uttering political criticism by cultural means.

[19] Böhm, '*Gallica Gloria*', 301.
[20] Asher, *National Myths*, 93–4.
[21] For the following, see Roelcke, 'Der Patriotismus', and Stukenbrock, *Sprachnationalismus*.

Some old arguments were good enough to serve this new purpose. After a long absence, the German Adam made another appearance, as did the claim that 'the German language is older than the Greek and Latin, which are only dialects of German'.[22] However, the genealogy of languages was now more closely linked to the genealogy of nations. Philipp von Zesen (1619–89), author of the above quotation and founder of a 'German-minded Confraternity' (*Teutschgesinnte Genossenschaft*) in Hamburg in 1643, added to his linguistic observations with the comment that the Greek and Latin peoples, too, 'sprouted from' the Germans (*von dem Deutschen volke entsprossen*).[23]

The German-speaking Adam also found himself in hitherto unfamiliar ideological territory. Georg Philipp Harsdörffer (1607–58), a Nuremberg patrician and poet, integrated God's first creature into a detailed portrayal of German as nature's own voice. In his *Treatise to Protect the Work on the German Language* (*Schutzschrift für die teütsche Spracharbeit*) of 1644, he asserted that German 'speaks with the tongues of nature', articulately expressing all its sounds:

It thunders with the heavens, flashes lightning with the fast clouds, patters with the hail, dashes with the winds, booms with the waves, creaks with the locks, resounds with the air, bangs with the cannons; it roars like a lion, lows like an ox, snarls like a bear, bells like a stag, bleats like a sheep, oinks like a pig, barks like a dog, neighs like a horse, hisses like a snake, meows like a cat, cackles like a goose, quacks like a duck, hums like a bumble bee, clucks like a hen, clatters like a stork, caws like a crow, coos like a swallow, chirps like a sparrow.[24]

To identify one's national language with animal noises was a risky strategy of claiming authenticity because it could invite foreign authors to read it as a confirmation of German's linguistic primitivism and barbarian sound. In Harsdörffer's treatise, though, naturalness had the connotation of absolute clarity, maximum richness and oldest age. This is why the German-speaking Adam was a welcome figure to him:

Nature speaks our German language in all things which make a sound. Thus, quite a few wished to think that the first man, Adam, had only been able to name the birds and all other animals with our words, because he expressed every innate sound according to its nature; it is no surprise, therefore, that most of our root words conform to the sacred language.[25]

German was not only the language spoken by Adam; it was the sound of the whole Garden of Eden.[26] By claiming to restore the original

---

[22] Zesen, *Rosen-mând*, 230.   [23] Ibid.
[24] Harsdörffer, *Schutzschrift*, 355.   [25] Ibid.
[26] Newman, 'Redemption in the Vernacular', 24.

German language, Harsdörffer and other language reformers could congratulate themselves on re-establishing a part of Paradise. Of course, no other nation was able to accomplish an equal task.

Harsdörffer was not alone in his attempt to sell German as a pure reflection of things – in modern words, as a language whose signifiers were identical with the signified. In more abstract terms, Justus Georg Schottelius (1612–76) expressed the same idea when saying that German was 'at the behest of the innermost essence' (*Geheiß der innersten Eigenschaft*) of all things.[27]

If one's own language possessed such singular qualities, its notorious susceptibility to foreign words had to be a cause of great concern. Quite a few authors treated foreign vocabulary, especially that of Latin and French origin, as an impairment to the clarity of the German language, as a threat to the purity of German morals and as a restriction of German liberty. Those countrymen guilty of using them were decried as 'traitors to their innate language' (*Verrähter ihrer angeborenen Sprache*) and considered worse than any other 'un-German German' (*Unteutschteutsche*). 'The Frenchman', the Erfurt-born philologist Kaspar Stieler (1632–1707) ranted, 'may take German soldiers and pay them, but he does not accept any German words anymore'.[28] The Germans, he insinuated, did it the other way round.

Some writers described foreign words as illegal immigrants that had 'sneaked' (*sich eingeschlichen*) into the mother tongue and now needed to be detected and deported. Consequently, they preferred to create German neologisms instead of adopting established terms with Latin roots. Von Zesen was probably the most effective in doing so. Among his successful inventions are 'Augenblick' (instead of *Moment*), 'Abstand' (instead of *Distanz*), 'Bücherei' (instead of *Bibliothek*), 'Gesichtskreis' (instead of *Horizont*), 'Grundstein' (instead of *Fundament*), 'Leidenschaft' (instead of *Passion*), 'Rechtschreibung' (instead of *Orthographie*) and 'Trauerspiel' (instead of *Tragödie*). Some of his other creations, such as 'Krautbeschreiber' (for *Botaniker*), 'Frauenburg' (for *Harem*) and 'Gesichtserker' (for *Nase*), did not last long. Von Zesen even proposed to give up *Natur* for 'Zeugemutter', but here even his fellow nationalists may not have given their consent.[29] Anyway, if the goal of this word-coinage had been to replace the German vocabulary of Latin origin by cross-breeding lexical material of pure Germanic pedigree, then the

---

[27] Schottelius, *Ausführliche Arbeit*, 60; for more examples, see Stukenbrock, *Sprachnationalismus*, 112–17.
[28] Stieler, *Der Teutschen Sprache Stammbaum und Fortwachs*, Y.
[29] Polenz, *Deutsche Sprachgeschichte*, II, 121.

whole operation failed. Even those neologisms that are still in use today did not manage to extrude the words they had been set against. They increased the stock of German words; they did not 'clean' it.

More moderate nationalist scholars proposed a procedure to grant 'German citizenship' (*Teutsches Burgerrecht*) to some linguistic incomers from abroad.[30] According to Harsdörffer, three conditions had to be met for 'naturalisation': there had to be no equivalent word in the German language; the word had to be familiar to everybody, and it had 'to behave civilly' (*sich Burgerlich halten*), that is, to take on German spelling and endings. This is how he could imagine his language being purified and enriched at the same time.[31]

On the whole, the German language reformers of the seventeenth century simultaneously deplored the corrupted state of their mother tongue and praised it as the most perfect of all languages. While the first judgement referred to a temporary situation soon to be overcome, the second asserted an indestructible, timeless superiority.[32] Harsdörffer deemed German 'richer in words than Hebrew, more flexible in compounds than Greek, more powerful in significances than Latin, more splendid in pronunciation than Spanish, more graceful in charm than French'.[33] Contrary to most Renaissance humanists a century before, he was emphatic about both its pivotal role in the competition for national honour and in the preservation of the national past:

It is the honour and tenet of Germans. It is the treasure and shelter of Germans. It is the pledge and tie of German loyalty, and, in short, it is the highest glory and the rightful property of our fatherland, through which all memorable deeds have been perpetuated, saved from oblivion, protected and splendidly preserved.[34]

The great majority of scholars engaging in this nationalist armament of the German language were Protestants writing either during or shortly after the Thirty Years' War (1618–48). Although they predominantly tried to hide the deep confessional divide within their own country, one important function of their work was actually to demonstrate that the 'un-German-Germans' were mostly to be found in the Catholic camp. Indeed, Catholic scholars in Germany were far less inclined to pit German against Latin. In practice, though, they used both languages for different purposes – in a similar way to their Protestant counterparts.

---

[30] Stukenbrock, *Sprachnationalismus*, 86–7.
[31] Harsdörffer, *Frauenzimmer Gesprächsspiele*, II, 196–7.
[32] Roelcke, 'Der Patriotismus', 162–3.
[33] Harsdörffer, *Schutzschrift*, 358.
[34] Idem, *Lobrede*, 39.

As a matter of fact, just as many *bons François* of the sixteenth century had continued to write and publish in Latin, the German language reformers of the seventeenth century hardly gave up using Latin (or even French); some of them, such as Martin Opitz (1597–1639), actually belonged to the best Latinists of their time.

Later German men of letters liked to laugh at the fanciful philology produced by the language reformers of the Baroque era. However, they often just laughed away the lasting impact of the very same scholars on their own works. One of them was Gottfried Wilhelm Leibniz (1646–1716), who was just a generation younger than von Zesen and his contemporaries. He treated the account of the German Adam and the linguistic purism with mocking irony, while passionately confirming the belief of a profound relation between standardised language and national wellbeing. In his *Exhortation to the Germans to better use their Mind and Language* (*Ermahnung an die Teutsche ihren Verstand und Sprache besser zu üben*), written in 1679, he maintained:

The bond of language, customs and even of the common name unites humans in such a strong, yet invisible way and creates, as it were, a kind of kinship. A letter or a journal concerning our nation can offend or delight us.[35]

Leibniz did not treat language as a component, but rather as a condition of national honour. It helped create a strong solidarity between strangers, thereby enabling them to care about their common honour and welfare. To strengthen his case that successful nation-building was intimately linked to language cultivation, Leibniz referred to ancient history. 'The Greeks and Romans', he explained, 'reached the height of their power, when Demosthenes lived among the former and Cicero among the latter'. Their most zealous students among contemporary nations were the French. According to Leibniz, they used 'a form of writing ... almost Ciceronian, which is why the [French] Nation excels so unexpectedly and almost incredibly in both war and peace'.[36]

So, the first lesson to be learned from the French was: 'it is better to be a genuine German than a copy of a Frenchman.'[37] More challenging was the second lesson: Germans had to study and cultivate their mother tongue according to the guidelines given by a 'German-minded Society' (*Teutschgesinte Gesellschaft*) – a yet-to-be founded community of scholars dealing with everything that could 'sustain or also re-erect the German glory'.[38] This was a pedagogical programme designed for

---

[35] Leibniz, *Ermahnung an die Teutsche*, 2.
[36] Ibid., 19.   [37] Ibid., 22.   [38] Ibid., 23.

all members of the nation, men and women, rich and poor, educated and ignorant, based on a general principle formulated towards the end of the *Exhortation*:

In those societies (*Völckern*) where happiness and hope thrive, the love of the fatherland, the honour of the nation, the reward of virtue, a quasi enlightened mind and thus fluent linguistic accuracy have descended even to the common man and are to be felt almost everywhere.[39]

A few lines further down, the polymath Leibniz, who would later achieve fame with philosophical and scientific works mainly written in French and Latin, outlined a theory about the significance of a standardised vernacular for a nation's welfare, which would eventually, through other channels, have an enormous impact on modern nationalist culture. Leibniz's *Exhortation to the Germans* was published only in 1846, almost 170 years after having been written, but it could hardly have been more relevant. In the second half of the nineteenth century, many European governments, among them the united Germany under Prussian rule, tackled sweeping educational reforms inspired by a linguistic nationalism very much in line with Leibniz's thoughts. A nation, so they believed, could only be united and strong with a people speaking and writing a standardised language of its own.

6.4   The limited originality of Romantic nationalism

If we consider the whole spectrum of ideas about language and nation developed and discussed between the mid-fifteenth and late-seventeenth centuries, we are drawn to the conclusion that the main intellectual work had already been done by the time the Romantics entered the stage in the late eighteenth century. Those Romantic thinkers, who turned linguistic nationalism into a weapon against the (alleged) universalism of the Enlightenment, had no need to create a profoundly new relationship between language and nation. Johann Gottfried Herder (1744–1803) was not particularly original when proclaiming in 1795 that 'through language a nation is brought up and educated; through language it cares about order and honour, is well-behaved, decent, sociable, famous, industrious and powerful'.[40] Neither was Johann Gottlieb Fichte (1762–1814) conquering new ground in his *Addresses to the German Nation (Reden an die deutsche Nation)*, given in Berlin in 1808

---

[39] Ibid., 22–3.
[40] Herder, *Briefe zur Beförderung der Humanität*, 287. For another, more detailed proof of Herder's close proximity to Leibniz, see his *Idee zum ersten patriotischen Institut für den Allgemeingeist Deutschlands* of 1787, especially § 3.

under French occupation, when calling German the 'original language' (*ursprüngliche Sprache*) and the Germans the 'original people, the people per se' (*das Urvolk, das Volk schlechtweg, Deutsche*).[41] With such statements, both Herder and Fichte were, without acknowledging it, standing on the shoulders of seventeenth-century language reformers.[42] In the case of Fichte's secularised linguistic nationalism, one could even argue that the ghost of the German Adam was still rattling around.

Although the German Romantics did not radically redefine the ideological impact of the language on the nation, they transformed linguistic nationalism considerably. One reason for this was that they narrowed the gap between ideological radicalism and practical laxity. Hardly any Romantic poet, philosopher or philologist was inclined to write, let alone publish in Latin or French any more, although many had still learned both languages thoroughly. They created and canonised a literary history made up of vernacular texts only. This led to the banishment of the vast majority of works written by German authors from the nation's 'literary archive' and to the discovery of a few hidden treasures, such as the *Nibelungenlied*, which was soon lauded as the 'Ilias of the North'.[43] By enforcing this sweeping change, Romantic scholars founded a new 'German Antiquity' (*Deutsches Altertum*) in the High Middle Ages, characterised by heroic poetry, gothic architecture and urban industriousness.

Another transformative aspect of Romantic linguistic nationalism was the effort made to historicise the study of language thoroughly. Romantic philologists constructed a language history that accentuated irreversible sound shifts, according to which languages were separated from one another at specific moments or elevated to a new evolutionary level. The 'Grimm's Law' (*Lautverschiebung*), named after the Romantic nationalist and philologist Jacob Grimm (1785–1863), probably proved the most influential and long-lasting concept of this enterprise.

Of far greater consequence, however, was a third innovation by Romantic nationalism: spreading the word. More than anything else, this constituted its modernity. Many leading Romantic scholars spent a significant amount of their lives at universities, and those who built a reputation as speakers regularly gave lectures to mixed audiences of students, bureaucrats and urban elites. In other words, they not only had the occasion to indoctrinate the next generation of scholars, teachers and journalists, but also those already exerting political and economic

---

[41] Fichte, *Reden an die deutsche Nation*, 105–7/184.
[42] For more examples, see Stukenbrock, *Sprachnationalismus*, 248–56.
[43] Hirschi, 'Mittelalterrezeption', 613–14.

influence. Thus, in a few decades, the core ideas of linguistic national-ism spread to the educated public throughout the German lands. And finally, as public beliefs were of bigger political relevance than before, the German rulers needed to adapt to the changing ideological land-scape in some way or another, if they wanted to be accepted as legitimate national leaders.

7   Humanist nationalism

Of course, every Frenchman is a Barbarian, but not every Barbarian is a Frenchman.

Petrarch, Invective against the One who Maligns Italy, 1373

Ours are the triumphs of the Goths, the Vandals and the Franks. Ours is the glory and honour of their empires founded in the most illustrious Roman provinces and even in Italy and Rome, the Queen of all cities.

Beatus Rhenanus, Letter to Bonifaz Amerbach, 1531

Not many people today would say that the terms humanism and nationalism make a good match. Quite the opposite, most would think that the two words completely contradict each another. Such a judgement seems correct, if we take the general understanding of humanism as a benchmark. In recent decades, 'humanism' and 'humanist' have become positively associated with a wide variety of ideas and actions linked to the promotion of human welfare, to the affirmation of human dignity or to the belief in the human capacity for self-improvement through education. Thanks to such fuzzy semantics, candidates for the honorary title of humanist can be taken from a diverse pool of people, including humanitarian aid workers, elder statesmen and intellectuals. The only conditions these candidates usually have to meet are a public presence, an altruistic attitude – and an anti-nationalist stance. Indeed, the caricature of the self-absorbed, morally indifferent and boneheaded nationalist helps to define the modern-day humanist *ex negativo*, thereby compensating for the lack of a distinctive profile of their own.

From a historian's point of view, the modern assimilation of humanism to humanitarianism and the fashioning of humanists as do-gooders and multiculturalists are not necessarily objectionable. They only become problematic when confused with the historiographical term of 'Renaissance humanism'. Unfortunately this happens all too often because modern defenders of 'humanist' values like to refer to a genealogy of great minds, whose intellectual legacy they claim to uphold. Among the 'usual suspects' they invoke are Giovanni Pico della

Mirandola (1463–94), Thomas More (1478–1535) and – above all – Desiderius Erasmus (1466/69–1536). In general, the pictures they paint of these Renaissance humanists are not entirely wrong; however, they tend to be very selective. What is lacking most is historical context.

When Erasmus, for instance, is portrayed as a peace loving anti-nationalist, who deplored the bellicosity of Europe's political elite, there is mostly no mention that his criticism also targeted fellow humanists, who glorified warriors as national heroes. Neither do defenders of modern-day humanism point to the fact that Renaissance humanists hardly ever praised Erasmus for what they do today. His fellow scholars venerated him as an elegant Latinist and as an excellent philologist, some as a great theologian, too. His political thinking, though, made him more enemies than admirers; it marked him as an outsider among his own followers and was thus no big source of personal prestige during his lifetime. Ulrich von Hutten (1488–1523), another elegant humanist poet and polemicist, even treated Erasmus as a 'German-French' bastard because he refused to declare openly his national allegiance.[1]

Considering all of this, if we want to use the term 'humanism' to describe the literary and scholarly movement of the Renaissance, we have to separate its meaning from the one used in today's public speech, media and moral philosophy. As soon as this distinction has been made, we will also be able to redefine the relationship between humanism and nationalism in European history. Ironically, the historical link between the two was just about the opposite of what modern-day humanists would like to believe. When the Alsatian humanist Beatus Rhenanus (1485–1547) proudly declared that the barbarian invasions by the Goths, Vandals and Franks into the Roman Empire were all accomplishments by the German nation, he was much more representative of humanist political culture than his good friend Erasmus.

To pack the historical relationship between humanism and nationalism into the shortest possible formula, we can borrow the other citation quoted at the head of this chapter, keep its structure and change its content: every nationalist in the Renaissance was a humanist, but not every humanist was a nationalist.

This chapter will start with a discussion of Renaissance humanism to enable a clear understanding of its historical particularity and significance. It will give special attention to the self-fashioning of humanists as public leaders and to the remarkable gap between the political roles they claimed and the roles they were given by political elites. This gap will later serve to explain why humanists expanded

---

[1] Hutten, *Cum Erasmo Roterodamo, Presbytero, Teologo expostulatio*, 239.

the already existing national discourse to nationalism (for my definitions, see Chapter 3.5). The development of humanist nationalism will be described in two steps. I will first analyse how humanists in Renaissance Italy constructed the relationship between their homeland and foreign countries; then I will examine how humanists from foreign countries reacted to this construction. The main thesis will be that it was only the reaction by French and German humanists to their Italian counterparts which brought about the concept of a multipolar competition of autonomous nations – in other words, which led to the emergence of nationalism.

7.1   Renaissance humanism – an innovative anachronism

In the exposition of my theoretical argument in Chapter Three, I related the origins of nationalism to the legacy of the Roman Empire in Western European history. The point was that this legacy brought about a persistent and powerful anachronism because it maintained an imperialist political culture, adhering to the ideal of a single universal power, within a fragmented territorial structure, where each of the major powers was of similar strength. On the following pages, I would like to show that Renaissance humanism can be regarded as both the culmination and the most profound transformation of this anachronism.

Humanists, more than any previous scholars and rulers, stressed the exemplariness of Roman culture and urged its re-establishment on the broadest possible basis. Most of them saw their own literary efforts as just one segment of a much larger dream to create a future of ancient greatness. Yet, because they carried the imitation of the Romans so far, they were forced to address the huge difference between the ancient past and the present more clearly. A popular, but not very productive, way was to renounce the present as a world upside down and to retreat into the 'splendid isolation' of classicist purism; another option was to attune the ancient model at least partly to contemporary circumstances in order to have a certain impact beyond the small group of one's own fellow campaigners. The construction of nationalism can be attributed to the latter option. One could even say that humanist nationalists reacted against other humanists, who preferred to perceive the present as a perversion of the ancient past. They tried to reconcile an anachronism gone to the extremes with the present, thereby creating new tensions between cultural and structural realities, which would later become a driving force of modern history.

Definitions of Renaissance humanism in the last few decades have been predominantly based on the work of the German-born American philologist and philosopher Paul Oskar Kristeller (1905–99).[2] Kristeller identified humanism with five subject areas that belonged to the liberal arts of the medieval educational curriculum: grammar, rhetoric, poetry, moral philosophy and history.[3] The most important of these areas was rhetoric. According to Kristeller, humanists were 'writers and critics, who wished not only to say the truth, but to say it well, according to their literary taste and standards'.[4] He called them 'professional rhetoricians' and regarded them as successors to the medieval *dictatores*, experts of official letter writing (*ars dictaminis*), who had utilised classical oratory for written rhetoric.

By proposing his definition, Kristeller made an early attempt to free the historical term 'humanism' from the semantic fog surrounding its modern-day use. His reference to the five subject areas was based on an explanation of the *studia humanitatis* by the Italian humanist Tommaso Parentucelli (1397–1455). Kristeller's suggestion to historicise and specify our historical understanding of humanism was well founded, not least because there was a long and powerful tradition within Renaissance studies to overemphasise the modernity of humanism, especially its contribution to modern republicanism. However, the success of his definition came at a price for humanism studies. Instead of offering new answers about the significance of humanism for modernity or about the impact of Renaissance humanists on contemporary politics, Kristeller gave up asking these questions altogether. Thus, while making the study of Renaissance humanism more serious, Kristeller made it less relevant, too.

Besides, Kristeller's identification of humanism with five subject areas hardly reflects the contemporary perception of humanists – neither by themselves nor by others. Apart from Parentucelli, most humanists chose different criteria to describe themselves. They often called each other *poetae et oratores*, thereby appearing as experts of elaborate speech and writing, not as specialists of certain subjects. This is how humanists were seen and used by the ruling classes, too. They were given the task of composing official letters, treatises and speeches no matter what the topic was. At the same time – and this is another flaw of Kristeller's approach – only a minority of humanists were 'professional' rhetoricians in the sense that they made a living from rhetoric or had an official post as rhetoricians. Humanism was never linked to a specific profession, education or rank. One could be jurist or theologian, layman or cleric, nobleman or commoner, and still count as a humanist.

---

[2] For an overview on Kristeller's work and legacy, see Monfasani (ed.), *Kristeller Reconsidered*.
[3] Kristeller, *Renaissance Thought*, 24.   [4] Ibid., 26.

Ronald G. Witt, one of Kristeller's many pupils, has recently proposed an alternative definition, which reflects the general perception of humanists more accurately and has the additional advantage of being simpler, too. For Witt, the 'litmus for identifying a humanist was his intention to imitate ancient Latin style'.[5] Being a humanist was first of all a question of linguistic behaviour, and recognising a humanist was, for the privileged few trained in Latin, a matter of a few seconds of reading or listening. One can hardly imagine a collective trademark of better perceptibility.

Consequently, Witt centred his discussion of the origins of humanism on the stylistic changes in Latin poetry and prose between the second half of the thirteenth and the first half of the fifteenth century. His account ends with the establishment of humanism as the dominant literary and political culture of the Florentine and Venetian patriciate. By then the leading model of ancient style was Ciceronianism. From the beginning, humanist Ciceronianism was more than a question of literary or oratorical style. According to Witt, it had a republican flavour for quite a while and therefore 'little to say to the great merchant families of signorial cities'. Only when humanistic education came to be identified 'with high social status would humanism find a significant number of adherents' outside the leading republican communes.[6] Even then it served a political purpose of long-lasting importance: 'Learning to imitate Ciceronian style through the medium of Cicero's writing, the student, whether residing in a republic or lordship, submitted to an indoctrination in civic values'.[7]

With this understanding of Renaissance humanism, Witt offers a modified and amplified version of Hans Baron's (1900–88) famous theory, first formulated in the late 1920s, that the 'civic humanism' developed by the Florentine Ciceronian Leonardo Bruni (1369–1444) was the origin of modern Western republicanism.[8] In other words, Witt's criticism of Kristeller's definition of humanism finally leads him back to an understanding of humanism that has, in turn, been the target of Kristeller's criticism.

This book adopts Witt's definition of Renaissance humanism, and it shares his conviction that humanist Ciceronianism was much more than a phenomenon of stylistic imitation. However, it takes a different stance regarding the political functions of humanism. It claims that its

---

[5] Witt, *In the Footsteps of the Ancients*, 22.
[6] Ibid., 477.   [7] Ibid., 493.
[8] On Hans Baron and his concept of 'civic humanism', see Hirschi, 'Höflinge der Bürgerschaft'; Hankins (ed.), *Renaissance Civic Humanism*.

main purpose was not to teach civic values to the ruling classes and even less to promote republicanism, but to establish a new political role for scholars modelled on Cicero's ideal of the 'learned orator' (see Chapter 4.1). It further maintains that there was no adequate place for this role in the political culture of Renaissance republics or principalities; the gap separating it from the ancient Roman republic was far wider than most humanists – and with them many modern historians – were ready to admit. And finally, it makes the point that the rapid and lasting success of humanism with the European ruling classes cannot be related to a practical suitability for government, but rather to a shared illusion about the exemplariness of Roman politics.

As a starting point of our approach to Renaissance humanism, I propose to ask the question: how did one become a humanist? The following answer will be short and in many ways insufficient, but its purpose is to outline the setting in which aspiring and established humanists operated. In order to enjoy the reputation of a *poeta et orator*, it was not sufficient to versify and speak like the ancient Romans. In addition, one had to practise a particular handwriting – mistakenly – believed to be classic (it was Carolingian); one had to train in special communicative rituals, such as letter-writing; one had to make friends with men already acknowledged as humanists; and one had to demonstrate publicly affiliation to and acceptance by them. All these practices leading to public recognition as an expert of the *studia humanitatis* were very informal. No official procedure was involved, and no institutionalised rites of passage established. A humanist had not gone through a certain school curriculum, nor completed specific university studies, nor occupied a particular post; he had mingled with other humanists, learned their linguistic and scholarly skills and adopted their behaviour.

The double lack of an institutionalised recruitment procedure and an official title, which separated humanists from scholars at medieval universities, was not necessarily a disadvantage. It enabled humanists to be fruitful and multiply outside the existing scholarly institutions, instead of being blocked by the traditional elites in control of them. Humanist studies thus expanded despite the fact that most European universities took their time to warm to this area and even then only allowed humanists to do some preparatory teaching for students aspiring to the higher faculties of Theology, Law and Medicine. As humanists quickly gained the patronage of the urban ruling classes, they could challenge the representatives of institutionalised learning from a position close to government, arguing that they were more helpful to those in charge of public welfare.

However, the extreme informality of humanist education and sociability had its downsides, too. In contrast to traditional men of learning at universities, monasteries or chancelleries, humanists suffered from chronic insecurity about their social status and scholarly standing. As a consequence, they felt the need to relentlessly persuade themselves and others of their own merit and importance and to simultaneously belittle competing scholars. The abundance of exuberant compliments and verbal slander in humanist discourse can at least partly be explained by this systemic insecurity.

The informal status of the *studia humanitatis* further complicated the drawing of boundaries between welcome and unwelcome types of scholars and scholarship. In other fields of learning, the conferring or refusing of personal certificates, titles and posts served this purpose effectively. In humanist circles, less authoritative and more delicate means had to be applied. Of crucial importance were the correspondence networks set up by early humanists. A letter written by an established figure could be an entry ticket into the humanist community or a sentence to permanent exile. In the early fifteenth century, there was no better confirmation of an established position within the humanist network than receiving mail from Erasmus. The document was passed around, copied or even published. Often enough, it had to be earned through persistent begging and lobbying by intermediaries. In contrast, becoming an object of ridicule or contempt in the correspondence of a distinguished humanist could lead to relegation from the community, especially when one's status was not high.[9]

Given all these informalities and insecurities, humanists relied heavily on the ruling classes to build up their public authority. Thus, the behaviour towards men in power was a central aspect of their self-fashioning. As I have indicated in Chapter Four, there were two principal roles open to medieval scholars allowing them to underline their authority in political matters.

One was that of the *functional elite*. It required the development of measures which were suitable for government, but too complicated to handle by the governing themselves – such as the adaptation of Roman law to contemporary politics by legal experts. Functional elites acted as servants in close proximity to their rulers and patrons, not as independent authorities in matters of politics. In order to exert political influence they did not necessarily need a public profile.

The other role was that of the *spiritual elite*. It implied teaching 'the truth' to the powerful by claiming a higher authority and integrity than both governing and governed – as did priests when acting as preachers. Spiritual elites had to appear as independent scholars, distant from the

---

[9] For a telling example of such an exclusion, see Müller, *Habit und Habitus*, 71.

halls of power and averse to material goods, in order to demonstrate that they did not soil their hands with earthly matters. In order to be of political consequence, they depended on an audience. They did not deliberate, but praised and blamed, demanded and warned. In the late medieval period, mendicant preachers were probably the most seminal spiritual elites.

Although these two roles were in many ways opposed to each other, certain scholars, such as legally trained priests, were able to switch between them. More importantly though, functional and spiritual elites had one thing in common: they treated government and scholarship as clearly separate fields. Medieval lawyers and priests rarely fashioned themselves as members of the ruling classes or urged rulers to become scholars like themselves.

Humanists, from early on, attempted to tear down this medieval separation of learning and governing and to replace it by a mutual assimilation of scholars and rulers. The goal was to create a new political sphere for scholarship combined with a new political role for scholars. Reviving the double meaning of *humanitas* as political expertise and human perfection in Cicero's writing (see Chapter 4.1), humanists promised rulers that they could once again become political heroes of ancient greatness if they accepted a classical education.

The civilising mission, targeted at their own patrons, was accompanied by a display of higher complicity between wit and power, literary and political heroism. When speaking to rulers, humanists adopted a new tone. Petrarch set an example by addressing both the Pope and the Emperor informally and by pretending to be on a par with them. In a letter to Emperor Charles IV of 1361 he wrote: 'You are summoning me to Germany; I am summoning you to Italy! You are superior to me in authority; I am to you in matter.'[10]

In the fifteenth century, humanists started to promote themselves as authoritative politicians according to Cicero's ideal of the learned orator. Leonardo Bruni composed a *Life of Cicero* (*Vita Ciceronis*), also known as *New Cicero* (*Cicero novus*) in 1415 – the same year he was awarded the citizenship of Florence. The scholarly parvenu particularly emphasised his hero's combination of scholarship and statesmanship. Cicero, through his deeds in 'public and private matters', was not only to be called 'the father of his fatherland', but also 'the father of our oratory and letters'.[11] Bruni maintained that Cicero's extraordinary

[10] Petrarch, *Epistolae de rebus familiaribus*, 23, 8.
[11] Bruni, *Vita Ciceronis*, 468.

achievements in both state and scholarship were based on 'the same stock of philosophy'.[12]

In 1428, one year after he had ascended to the chancellery of Florence, Bruni wrote his famous funeral oration on the Florentine patrician and condottiere Nanni Strozzi (*Oratio in funere Ioannis Stroze*), using the occasion to present the *studia humanitatis* as an integral part of Florentine political culture. They were 'most adequate to the human intellect' and 'indispensable for the private and public life'.[13] In Bruni's eyes, the revival of humanism by the Florentine patricians and citizens proved the city's status as the true successor to the ancient Roman Republic.

In republican city-states, such as early fifteenth-century Florence, humanists did not meet many obstacles when promoting themselves as members of the ruling classes. The same cannot be said about principalities. Here, it was easier to start the process of assimilation the other way round – by turning rulers into humanists. Different procedures were tried out to achieve this effect. The Franconian humanist Conrad Celtis (1459–1508) listed Emperor Maximilian as a member of his highly abstract 'Literary Sodality for Germany' (*Sodalitas litteraria per Germaniam*).[14] Johannes Trithemius (1462–1516), a humanist abbot of a Benedictine monastery in the Palatinate, composed a biographical catalogue of German men of letters (*Catalogus illustrium virorum*), in which he listed Charlemagne and described him as a great humanist – proficient in Latin, Greek and Hebrew, engaged in bibliophilic projects and in the study of the liberal arts. Rather than portraying a single ruler as a humanist, the Italian poet laureate Girolamo Amaseo (1467–1517) postulated that there was no other education as appropriate to a ruler as the *humanità*:

> The study of humanity (*humanità*) contains all sciences of the world, and no science or profession is more political (*più politica*) and more proper to a lord, a prince or a King; ... in Antiquity, teachers of the liberal arts and jurists have all been highly erudite humanists (*dotissimi humanisti*) and most of all the princes and the whole nobility.[15]

However, even in principalities and kingdoms, humanists found ways to align themselves as learned speakers with the prince or king. One such way was the laurel coronation, a public act loaded with symbolic references. It was Petrarch who had reintroduced the ritual on the Capitoline hill in 1341. At his coronation, he wore the royal purple of

---

[12] Ibid., 470.   [13] Daub, *Leonardo Brunis Rede*, 288.
[14] Klaniczay, 'Die Akademie', 13.
[15] Quoted in Rüegg, 'Die Funktion des Humanismus', 18–19.

King Robert of Naples, which he had acquired specially for this occasion. In his coronation speech, Petrarch asserted that in ancient Rome, poets and triumphators had been crowned in the same way.[16] This observation could have hardly been sourced from classical documents. It was an exemplary invention of tradition, and it was far too attractive for later humanist generations to be critically examined.

Enea Silvio Piccolomini, who, in 1442, was the first humanist to be crowned with the laurel north of the Alps, adopted the argument in a letter discussing the art of poetry,[17] and Conrad Celtis, who was the first German humanist to be given the laurel in 1487, again repeated that poets and victorious commanders had been awarded equal prizes (*aequis praemiis*) in ancient Rome.[18] Just like Enea Silvio, Celtis was crowned by Emperor Frederick III, but he gave much more weight to the political significance of the ritual than the Italian laureate. At the ceremony, he committed himself to promote the Emperor's political agenda with public praise 'here and everywhere'.[19] Furthermore, he staged a reversal of roles between Emperor and humanist when acting officially as Poet Laureate. In 1501, Maximilian, Frederick's son and successor, endowed a 'College of Poets and Mathematicians' (*Collegium poetarum et mathematicorum*). It was tailor-made for Celtis, who was now granted the privilege of crowning the graduates with the laurel *in place of* the Emperor. With his right of coronation, Celtis claimed to draft and deliver Imperial documents on his own. While he counted Maximilian among his humanist peers in his concept of a German literary sodality, he arrogated to himself a share of the Imperial dignity[20] (see Figure 8).

The political significance attached to the laurel had the contradictory consequence that the ideal candidate profile corresponded much more to the learned speaker than to the poet. In Florence, this contradiction had already become manifest by the mid-fifteenth century. Here, contrary to custom in the Imperial court, coronation ceremonies were part of state funerals for humanist officeholders. Laureate Florentine men of letters, such as the chancellors Coluccio Salutati (†1406), Leonardo Bruni (†1444), Carlo Marsuppini (†1453) and Poggio Bracciolini (†1459), did not make their name as poets, if they had written poetry at all. When Giannozzo Manetti (1396–1459) wrote his funeral oration

[16] Wilkins, 'The Coronation of Petrarch', 161; idem (ed.), 'Petrarch's Coronation Oration'; Kantorowicz, 'The Sovereignty of the Artist', 362–3; Worstbrock, 'Konrad Celtis', 15–16.
[17] Piccolomini, *Briefwechsel*, vol. I, no. 144, 326–31.
[18] Worstbrock, 'Konrad Celtis', 15.
[19] Mertens, 'Maximilians gekrönte Dichter', 107.
[20] Idem, 'Celtis ad Caesarem', 79.

Figure 8 The memorial portrait of Conrad Celtis, produced by Hans
Burgkmair in 1508, gives an idea of the intertwined relationship
between politics and scholarship in Renaissance humanism. The
whole arrangement is modelled on Roman portrait tombstones. Celtis'
humanist status is not only emphasised through his books, but also
through his Imperial prerogatives. The band on his right upper arm
with Maximilian's monogram – as it appears on the Emperor's deeds –
probably refers to Celtis' privilege of personally awarding the laurel
to students of his 'College of Poets and Mathematicians'. Celtis' own
laurel is depicted twice, once on his head, once like a halo above him;
the tiny coat of arms pinned on it shows the double-headed imperial
eagle, which further highlights the self-image of the humanist scholar
as an autonomous authority on the stage of German politics.

for Leonardo Bruni, he tried to present the poet, referring to Cicero's *De oratore*, as the closest relative to the speaker; apparently not so convinced of his own argument, he added that Bruni, just before his death, had planned to publish a collection of his poems.[21] None of them has ever been seen.

To legitimise the creation of poet laureates without any poetic achievements, humanists could also draw on Petrarch's portrayal of the crowned writer as a reviver of Roman virtue.[22] With this, they applied another popular method to assimilate scholars and rulers. Following Cicero's example, humanists propagated largely identical values for men of the pen and men of the sword (see Figure 9). *Civilitas, urbanitas, gravitas, virtus, honor* and *laus* were meant to be guidelines for both the battlefield and the study room. This also allowed for comparisons of contemporary men of letters with ancient rulers and warriors, when humanists praised their peers. Even Erasmus, who otherwise liked to distance himself from military heroes, practised this kind of assimilation. When he drafted a short biography of his friend Thomas More in a letter to Ulrich von Hutten of 1519, he started with the preliminary consideration: 'It is neither, I reckon, easier to draw a picture of More than of Alexander the Great or of Achilles, nor have they merited immortality more than he has.'[23]

The humanist who developed arguably the most elaborate and successful self-image as a learned politician in Cicero's footprints was also the one who would become most influential in stimulating humanist nationalism outside Italy. This was Enea Silvio Piccolomini, elected Pope Pius II in 1458. He kick-started his political career at the Council of Basle (1431–49), where he attracted attention as an excellent speaker. In 1443 he entered the service of Frederick III. In the same year, he published the *Pentalogus*, which I have introduced in Chapter Four, referring to its innovative combination of patriotic and nationalist language.

The text was remarkable in other respects, too. It was a fictive dialogue between five actual exponents of German politics at the time: the Emperor, the bishop of Chiemsee Nicodemo della Scala, the Bishop of Freising Silvester Pflieger, the Imperial chancellor Caspar Schlick and Enea Silvio himself. The author made them look like Roman statesmen discussing Imperial politics.[24] They all addressed each other informally, according to the classical ideal of conversation. In addition, the

[21] McManamon, *Funeral Oratory*, 135.
[22] Rüegg, 'Der Humanist als Diener Gottes', 159–60.
[23] Erasmus, *Opus epistolarum*, vol. IV, 13.
[24] Piccolomini, *Pentalogus*.

CICERO.

Figure 9 How did Cicero receive his laurel wreath? The artist of a late
sixteenth-century portrait series of men of letters probably modelled
him on copies of the ancient marble bust (see Figure 5). However,
with the laurel wreath, he added an attribute which Cicero had never
worn and which no Roman would have associated with him. The
laurel could only appear on Cicero's head due to its transformation
from a mark of military triumph in Antiquity to a symbol of humanist
political power in the Renaissance. In the accompanying text, Cicero
is described as the perfect scholar-cum-politician: the most famous
orator, best teacher, liberator of the state and Father of the Fatherland.
Tellingly, the portrait of Cicero is directly followed by those of Dante
and Petrarch, both of whom are presented with laurel wreaths, too.

author's alter ego, by far the lowest in rank of the five, clearly dominated
the dialogue with his statements. He urged the Emperor, in an imperi-
ous tone, to give a speech to the assembly of the Imperial Diet and to
persuade the German princes to recapture Italy for the Empire. The

literary Enea even presented a draft for the speech, which was packed with the nationalist rhetoric mentioned above.

While the real Frederick was unimpressed by the humanist attempt at persuasion and refused to act as a public speaker, Enea Silvio, after being promoted to Bishop of Siena and Imperial secretary, acquired for himself the opportunity to address the Imperial Diet in deliberative speech in Frankfurt in 1454, acting as a substitute for the Emperor. His oration *On the defeat of Constantinople* (*De Constantinopolitana clades*), which called for immediate military action against the Turks, emulated Cicero's famous speech *De lege Manilia* of 66 BC, whose purpose had been to give Pompeius supreme command in the fight against Mediterranean pirates. With his speech, Enea Silvio initiated a new period of deliberative oratory in German Imperial politics, which eventually generated an Imperial speaker, too. Maximilian, contrary to his father, liked to deliver public speeches, thereby counteracting traditional convictions about princely dignity. Apparently, he was even blessed with talent. His performance at the Diet of Constance in 1507 did not fail to impress contemporary humanists nor the great nineteenth-century historian Leopold von Ranke (1795–1886), who was so stunned by the Emperor's patriotic rhetoric that he mistook the speech for a 'Livy-style fiction'.[25]

When Enea Silvio completed his life as Pius II on the Papal throne, his former clients were given the task of perpetuating his image as a learned speaker and successful politician. The leading role in this enterprise was taken by the Curial humanist Gian Antonio Campano (1429–77), who would later also provoke heavy nationalist reactions against Italian humanists in Germany. Campano composed no fewer than three works commemorating the humanist Pope – a *Funeral Oration*, a *Life* and *Commentaries* to his speeches and writings.[26] In the biography, he decided to paint Enea Silvio as an emperor-like figure by following the model of Suetonius' *The Twelve Caesars* (*De vita Caesarum*) of AD 121.[27] In the comments on Enea Silvio's works, however, he drew on Bruni's *Cicero novus* and its propagation of the *vita activa*: that is, a scholarly existence in service of the public good.[28]

In contrast to Bruni, Campano did not content himself with presenting his hero as a new Cicero. Now the copy had to be better than

[25] Maximilian, 'Denkschrift an die Reichsversammlung in Konstanz 1507', in Wiesflecker-Friedhuber (ed.), *Quellen*, 152–9; Helmrath, 'Rhetorik', 440; Hirschi, *Wettkampf der Nationen*, 169–72.

[26] Campano, *Oratio in Funere Pii II*; idem, *Pii II pontificis maximi vita*; idem, *De Pii II, Pont. Max. Commentariis historicis*.

[27] Enenkel, *Die Erfindung des Menschen*, 345–54.

[28] Widmer, *Enea Silvio Piccolomini*, 20.

the original. The humanist Pope, he insisted, had surpassed his idol, Cicero, both as a statesman and as a scholar. Campano's comparison was based on criteria such as the number of public speeches, the importance of the topics discussed and the size of the audiences addressed. The result left no doubt: Cicero, Campano reported, had almost exclusively given private speeches, Enea Silvio only public ones; Cicero had addressed minor matters, Enea Silvio major ones; Cicero had appeared on few political stages, Enea Silvio 'on every forum, in every assembly of the world' (*in omni foro, in omni contione orbis terrarum*). In order to describe Enea Silvio as the 'more public' speaker, Campano related the adjectives *privatus* and *publicus* to the motivations of the two. While alleging that Cicero had, apart from his orations against Catiline and Verres, always followed personal interests when speaking publicly, Campano asserted that Enea Silvio had always and only pursued 'the common benefit of peoples' (*communis gentium utilitas*).[29] The Roman ideal of the learned politician, the *Commentaries* claimed, had finally found its personified perfection in the humanist Pope Pius II.

By the mid-fifteenth century, the success of Renaissance humanism was evident throughout Italy. Starting with Florence, Venice and Rome, the classical education of political elites had reached an unprecedented quality in a short time. In the sixteenth century, the countries west and north of the Alps followed suit. For the whole early modern period, the figure of the seemingly effortless and universally educated humanist virtuoso became the leading role model for male aristocrats and diplomats at princely and royal courts.[30]

Humanists were successful as public speakers, too. In most Italian territories, humanist oratory was well established by 1450, not only in republics, but also in principalities and at the Roman Curia. A few decades later, thanks to the unmistakable presence of Italian humanists at the Councils of Constance and Basle, the political elites of many European countries warmed to humanist oratory, too. In Germany, it reached its zenith after Maximilian's accession to power in 1493 with the newly crowned poet laureates calling the tune.

Finally, many humanists climbed up the social ladder from relatively modest origins, and quite a few even ascended to political offices with significant prestige and influence. In Florence, the chancellery became a humanist stronghold as early as 1375, when Coluccio Salutati (1331–1406) was elected chancellor of the Republic. From then on, the

---

[29] Campano, *De Pii II, Pont. Max. Commentariis historicis*, 8–9 / 11.
[30] Burke, *The Fortunes of the Courtier*.

official correspondence by the city-state became characterised by an elegant Latin prose that added to the reputation of Florence as a centre of Roman education. In Germany, the humanist lawyers Conrad Peutinger (1465–1547) and Sebastian Brant (1458–1521) occupied the chancelleries of the big Imperial cities Augsburg and Strasbourg around 1500. Both bore the title of 'Imperial counsellor' (*kaiserlicher Rat*), too, and cultivated close ties with Maximilian and his court, where another humanist lawyer, Johannes Cuspinian (1473–1529), acted as a leading adviser and envoy.

The biggest career opportunities for humanists beckoned at the Roman Curia, though. In 1447, eleven years before Enea Silvio was raised to the Papacy, the College of Cardinals elected Tommaso Parentucelli, a humanist of humble birth, to become Pope Nicholas V. Not least because of his active patronage, there was a regular promotion of humanist clerics to the Cardinalate during the late fifteenth and early sixteenth centuries.

Nevertheless, despite the long-lasting success of the humanist 'civilising' mission with the ruling classes and despite the rapid rise of humanist scholars into prestigious political positions, humanists never occupied political roles anywhere which corresponded to the positions taken by their ancient Roman role models. Their favourite role of public speaker, as one who persuaded his audiences of the right political decisions, thanks to his mastery of Latin and to his profound knowledge, remained an illusion. The actual political functions played by humanists were of a very different sort.

In order to explain this contradiction of a failure within success, we have to consider the humanist myth about their successful revival of Roman political culture with the late medieval political reality they emerged and acted in.[31] The public functions of humanists grew out of two scholarly traditions in medieval Italy, both of which professionalised the official communication of the state.

The better-known tradition is the *ars dictaminis*, which has already been mentioned here when discussing Kristeller's understanding of humanism. It can be described as a method of official letter-writing drawing on Cicero's instructions for the composition of a deliberative speech.[32] Its origins lay in the late twelfth-century Papal States. Following the example of medieval poetics, the *ars dictaminis* deepened the rupture with ancient rhetoric by transferring a technique for oral communication to written

---

[31] For a broader theory on the origins of Renaissance humanism, including the fields of grammar and poetry, see Witt, *In the Footsteps of the Ancients*.
[32] Camargo, 'Ars dictaminis'.

use.[33] Thereby, the letter became a persuasive medium, whereas it had been regarded as a dialogical medium in Antiquity.

The *dictatores*, the teachers and practitioners of *ars dictaminis*, were typical functional elites. They developed and mastered tools for political use, which could not be handled by the power holders themselves. While a Cicero or Caesar had written or dictated their letters personally, most medieval rulers depended on other people's words and pens to communicate with each other over distance.

The second tradition of scholarship paving the way for the political functions of humanists was the *ars arengandi*. It constituted a method for public addresses on official occasions and had been in use since the middle of the thirteenth century.[34] Similar to the *ars dictaminis*, it offered ready-made formulas for different public purposes, thereby abandoning the general instructions of ancient rhetorical treatises. The *ars arengandi* was suited to the politics in Italian city-states. Before it was introduced, the popular assembly with the telling name *concio* – referring to the Roman *contio* (see Chapter 4.1) – had been the main institution for public speech. Here, lay speakers were able to address their fellow citizens to deliberate on political decisions.

As this system was not exactly made for stemming the chronic violence and factional strife in late medieval city-states, the political competence of the popular assembly was continually reduced in favour of elected committees. The introduction of the *ars arengandi* took place in this context. It formalised and ritualised public rhetoric and replaced the civic lay speakers with rhetorically trained officials. Thus, the process of political decision-making slowly disappeared behind the public scenes, and public oratory took on a mainly celebratory function, despite preserving some deliberative forms.[35]

At the end of the fourteenth century, when the first humanists held offices in Florence and other Italian city-states, this process of political disciplining and formalising had long been under way. The humanists of Salutati's and Bruni's generations not only became part of it, but actively helped to direct it towards a durable oligarchic rule. At the end of this process, in mid-fifteenth-century Florence, even the elected committees lost their power to take decisions, as political decisions were now made in informal circles controlled by the Medici family.

In their official functions, humanists combined the tasks of the medieval experts on *ars dictaminis* and *ars arengandi*. They drafted and

[33] Boureau, 'The Letter-Writing Norm', 25; Murphy, *Rhetoric in the Middle Ages*, 194–5.
[34] Koch, 'Ars arengandi', 1033.
[35] Klein, 'Politische Rede', 1482–3.

executed the official correspondence of urban governments and princely courts, and they delivered public speeches on celebratory occasions, such as state funerals or official receptions of foreign rulers or envoys. In many respects, humanists continued the tradition of medieval rhetoric in these functions. The genres of official letter and official speech, for instance, remained closely related to each other, both formally and functionally. Many humanist 'orations', including Bruni's *Oratio* on Nanni Strozzi and Campano's *Oratio in funere* on Enea Silvio, were not only never delivered, but deliberately addressed at a reading public. Some written 'speeches', such as Bruni's *Praise of the City of Florence* (*Laudatio Florentinae urbis*), were also used by governments as propaganda tools in foreign relations. Official humanist letters in turn were often fashioned as a speech sent in writing and, indeed, read out aloud to the recipients. When the Florentine chancellor Poggio Bracciolini sent King Alfonso V of Aragon (1396–1458) a letter of congratulations on the peace agreement of Lodi in 1455, humanists at the court of Naples first copied the text on a precious scroll of parchment and then recited it in front of the King and his courtiers.[36]

However, humanists promised rulers much more than their medieval predecessors had done. Writing official letters and speeches in allegedly ancient style was just meant to be a small part of a great project to turn political patrons into heroes of Roman stature. The renewal of classical Latin, so the logic went, would offer the potential to re-establish a Roman-like power by Roman-like rulers. This was an attractive message for the political elites of the Italian city-states, who had long been competing against each other for the official succession to Rome. And it was to become equally appealing to the European monarchs, especially the Emperor and the King of France, who overran Italy after 1494 in their pursuit of a universal Empire. In other words, the extreme anachronism of humanist political thinking could be credible and desirable because it stimulated the political elites' own anachronistic political dreams.

But even if Renaissance rulers and their entourage believed some of the humanist promises and agreed to accept a 'civilising' treatment under their guidance, they could not grant them a political role that corresponded to the ancient learned speaker. In no late medieval state – republic or principality – were political decisions taken in public deliberation, and thus there was no official place for public orators in the decision-making process. If humanists claimed to lead the *vita activa* of ancient learned men, such as Cicero and Sallust, they were deeply

---

[36] Harth, 'Überlegungen zur Öffentlichkeit', 136.

mistaken, because even if they occupied public offices, they could not act as statesmen in their own right.

This particularly applies to the so-called 'civic humanists' of Florence – Salutati, Bruni and their peers. Many historians of political thought have taken their self-promotion at face value, leaving its ana-chronistic quality unnoticed. Quentin Skinner, for instance, ascribes to Florentine humanists a concept of liberty 'in the sense of being free to take an active part in the running of the commonwealth'; he does not clarify, however, that these humanists did not 'run' anything, unless they were born to the ruling families.[37] They were carrying out orders, or, if they were trusted by their patrons, acting in the name of the prince or the patriciate. With few exceptions, such as Enea Silvio on the Papal throne, Renaissance humanists remained, as far as their official functions were concerned, confined to the scholarly role of functional elites.

The profound discrepancy between the pretended role and the proper position of humanists is reflected in some of their favourite gen-res, too. Most humanist speeches were epideictic. This genre – often described as rhetoric of praise and blame – was most suitable for the use of humanist orations as propaganda tools, as festive additions to public ceremonies or as educational texts.[38] Yet, it was the very genre which had been attributed the least prestige by ancient Roman authors. In Cicero's view, there were 'both graver and more common genres of oratory' (*sunt orationum genera et graviora et maioris copiae*) than the *laudatio*, and with regard to the eulogy he made the even more disparaging judgement that it was not at all capable of adding to the prestige of oratory (*ad orationis laudem minime accommodata est*).[39]

Compared to the other two genres of classical rhetoric, forensic and deliberative speech, epideictic rhetoric seemed much less suited to dem-onstrate the power of oratory and the impact of the orator. In republican Rome, oratorical fame was achieved by persuading a doubting public of one's own standpoint. For this, the appropriate tools were foren-sic and deliberative speech. Epideictic rhetoric, in contrast, dealt with certainties (*res certa*) and was thus meant to strengthen a pre-existing consensus between speaker and public. Therefore, if we were to look at Renaissance humanism with Roman eyes, we would hardly see the oratorical production of Renaissance humanists as a sign of political impact, let alone success.

---

[37] Skinner, *The Foundations*, vol. I, 77.
[38] Mertens, 'Die Rede', 412–13.
[39] Cicero, *On the Ideal Orator (De oratore)*, II, 341.

Even when humanists tried to imitate forms of deliberative speech, the oratorical function regularly remained epideictic. The draft for Frederick's address to the Imperial Diet, which Enea Silvio composed in his fictive dialogue *Pentalogus*, contained deliberative vocabulary void of any deliberative sense. The Emperor was supposed to tell his audience: 'If you indeed want to consult and help me, as I hope, the aim is to attack Italy.' Here, *consulere et auxiliari* did not mean weighing the pros and cons of an upcoming decision, but giving retrospective consent to a decision already taken by the superior.[40] Enea Silvio's deliberative language was mildly absurd, too, when the Emperor let the German princes and patricians know: 'I have convoked you so we can negotiate about the honour of our nation.'[41] This time, the audience was given a discretionary power, albeit in a matter where nothing needed to be negotiated. There was no point in deliberating over the choice between honour and shame.

Enea Silvio's Frankfurt oration of 1454 may be even more revealing, not least because it was actually delivered. Although he flaunted its deliberative structure by imitating one of Cicero's greatest political speeches, he never allowed the question for or against a war on the Turks to appear as doubtful and thus debatable.[42] In this regard, his audience completely agreed with him, just on opposite sides. The German princes and patricians could not imagine participating in a war on the Turks and saw no reason to debate the issue at all. They listened to Enea Silvio's classical Latin for two hours, probably experiencing it as authentically Roman, as most of them could hardly understand a word. Afterwards they were given a German paraphrase, from which they learned that the humanist speaker had not made a single specific proposition to be discussed. While they were still expressing their disappointment, Enea Silvio distributed written copies of his speech, thereby laying the foundation for its later fame. The fact that his oration proved a literary success, despite its complete political failure, indicates that his humanist followers were willing to pursue the imitation of Roman orators even at the cost of a departure into escapism.

A similar story can be told about humanist historiography. As writers of historical works, humanists claimed a new political competence, too, referring to the public authority of Roman historians. In Republican Rome, historiography had originally been associated with the senatorial office of the censor, who, among other things, had to preserve the dignity of the senate and public morals by reminding his contemporaries of their ancestors' deeds and customs. Although in the late Republic

---

[40] Piccolomini, *Pentalogus* (ed. Weinrich), 260–1.   [41] Ibid.
[42] Helmrath, 'Der europäische Humanismus', 39–40.

writers of Roman history loosened their ties to the office of the censor, they still treated the genre as the storage of official memory and thereby positioned it against 'partisan' media, such as the archives of senatorial families with their family trees and wax masks. The historian was expected to be a judge, not an advocate for political leaders, and thus historiography was supposed to be anti-panegyrical and anti-dynastic.[43] This claim to impartiality was still upheld by historians of the Principate and found its classic expression in Tacitus' *Annals* of the early second century AD. The author, who was also a senator, assured his readers at the beginning of his work that he had written it 'without anger and fondness' (*sine ira et studio*).[44]

Although Renaissance humanists were eager to renew the image of the historian as an impartial authority in political and moral matters, they were unable to carry out this role if they wanted to remain integrated into the political culture of the ruling classes. As historians, humanists were first and foremost supposed to raise and preserve the fame of a prince, a town, a region or a nation. Humanist historiography was thus overwhelmingly panegyrical and rarely anti-dynastic. To write history *sine ira et studio* was hardly possible under these circumstances (if it had ever been), and so Tacitus' sentence mainly served as a polemical weapon against other historians, whose partiality clashed with one's own partiality.[45]

As letter-writers, too, humanists largely failed to enforce the public image to which they aspired. After Petrarch had made the informal address of recipients, including high dignitaries, fashionable, Salutati tried to introduce classical salutations in the singular form to the official correspondence of the Florentine Republic. The ruling families did not like it and so he had to give it up.[46] Later humanist generations maintained the pretence that they were communicating with high-ranked personalities on an equal level, thereby living up to Cicero's description of the exchange of letters as a 'conversation between absent friends' (*sermo amicorum absentium*). Poggio Bracciolini assembled three letter collections during his lifetime, in which he greeted his correspondents informally, regardless of office or rank. When modern scholars found some of Poggio's originals, though, they discovered that the humanist had engaged in some inventive philology. In the original letters, high dignitaries were addressed in the common majestic plural.[47]

[43] Wittchow, 'Von Fabius Pictor zu Polydor Vergil', 52.
[44] Tacitus, *Annals* (*Annales*), I, 1.   [45] Ibid., 48.
[46] Witt, *Coluccio Salutati*, 25–6.
[47] Harth, 'Überlegungen zur Öffentlichkeit', 129–31.

Only a few Renaissance humanists realised the impossibility of walking in Cicero's footsteps through Renaissance Europe. One of them was Erasmus. In his invective against Ciceronian humanists of 1528, he asked critically: 'Even if we allow that Cicero's eloquence served some purpose in its time, what use is there for it today?'[48] His answer was devastating. In the law courts, he explained, business was conducted 'by means of clauses and sections and legal terminology' and thus there was no place for Ciceronian forensic speech. Neither was it of use in council chambers (*concilia*), where 'individuals put forward their views to a small group' in their mother tongues. Their statements were of no big consequence anyway, as most political decisions 'are now taken by privy council, attended by at most three men, usually of no great education; everyone else is merely informed of their decisions'. Finally, there was no point in addressing public assemblies (*contiones*) with Ciceronian oratory, because 'the public does not understand the language of Cicero, and no matters of state are discussed with the public'.

So was there any use for Ciceronian Latin at all in Erasmus' eyes? Yes, there was, though on a very limited scale. On the one hand, a humanist could deliver 'platitudes' and engage in 'flattery' at ceremonial occasions, for which he 'deserves no credit except for the stamina in recitation'. On the other hand, he could write letters in Ciceronian style – 'to whom? To learned men'.

Erasmus' answer was, of course, sardonic but his observation can also help to acknowledge the degree of innovation which Renaissance humanists provoked in the pursuit of their anachronistic agenda. If Erasmus was right that politically ambitious humanists set an entire political stage in Roman décor just to end up performing a farce in classical Latin to each other, then one may say, too, that they involuntarily acted as a political avant-garde. Instead of restoring the political order of Ancient Rome and conquering the role of the learned statesman, they created a literary sphere, detached from the constraints of contemporary politics. In this sphere, they could let their imagination run free and carry their political daydreams much further than those scholars who fashioned themselves according to their official functions. This is how the illusions of Renaissance humanists about their contemporary place in politics released a utopian energy that eventually came to shape the reality of modern Europe considerably.

Helped by the invention of the printing press, humanists fashioned an egalitarian community of learned men that had already implemented the ancient ideals of public deliberation and polite conversation. Published

[48] Erasmus, *The Ciceronian*, 405–6.

correspondences and literary dialogues created an image of humanist communication as an autonomous discourse among civilised human beings in search of truth and the right decisions. And by congratulating each other on their civilising successes in the dedicatory letters of their published works, humanists presented their scholarly community as an expanding sphere, which would eventually transform the whole political culture according to its ideals.

To label their scholarly community, humanists used different terms; they frequently called it *coetus eruditorum* and *sodalitas literaria* and very occasionally *res publica literaria*. However, it was the latter term that had the biggest impact on early modern scholarship. Unlike the two other terms, *res publica literaria* described men of letters as citizens of an alternative state. This peculiar and in many ways distorting metaphor only became widespread and influential in the second half of the seventeenth century, when scholars of different fields and countries attempted to draw a rhetorical line of demarcation between religious controversy and learned disputes. Once again, the language they used for this purpose was largely drawn from Cicero, this time more from *De re publica* than from *De oratore*.[49] The term *res publica* designated a realm of high independence and high morality, inhabited and governed by virtuous men. In the early modern period, *res publica* could, contrary to Roman Antiquity, signify both state and republic, and consequently, it could be presented as a counter-model to the monarchical governments of most European states. In this sense, it symbolised an egalitarian and meritocratic commonwealth, whose citizens shared their intellectual treasures, and celebrated and criticised each other publicly.

Now the same utopian energy that enabled the imagination of an independent scholarly community transcending all political boundaries also made possible the fashioning of the nation as an autonomous community, engaging in an intensive competition of honour with other nations. In this sense, modern internationalism and modern nationalism have their origins in the same cultural setting, the humanist literary sphere constructed as a political stage. On this stage, humanist nationalists were able to address an imaginary public that far outnumbered their actual audience. When Conrad Celtis delivered a speech at the University of Ingolstadt in 1492, he did not really address the members of the Faculty of Law sitting in front of him, but the whole nation. Speaking to the 'free and strong people' of Germany (*liberus et robustus populus*), he urged in an authoritarian tone: 'Assume, O men of Germany, that ancient spirit of yours, with which you so often

---

[49] Jaumann, 'Respublica literaria', 80–1.

confounded and terrified the Romans!'[50] The publication of the speech after its delivery was meant to sustain the claim that Celtis' true audience was the German nation.

Although the appeals to the whole nation defied the scope of humanist writings, they clearly prepared the ground for the construction of a national public in the modern period. Thirty years after Celtis' oration in the Bavarian university town, this rhetoric expanded its scope massively. One of its first and most seminal students outside the small community of humanist nationalists was Martin Luther. In his popular writings, he regularly addressed his audience as 'my beloved Germans' (*meine lieben Deutschen*) and he even continued doing so when it became obvious that his theology was refused in large parts of Germany and that the Reformation could only continue as a territorial, not as a national affair.[51]

When acting as admonishers and preceptors of the nation, humanists could make use of their favourite rhetorical genre, epideixis, again. With it they could combine panegyrics with pedagogics, celebrate national honour and teach patriotic lessons. In such situations, however, they occupied the classical role of spiritual elites. Renaissance humanists thus provided the first exemplars of a scholarly species, which would happily multiply in the modern age – the 'national priest'.

7.2   Barbarising the French or how Italian humanists successfully fought reality

Fighting barbarism was a prime duty of every humanist. He had to do it with a missionary zeal, acting as an apostle of classical education. However, what *barbaries* and *barbarus* precisely signified, often remained unclear and varied considerably. It could refer to complete ignorance or to a sophisticated, but useless, education; it could diagnose a temporary lack of civilisation or a total incapacity to leave the state of savagery; it could be limited to Latin speech and writing or comprise the whole human appearance, including manners, gestures, clothes and smells; and it could stigmatise a small group of countrymen or all foreign people. Despite all these different significations, one meaning always remained the same: *barbaries* was the exact opposite of *humanitas*.

The creation of a bipolar opposition between barbarism and humanism served the self-promotion of Renaissance humanists as revivers of

---

[50] Celtis, *Oratio in gymnasio*, 47.
[51] Hirschi, *Wettkampf der Nationen*, 428.

Roman greatness. Humanists, though, adopted a different tone when speaking about barbarism than their ancient role models, thereby creating tension-filled situations. The way Italian humanists treated foreigners as barbarians is exemplary in this respect.

In ancient Greece and Rome, βάρβαρος respectively *barbarus* was a term predominantly, though not exclusively used to label foreigners, who were identified as speakers of alien languages. While it was normal to use the word pejoratively in order to express one's own alleged superiority as a civilised people, it was not uncommon to make neutral or even positive statements about 'barbarians', most notably in the genre of ethnographic description. Ancient discourses on foreign barbarians thus varied remarkably. Nevertheless, they had one thing in common: they were usually set in a communication situation, from which those labelled barbarians remained excluded. There was no need to persuade foreigners to perceive themselves as 'barbarians', unless they wanted to adopt one's own culture (such as the Romans the Greek) or unless they were conquered and integrated into one's own territory (such as the Gauls by the Romans). In both cases accepting the stigmatisation as 'barbarians' was meant to be a transition into a civilising process. So, although the description of foreigners as barbarians in ancient literature was predominantly pejorative, it was rarely polemical, because discourses of barbarism were hardly ever addressed at 'barbarians'.

In the Renaissance, it was quite the opposite. When Italian humanists started to call non-Italians 'barbarians', their discourse was not only invariably pejorative, but extremely polemical. It was reintroduced as an attack on the honour of non-Italians and thus targeted an audience of both countrymen and foreigners. In other words, those excluded from civilisation were included in the communication. They were treated as ignorant brutes, but supposed to understand insults in elegant Latin.

So, while the rhetoric suggested that there was no common ground between Italians and foreigners and thus no possibility for an affair of honour, the communication situation provoked a defence of honour by foreign scholars and eventually proved an excellent catalyst of nationalism. One could even say that the anachronistic attempt to re-establish a bipolar opposition of civilised and barbarians triggered a premature development of a multipolar competition of nations. It released a cultural energy to transform the relationship between collectivities, which the much slower political changes of the time could not yet provide.

Given the communication situation, it is not surprising that Italian humanists used a literary genre very untypical of classical writings on foreign barbarians: the invective. Some of them must have realised that they were not exactly following the example of the ancients, and so they tried to reconcile the polemical tone with the classical discourse of bar-barism. This is why they wrote texts such as Petrarch's invective *Against the One who Maligns Italy* (*Contra eum qui maledixit Italie*) of 1373 – a piece of unrestrained slander against the French, scantily disguised as an ethnographic description.

Petrarch composed this polemic as an old and famous man one year before his death. Before we can discuss it, we have to take a closer look at its historical and personal background. During his later years, Petrarch had aggressively pushed for a relocation of the Imperial pow-ers – the Empire and the Papacy – to their original place, the city of Rome. Equally aggressively, he had claimed that Italy owned, owing to its climate, its inhabitants and its history, a monopoly on Roman civil-isation. Consequently, he rejected the medieval doctrines of *translatio imperii* and *translatio studii* (see Chapter 3.3) as completely ludicrous. 'If the Roman Empire is not in Rome', he asked snidely, 'where is it then?'[52]

Petrarch could neither accept the idea of a Frenchman being Pope nor a German being Emperor; if they were, as was the rule during his lifetime, he either attacked them as barbarians or turned them into Italians. In 1351, for instance, he informed Emperor Charles IV: 'The Germans may claim you for themselves; we, however, regard you as an Italian.'[53] Of course, this meant that the Emperor had to live in Italy, too.

Although Petrarch had exchanged a few personal letters with Charles IV and spent many years at the Curia enjoying direct access to the Pope, his efforts were in vain. Apart from a short interlude (which we will touch on further down), the seats of Roman power remained in 'barbarian' hands – the Imperial court at Prague, the Papal Court at Avignon, where it was protected and controlled by the King of France. To Petrarch, his inability to bring them back to where they belonged came as proof that he lived in a topsy-turvy world, ruled by the blind *Fortuna*. And so he lamented that since the fall of the Empire into bar-barian hands, the Queen of the World, Rome, had been treated as a maid, and Italy, badly wounded by barbarian swords, had been pining away with fever.[54]

It was this perception of the present as a perverted place, which ena-bled Petrarch to attack scholars and rulers who shared his culture, read his writings and even communicated with him, as uncivilised brutes.

---

[52] Petrarch, *Book without a Name* (*Liber sine nomine*) *IV*.
[53] Idem, *Epistolae de rebus familiaribus*, x, 1.
[54] Idem, *Rerum vulgarium fragmenta 128*, 1–6.

The world, as it appeared in his eyes, was false; its true order was invisible, hidden in old Roman scriptures. With his concept of a world upside-down he also created a communication situation upside-down.

When Petrarch wrote the invective *Against the One who Maligns Italy*, he had special reason to be in an escapist mood. The text was his last word in a long and heated exchange. A few years before, in 1367, Pope Urban V had made an early attempt to move the Curia back to Rome, pushed forward by the Emperor and pulled back by the King of France. His step was also accompanied by fierce wrangling between scholars with close links to the Curia. And even then, Petrarch was one of the prime agitators on the scene.

In August 1366, he sent a letter to the Pope asking him directly to return to Rome. Addressing Urban as a born Frenchman, Petrarch used the opposition of earthly and celestial fatherland: 'You will glory in the fact', he promised, 'that you turned your back on the earthly fatherland, whence you come, for love of the celestial fatherland toward which you proceed.'[55]

It was not long before his writing circulated among the courtiers and cardinals at Avignon. Soon after, Anseau Choquart (†1369), a Professor of Canon Law at the University of Paris, was sent on a diplomatic mission by his King, Charles V. At the beginning of the following year, Choquart delivered a speech to the Pope and the French cardinals.[56] He contrasted the security, peace and supply of excellent food and drink in France with the chaos and chronic warfare in Italy. He referred to the piety of Frenchmen and to the persecution of Christians by the Romans. He stressed the central position of Avignon within the Papal Church and warned against the 'democracy' of Italian states. His most provocative statement though, at least to Petrarch, was about Avignon's proximity to the University of Paris, where the sciences had their seat since the *translatio studii* under Charlemagne – prefigured by the Gallic druids![57]

Petrarch answered Choquart's speech with another public letter to the Pope, in which he strongly denied the French claim to own the sciences. At best, he maintained, they managed to imitate the Italians, and so it was 'ridiculous to argue about the differences in intellect':

Tell me, what of the liberal arts, of the cognitive, natural or historical sciences (*de rerum cognitione seu naturalium seu gestarum*), of wisdom, of eloquence, what of ethics and any part of philosophy in Latin was not practically all discovered

[55] Idem, *Letters of Old Age* (*Epistolae rerum senilium*), VII, 1, vol. I, 246.
[56] Simone, *Il rinascimento*, 47–9; Saccaro, *Französischer Humanismus*, 148–9.
[57] Ouy, *Paris*, 81–2.

by the Italians? If any foreigners ventured to handle any of these subjects successfully, they either imitated Italians or they wrote in Italy or they studied in
Italy.[58]

Of the four Church Fathers, Petrarch continued, none had been French,
and none had been educated in France (*Nullus est gallus, nullus doctus in
Gallia*). Nor were there any Latin 'poets and orators' to be found outside
Italy – 'they were all either born here or educated here'.[59]

Petrarch was only able to make such a broad-brush claim because
he strictly referred to the past, turning ancient Roman authors into
Italians. Comparing the present state of learning in the two countries
had no validity for him, given the general degree of degeneration and
barbarisation. His main point, however, was that the sciences could
only flourish again – if at all – where they had flourished before: in
Italy.

On the whole, Petrarch's initial response was still restrained compared to the follow-up one, because he thought he had history on his
side for once. Now, the Pope was residing in Rome, while the French
cardinals, who remained in Avignon, desperately tried to bring him
back. In a triumphant gesture, Petrarch opened his letter with a biblical
quote: 'When Israel went out of Egypt, the house of Jacob left a barbarian people' (*In exitu Israel de Egipto, domus Iacob de populo barbaro*).[60]
This chauvinist comment that equated Italy with the Holy Land and
the French with barbarians, provoked another response by the vindica-
tors of Avignon. They used the opportunity to repeat their case, show-
ing particular indignation at the Italian's attempt to barbarise all the
French.

The author of the riposte was Jean de Hesdin, a little-known theologian and client of the influential French Cardinal Gui de Boulogne. In
1369, he completed a *Letter against Francesco Petrarca* (*Contra Franciscum
Petrarcham Epistola*).[61] Hesdin repeated some of the points made by
Choquart, such as the political stability and the good supply situation
in Avignon. Besides, he enumerated learned Frenchmen past and present, all philosophers and theologians; citing Plato's contempt of poets,
he maintained that the French did not have to regret their absence.[62]
The conclusion of these deliberations was: *nullus doctus in Italia*.[63]

---

[58] Petrarch, *Letters of Old Age* (*Epistolae rerum senilium*), IX, 1,5, vol. I, 312 (translation revised by Hirschi).
[59] Ibid.
[60] Vulgata, *Psalmi*, 113,1 (in modern Bibles, *Psalms*, 114,1).
[61] Hesdin, *Contra Franciscum Petrarcham Epistola*, 112–39.
[62] Ibid., 131–4; Wilkins, *Petrarch's Later Years*, 235–6.
[63] Hesdin, *Contra Franciscum Petrarcham Epistola*, 132.

Hesdin also criticised his opponent's ahistorical glorification of Rome. There was no other city in human history (*in rebus humanis*) as 'inconstant and mutable' as Rome, he claimed, pointing to the contrast between its splendour in 'the time of Augustus' and the 'misery' of its present state.[64] In Hesdin's eyes, therefore, the appropriate biblical quote for the Pope's return to Rome was: 'A man was going down from Jerusalem to Jericho, and fell into the hands of robbers'.[65]

Despite his firm response, Hesdin's tone *vis-à-vis* Petrarch was respectful; he referred to him as a great man, while rejecting his attacks on France as unworthy of him. The same cannot be said about Petrarch's next reply. 'The one who maligns Italy' was, of course, meant to be Hesdin, but by refusing to call him by his name, Petrarch made clear that his opponent was a no-name to him. In the text he called him 'this barbarian' (*hic barbarus*), *Gallus noster* and *Galliculus*, which had the double significations of 'our Gaul' and 'our cock', respectively 'the little Gaul' and 'the cockerel'. So while his answer signalled that he accepted the Frenchman's challenge, his rhetoric indicated that he deemed the challenger far beneath him. The paradox of this situation left an imprint on the whole invective.

Petrarch replied to Hesdin's letter in March 1373. By then, the Italian humanist had found himself on the losing side again. Pope Urban V had not stayed in Rome for long. With the situation in Italy very much unsettled and his personal security in Rome under threat, he returned to Avignon after less than three years, where he died in December 1370. His decision to leave Italy had proven Choquart and Hesdin right; Avignon had indeed better security and food supplies than Rome, and there had been no sign that this would change in the near future.

Under these circumstances, Petrarch's invective amounted to an angry last word on a lost cause. However, this last word turned out to be just the initial spark of a much broader debate about barbarism and civilisation, about the French and the Italians. Petrarch did not witness this debate anymore, but in the end he was proven right in many respects – even by those who tried to fight off the stigma of barbarism.

The invective's main purpose was to portray the French as a faceless mass of barbarians and France as a cultural wasteland that would never become a fertile soil for civilisation. Italy, in contrast, had to shine as the only place on earth where Roman glory could revive again. Petrarch constructed a clear-cut bipolar and unequal opposition – and thereby accelerated the emergence of nationalist discourses outside Italy.

---

[64] Ibid., 113.   [65] Ibid., 112; Luke 10,30.

The dispute between him and Hesdin was elevated to a clash of two collectivities. The reaction to the Frenchman's letter in Italy, which Petrarch himself had acquired only three years after it had been written and only thanks to his good connections to the Curia,[66] was described as follows: 'How suddenly all of Italy was aroused!'[67]

Hesdin and his fellow countrymen were not only accused of 'barbarism bred in the bones', but also of its stubborn denial and clumsy pretence of civilisation. The French were in the state of a 'happy nation, which has the highest opinion of itself and the lowest of all other nations, and which is always cheered at least by a gratifying lie'.[68] *Natio*, in Petrarch's vocabulary, was still carrying the old connotation of 'barbarian', when used as a collective term (see the beginning of Chapter 5). There was no *natio Italica* in his vocabulary, whereas all non-Italians were assigned to *nationes*. The cultural differences between them were treated as minimal; Petrarch only felt compelled to distinguish between the nation usurping the Empire and the nation captivating the Papacy. About the latter's scale of self-misunderstanding, he elaborated:

> Truly, there is no tribe (*gens*) more prone to this than the Gauls. In any case, let him [Hesdin] believe as he pleases. They are still barbarians, and among the learned there has never been any doubt about this. Still, there is one thing I would not deny, nor do I think it can be denied. Of all the barbarians, the Gauls are the most effete.[69]

By pretending to be civilised, Petrarch argued, the French had just become decadent barbarians. Once they had been called 'Franks' because of 'their feral behaviour', but now they were a light-headed and light-hearted race, pursuing pleasures and spending their time playing, laughing, singing, eating and drinking.[70] Whatever attribute of civilisation they tried to adopt, they could not handle it. Instead of speaking Latin properly, they produced an awful noise; instead of drinking wine moderately, they drank to excess.

Wine, a symbol of both civilisation and salvation, was a matter of particular delicacy for Petrarch. At the time and for many centuries to come, Italian wines had no great reputation and were only drunk by the well-to-do *faute de mieux* – even in Italy. By contrast, France already had some of the most prestigious wine-growing areas; the most celebrated is known today as 'Burgundy'. When the Curia was moved to Avignon

---

[66] Wilkins, *Petrarch's Later Years*, 234.
[67] Petrarch, *Invectives*, 385.
[68] Ibid., 437 (translation revised by Hirschi).
[69] Ibid., 375 (translation revised by Hirschi).
[70] Ibid., 373.

in 1308, the popes and Cardinals made sure that large quantities were shipped to the new Papal city and thereby advanced the reputation of the region even more.

In his two letters to Urban V, Petrarch had already denounced the curial addicts of *vinum beunense* – the 'wine of Beaune' in the heart of Burgundy – accusing them at the same time of preferring alcoholic pleasures to the Church's well-being and of ignoring the great wines of Italy. 'If they at least judged rightly, which wine deserved the prize', he complained, 'they would not have long preferred Avignon above all other lands'.[71] Hesdin answered with a staunch defence of the 'precious wine' of his home country, stressing its health-enhancing qualities and calling Petrarch's criticism – because of its picturing of the Cardinals – a 'blasphemy'.[72] In his invective, Petrarch repeated his case again, this time by insinuating that the French loved Burgundy wine because they were barbarians. To his civilised self, it did not taste good at all.[73]

Considering all his arguments presented so far, Petrarch's endeavour to barbarise the French was, despite its aggressive tone, lacking bite, because he could only refer to the validity of a long-gone past and had to declare the present a complete sham. However, within this false present, he claimed to have found one true symptom to substantiate his diagnosis of French barbarism. This was Hesdin's Latin text. From its language and reasoning, Petrarch derived the entire character of its author plus the entire condition of his nation. The composition of Hesdin's letter was presented as follows:

This barbarian mixes his criticisms of my views with his own praise in a confused order that betrays more rage than anger. Unable to control his bile, he has vomited many charges against me, apparently considering himself someone great, who is licensed by the wickedness of our times to disparage the greatest men with impunity.[74]

Petrarch also offered an explanation as to why Hesdin's letter made such unpleasant reading. It was the French climate's fault. 'He may be excused', Petrarch reasoned with ironic generosity, 'by the charm of his native clime – a feminine charm, not a manly one – which, by the force of habit, wields great power over the affairs of men, especially the ignorant.'[75] The mild climate of France had made its inhabitants both decadent and overambitious. Hesdin in particular was a haughty nobody, who challenged a famous scholar with a clumsy piece of writing

---

[71] Petrarch, *Letters of Old Age* (*Epistolae rerum senilium*), IX, 1,3, vol. I, 308.
[72] Hesdin, *Contra Franciscum Petrarcham Epistola*, 125.
[73] Petrarch, *Invectives*, 399–403.   [74] Ibid., 375.
[75] Ibid., 377 (translation revised by Hirschi).

because he hoped to be awarded a bishopric by the French Pope for his flattery.[76]

In order to condemn Hesdin across the board, Petrarch interconnected literary ability, truthfulness and morality. He did the same, just with reverse effect, when speaking about himself. Within the invective, Petrarch presented himself as a modest and manly old savant, guided by 'experience and truth'.[77] He had no emotional bias and no ambition apart from defending the facts as they were. All his life he had 'preferred freedom to riches' and even refused bishoprics when offered to him.[78] His comments about France were not born out of hatred, but of close observation and historical knowledge. 'I am not condemning Gallic behaviour', he insisted, just as he was not favouring Italy.[79] In short, denying his own polemical tone, Petrarch tried to fashion himself as the embodiment of *humanitas*, the classical unity of profound learning, linguistic elegance and moral integrity. He was talented, rational and civilised and thus free of base motives.

Petrarch must have hoped to cause a great stir with his invective and yet he could not have foreseen its massive impact in the decades following its publication. When he died in 1374, there was no indication that Pope Gregory XI (1336–78) would start preparing the ground for a return to Rome just one year later. His legates in the Papal States were advised to secure the crop supply to the City of Rome by intervening in southern Tuscany, and when they did so, the Florentine republic reacted with aggressive panic. The result was the so-called 'War of the Eight Saints' (*Guerra degli Otto Santi*), lasting from 1375 to 1378. In Florence, the man executing the official war propaganda was Coluccio Salutati, the great admirer and friend of Petrarch, who had just been elected Chancellor. He quickly made use of Petrarch's polemical rhetoric against the French, though now for the opposite purpose.

In a frenzy of diplomatic activity, Salutati sent letters to the communes of the Papal States, trying to cause an uprising against the Pope's government. His main message was that the Holy Father's return to Rome was just a pretext for an invasion of the French barbarians, who wanted to destroy the liberty of Italy (*libertas Italiae*).[80] Salutati referred to the fact that the Papal throne and the Cardinalate were still in the hands of Frenchmen. So while Petrarch had barbarised the French to bring the Papacy to Italy, Salutati did the same to keep the Papacy out of Italy. His diplomatic offensive was of no avail, though. In January 1378, Gregory XI, after a successful war and an arduous trip, returned

[76] Ibid., 381 / 393.   [77] Ibid., 453.   [78] Ibid., 381.
[79] Ibid., 371.   [80] Langkabel, *Staatsbriefe*, 100 / 110.

to Rome. Furthermore, Salutati had to explain himself to the King of France, an old ally of Florence, who got wind of his anti-French propaganda.[81]

Pope Gregory did not enjoy his new residence for long; he died two months after his arrival in Rome. The Cardinals, pressured by the Roman populace, elected the Italian Bartolomeo Prignano (1318–89) as successor; he chose the name Urban VI. Following the conclave, however, most of the Cardinals left the unsafe City again and elected, this time pressured by the King of France, Robert of Geneva (1342–97) as Counter-Pope. Taking the name of Clemens VII, he soon returned with his followers to Avignon. What followed was the Great Western Schism that lasted for almost forty years until it was resolved by the Council of Constance in 1417 (see Chapter 5.2). With two rival Papal Courts, the tensions between Italian and French political scholars further increased.

The French writers who were engaged in debates with Italian humanists about the cultural state and status of France and Italy had close ties to the Royal Court of Paris or to the Papal Court of Avignon or to both. In 1389, the young theologian Jean Gerson (1363–1429) called for a history of great Frenchmen in order to fend off 'the biting and envious insults of the haters of the French name'.[82] His formulation directly referred to Petrarch's attacks against Choquart and Hesdin. A few years later, two other political writers, Jean de Montreuil (†1418) and Nicolas de Clamanges (1360–1437), set out to refute thoroughly the stigma of barbarism attached to the French by Petrarch and his Italian disciples. They pointed to elegant Latin prose by French authors, claiming that France's literary excellence had long outstripped that of Italy. Furthermore, they maintained that the French now had the lead in rhetoric, too; true eloquence was subordinate to wisdom (*sapientia*), and wisdom, so they argued, was not a forte of Petrarch and the Italians.[83] Thus, they concluded, the *translatio studii* to the French was perfectly justified.

Despite their seemingly self-assured tone, the public letters by Montreuil and Clamanges contained another message of very different content. Namely, their literary styles did not resemble Choquart's or Hesdin's scholastic Latin anymore; they rather showed, first of all in the case of Clamanges, a striking similarity with the classicist Latin of early Italian humanists. Indeed, ten years earlier, in 1384, Montreuil had begged Salutati in clumsy sentences to send him some of his letters in order to

---

[81] Herde, 'Politik und Rhetorik', 174.
[82] Ouy, *La plus ancienne œuvre*, 472.
[83] Furr, 'France vs. Italy'.

learn his art of writing. His plea was heard and so he imitated Salutati's Latin style, while at the same time damning Italy as the new Babylon, the kingdom of Pluto and a cave full of greed and haughtiness.[84]

Clamanges even went one step further.[85] He expressed disdain for Petrarch's literary legacy, asserting that he hardly paid attention to his works and that when he did, it was without profit. He treated Petrarch as a poser and chatterer, who mindlessly parroted his pagan idols. Within the same letters, however, Clamanges gave direct and indirect evidence of his thorough study of Cicero and Quintilian – and of his profound knowledge of Petrarch's works. Linguistically more talented than Montreuil, Clamanges aspired to the double reputation of 'Pétrarque français' and 'Anti-Pétrarque'.[86] Thereby, he presented himself as proof that the French were, on the one hand, on a par with the Italians and, on the other hand, completely independent of them.

Overall, the reactions by Montreuil and Clamanges show an ambivalent attitude towards Italian humanists. While rejecting their stigma of barbarism explicitly, they must have accepted it implicitly, which is why they tried to shake it off by proving their humanist credentials. Clamanges and Montreuil obviously felt obliged to play the Italian detractors of France at their own game in order to win the argument. And thus, Petrarch was, thanks to his literary authority and despite his own denial of reality, posthumously proven right.

Writing their public letters in 1394 and 1395, Clamanges and Montreuil did not yet have the language of national honour available; this only started to take shape twenty years later at the Council of Constance (see Chapter 5.2). However, the way in which they responded to Petrarch's barbarisation of the French turned out to be a prelude to the behavioural patterns by those Renaissance humanists outside Italy, who would eventually stage a broad competition for honour between nations. Towards the end of the fifteenth century, German, French, Spanish and English scholars fashioned themselves simultaneously as humanists of Italian greatness and as champions of a free and authentic nation. In both roles, they claimed to contribute to the honour of their nation.

7.3   The Emperor's independent supporters: humanist nationalists in Germany

Italian humanists of the fifteenth century, with only few exceptions, continued to paint non-Italians as 'barbarians' and regularly expressed

---

[84] Ouy, 'Pétrarque', 421–2; idem, *Paris*, 83–4.
[85] Cecchetti, *Petrarca, Pietramala e Clamanges*, 13–52.
[86] Ouy, 'Pétrarque', 429.

their amazement when being confronted with a foreign scholar who proved himself capable of writing a few correct sentences in classical Latin. They still targeted the French more than any other nation, although Rome was no longer under threat as seat of the Papacy after the end of the Great Western Schism. The French, though, still posed the biggest challenge to the Italians, who desired recognition of their homeland as a hub of European letters. The French were vilified the most because they were the least 'barbarian'.

This situation changed considerably when foreign rulers invaded Italy after 1494. German *landsknechts* helped to revive old stereotypes about the savage warriors from the north robbing the riches of the civilised and leaving behind nothing but death and destruction. While northern Italy was transformed into a European battlefield and the Germans became the focus of Italian polemicists, Maximilian I established himself in Germany. After his accession to the throne in 1493, humanism quickly took hold in the urban centres of southern Germany, many of which were strongholds of the Habsburg dynasty. This development may have helped Maximilian to acquire the unofficial title of *Hercules Germanicus* (see Figure 10).

Leading German humanists soon acquired a reputation as staunch defenders of German honour against foreign nations. Given the situation with the Italian Wars, they not only felt compelled to counter the louder barbarising rhetoric by the Italians, but also the hegemonic ambitions of the French and the self-determined military power of the Swiss. Their literary actions produced a multipolar discourse of national honour that expanded to all fields of comparison associated with prestige.

German humanists praised their nation for its achievements in warfare and territorial expansion, Christian piety and orthodoxy, public morals and hospitality, mechanical and liberal arts, secular and ecclesiastical architecture. They highlighted natural qualities of the German lands, such as the mild climate, the topographical variety, the mineral resources, the fertile soils and the excellent conditions for wine growing. And they did not forget to mention their own contribution to the national honour as commemorators of national history and authors of elegant literature.

With literary quality becoming a field of nationalist competition too, humanists could even turn into national heroes those of their peers who ignored or even opposed the competition between nations. Erasmus, who was born in the Burgundian Netherlands, was pressed by both French and German humanists to declare himself publicly a member of their nation, so that they could add his literary glory to their collective

Figure 10 In the upper portion of this woodcut broadsheet (*c.* 1500) Emperor Maximilian I is portrayed as the 'German Hercules', loaded with the attributes of the Greek original (club, lion skin, sword, bow and arrow). In the lower portion, though, he is depicted as 'the most glorious ruler of the world' (*Mundi Monarcha Gloriosissimus*), leading various nations, each identified with a banner, to war. The two compartments thus combine the nationalist and imperialist roles assigned to the Emperor according to different political circumstances.

honour. Unwilling to give up his cosmopolitanism, Erasmus disappointed his possessive admirers in both countries.[87]

Despite its far-reaching scope, the nationalist discourse of German humanists was in many respects related to the domestic propaganda of the Habsburg dynasty (see Chapter 5.6). Humanists not only borrowed the language of national honour from the German mandates and missives issued by the Imperial chancellery, they also presented themselves as strong supporters of the Emperor, urging German princes to follow his lead. Speaking for many of his nationalist friends, Wimpfeling, in a letter to Maximilian of 1492, declared his willingness 'to defend the honour and the splendour of your and our Germany's name' (*honorem ac splendorem nominis tui Germaniaeque nostrae defendere*).[88]

Quite a few humanist nationalists could even pride themselves on being in personal contact with the Emperor. Some, such as Conrad Peutinger of Augsburg, Willibald Pirckheimer of Nuremberg and Jacob Wimpfeling of Strasbourg, were sporadically asked to provide assessments on legal and historical questions; others, such as the Swabian professor Heinrich Bebel and the Franconian knight Ulrich von Hutten, had the privilege to be crowned poet laureate by the Emperor and to write a speech for the Imperial Diet; and a select few, such as Conrad Celtis, were even offered prestigious positions to raise Maximilian's fame.

However, none of the humanist nationalists belonged to the inner circle of the Habsburg court and none were included in the Emperor's decision-making. Maximilian did not even ask his humanist supporters to contribute to his own genealogical and literary projects of massive proportions. They were kept at a distance, both spatially and ideologically. And while humanist nationalists fashioned themselves as political preceptors of German rulers, the Emperor did not even grant his poet laureates a respectable position at court. He treated them as low functional elites, similar to heralds, who were used as official messengers for ceremonial occasions.[89]

Although Maximilian disappointed the expectations of humanist nationalists in many respects, they continued to venerate him as the leader of the German nation. What they did, however, was to redefine the national agenda in a direction quite different from the Emperor's own political priorities, which were dictated by dynastic interests. Instead of backing Maximilian's genealogical studies that traced the

---

[87] Hirschi, *Wettkampf der Nationen*, 294–5.
[88] Wimpfeling, Letter to Maximilian, 1492, in *Briefwechsel*, vol. I, 199.
[89] Mertens, 'Maximilians gekrönte Dichter', 108–9.

Habsburg dynasty back as far as the Trojans, they ridiculed all princely attempts to look for ancestors among the refugees of Troy and advocated a pure German origin for every German dynasty. And instead of calling the King of France at one time 'the hereditary enemy of us all' (*unser aller Erbfeind*) and at another time 'our dear brother' (*unser lieber bruder*), as the Emperor did according to political expediency,[90] they preferred to credit the Germans with a *genuinum odium in Gallos*, an 'innate hatred against the French', and continued treating France as 'the avowed enemy of the German nation' (*teutscher nation abgesagten feind*) in times of political peace.[91]

Looking at the relationship between the Emperor and the humanist nationalists from a different angle, one could argue that being kept at a distance from the Imperial court actually helped many humanists to develop a more consistent and comprehensive nationalist discourse. They used Maximilian's symbolic patronage through titles and honours to build up public authority, while pursuing their own literary and political projects concerning the German nation. Apart from a few incidents, the Emperor did not appear bothered by his independent-minded supporters; had he been worried, he probably would have been unable to sanction them severely anyway, as they were protected by local patrons, too.

To make a living, German humanists relied on various resources, among which the House of Habsburg's chronically empty treasury chest was a minor one. They could be endowed with a benefice, enjoy a pensioner's life, have an office at court or municipality, work as university professor or teacher. What they could not do, however, was make a living as a humanist writer. The *studia humanitatis* were not practised as a profession, but as a vocation.

7.4   The interdependence of nationalist isolation and assimilation

The nationalist discourse of German humanists was marked by two contrasting motifs, similar to those of Clamanges' reaction against the barbarisation of the French but much more extensive in content and claim. On the one hand, it described the German nation as either fully civilised or in need of civilisation, based on the principle that the Germans could only prevail in the competition with other nations

---

[90] Idem, *Reich und Elsass*, 120–1; Wiesflecker-Friedhuber (ed.), *Quellen*, 181–2; Janssen (ed.), *Frankfurts Reichscorrespondenz*, 793 / 828 / 897.
[91] Gebwiler, *Libertas Germaniae*, x, 225, 1; Aventinus, *Bayerische Chronik*, vol. v, 2, 495.

when possessing fine manners, elegant speech, mechanical inventions, literary and artistic masterpieces etc. On the other hand, it portrayed the German nation as completely authentic, justified by the idea that the Germans could only uphold their freedom and integrity if they stayed genealogically pure, were governed only by their own countrymen, cherished the values of their ancient forebears and refused foreign goods and morals.

A modern observer will probably note some ideological inconsistency when being confronted with these two intertwined motifs. How are we to describe their mutual relation, and how are we to explain the fact that humanist nationalists apparently did not perceive them as incompatible at all? Interestingly, this question has hardly been asked, let alone answered, by specialists of humanist nationalism. Some historians have dodged it by denying any notion of national authenticity in humanist discourses and by postponing its emergence until the era of Romanticism.[92] To find an elaborate approach to the topic, we have to go back to a pioneer of German-humanism studies, Paul Joachimsen (1867–1930). He treated the two motifs of authenticity and civilisation as symptoms of a deep rupture between humanist 'ethics' and 'aesthetics' that led to a 'period of national Romanticism' (*Periode der nationalen Romantik*) in classicist decor.[93]

Although Joachimsen showed an impressive awareness of the problem, he made the same conceptual mistake as those who completely denied it. Neither could contextualise the concept of 'national authenticity' because they were still under the spell of its Romantic fixation as a phenomenon rooted and expressed in the vernacular.[94] Authenticity, of course, can be constructed in various ways. As we have seen in Chapter Six, most humanists counted the vernacular among the characteristics of a nation, but not among the expressions of national character. It was thus impossible to demonstrate 'authentic' German behaviour by writing poems in German *Knittelvers* instead of Latin *Pentameter*. Instead, national authenticity was based on ideas such as pure blood, indigenous origin, traditional clothing and food, simplicity and absence of homosexuality.

Comparing humanist nationalism to modern nationalism may also help to better capture the relationship between the motifs of civilisation and authenticity. Although modern concepts of national authenticity

---

[92] Finsen, *Die Rhetorik*, 11–15; Muhlack, 'Die Germania', 138–9.

[93] Joachimsen, 'Der Humanismus', 443–5.

[94] For an extensive discussion of Joachimsen's theory, see Hirschi, 'Das humanistische Nationskonstrukt', 377–80; for a more elaborate criticism of Finsen and Muhlack, see idem, *Wettkampf der Nationen*, 320–4.

differ greatly from the humanist one, it is important to see that they were entangled with sharply contrasting motifs, too. German Romantics, for instance, presented their national language simultaneously as the source of German identity and as the origin of all languages. Similarly, they took the vernacular poetry of the Middle Ages for both the literary embodiment of German exceptionalism and for the foundation of a new 'universal' poetry. And when the 'classicist' Wilhelm von Humboldt called language the 'breath, the very soul of the nation' (*Der Odem, die Seele der Nation selbst*), he did it within a universal theory of comparative linguistics.[95]

So, what appeared to Joachimsen as a specific contradiction of Renaissance humanism, later resolved by Romanticism, in fact looks like a general condition for the construction of an 'authentic nation'. This observation fits well into our theory of nationalism. If the construction of different nations is as closely intertwined as I argue, then concepts of 'national authenticity' can only be developed within a complementary discourse that links a nation to other nations and thereby enables comparison and competition between them. What seems to be an ideologically incompatible marriage of isolation and assimilation is, in fact, a functional necessity; the humanist motifs of the civilised and the authentic nation are, functionally speaking, two sides of the same coin.

However, the authors and advocates of an 'authentic nation' inevitably put themselves in an awkward position: in order to develop their ideal of collective authenticity, they need to have an educational background that provides them with intimate knowledge of the cultures they reject as alien or inauthentic. In other words, they would have every reason to exclude themselves from the purist community they dream of. In this sense, Joachimsen was right to speak of an inherent contradiction in humanist nationalism, but he was wrong to assume that it could be resolved within the framework of nationalist discourse.

Tellingly, the humanist motifs of the civilised and the authentic nation were often incorporated side by side into the same texts. Both were embedded in historical arguments drawn on a variety of – mostly – literary sources. Exploiting them offered humanists an ideal opportunity to apply, display and refine their philological competence. They offered re-readings of well-known texts, such as Einhard's *Life of Charlemagne* (*Vita Caroli Magni*) of the early ninth century. They tried to enforce their interpretation of newly discovered writings, such as Tacitus' *Germania* of the late first century AD. They retrieved unknown

---

[95] Humboldt, *Gesammelte Schriften*, vol. III, 166–7.

literary treasures from German monasteries, such as the poetic and dramatic works by the Benedictine canoness Hrotsvit of Gandersheim of the late tenth century, which Celtis found around 1494 and edited in 1501. And they occasionally invented old German sources themselves, such as the *Chronicle of Hunibald* (*Duodecim ultimi Hunibaldi libri*) of the sixth century, a Carolingian history of the Franks 'found' by Johannes Trithemius, but never seen by anybody else – and still defended as a genuine document by the Romantic Joseph Görres (1776–1848) in Friedrich Schlegel's (1772–1829) journal, *Deutsches Museum*, in 1813.

Humanist nationalists followed mainly two criteria when collecting their source material of ancient and medieval origin. A document either had to contain information which could be interpreted as concerning the German nation, or it had to be by an author who could be identified as a German. The former were generally deemed the more valuable, the more flattering their information appeared, while the latter were regarded the more prestigious, the higher their literary quality was judged.

By assembling, rearranging and interpreting these sources, humanists constructed a 'history of the Germans' (*res Germanorum*), remarkably different from the medieval history of salvation in both form and content. They used typically humanist genres, such as the philological commentary and the epitome, and they replaced the teleological perspective on the end of time with the accentuation of Germany's glory in the present and near future. Even those humanists who stuck to the traditional genre of chronicle history often turned it into a vehicle for new nationalist ideas.

7.5   Germany – the (yet-to-be) civilised nation

To prove Germany's status as a civilised nation, humanists piled up diverse pieces of evidence. Trithemius established a catalogue of learned German men to expose those 'mendacious panegyrists of their own nation', who had called the Germans barbarians.[96] Bebel collected several hundred German proverbs, translated them into Latin and published them in 1508 as proof that the old Germans had possessed a public 'philosophy', too.[97] The Swabian humanist postulated that this philosophy must have been developed by a sage, who had taught the German populace 'prudent, pointed and elegant'

---

[96] Trithemius, Dedication of the *Catalogus illustrium virorum* to Jacob Wimpfeling, 1491, in Wimpfeling, *Briefwechsel*, vol. I, 165.

[97] Bebel, Dedication of the *Proverbia Germanica* to Gregor Lamparter, in *Opuscula nova*, fol. A ii[r–v].

sentences.[98] To demonstrate their quality, he juxtaposed them with comparable sayings by Roman authors.

Wimpfeling, besides praising the high standard of German scholarship, also highlighted the accomplishments of German artists and architects. Among painters, he deemed those the most distinguished who sold their works abroad. One of them was his contemporary, Albrecht Dürer (1471–1528), whom Wimpfeling called 'the most outstanding painter of our time':

He paints perfect pictures in Nuremberg, which are transported to Italy by dealers, where they are no less acknowledged by the most famous painters than the works of Parrhasios or Apelles.[99]

As to architecture, Wimpfeling just pointed out one part of one building to demonstrate that the Germans 'exceed all other peoples in the art of construction'. It was exactly the same building, which, 270 years later, was chosen for a similar purpose by the young Johann Wolfgang Goethe in his seminal treatise *On German Architecture* (*Über deutsche Baukunst*): the Cathedral of Strasbourg. Wimpfeling treated the tower as its finest component:

With its reliefs, statues, images and effigies of various things, it easily surpasses all other buildings of Europe. Its height exceeds the number of 515 cubits. It is a miracle that such a huge bulk can be erected so high.[100]

The cathedral of Wimpfeling's hometown was, indeed, one of the tallest buildings in Europe, but our humanist may have been carried away by both his nationalism and local patriotism when indicating its height. His number of 515 cubits was way off the mark. The tower, which was completed in 1439, measures 142 metres; with a cubit equalling between 53 and 60 centimetres in southwest Germany at the time, it has about 258 cubits – just half the size claimed by Wimpfeling.

There was probably no single accomplishment German humanists were more proud of than the invention of the printing press a few decades earlier. It was the centrepiece in their praise of Germany as 'fortunate inventor of arts' (*felix Germania inventrix artis*).[101] Celtis treated it as the most useful innovation of all time and as proof that the Germans had shaken off their old barbarian habits. Thus the Italians no longer had the right to 'blame the Germans for dull inertia, as they see that through our artistry Roman literature will continue to flourish

---

[98] Ibid., fol. A ii^v.
[99] Wimpfeling, *Epitoma Rerum Germanicarum LXVII* (*De pictura & plastice*).
[100] Ibid., *LXVI* (*De architectura Germanorum*).
[101] Idem, 'Epilogue to De laudibus sanctae crucis', 1502, in *Briefwechsel*, vol. I, 357.

for many centuries to come'.[102] To Brant, the invention of the letter-
press announced that the *translatio imperii ad Germanos* would soon be
followed by a *translatio studii*. Germany already now had a Cicero, a
Vergil and a Hesiod, he boasted, but before long it would have a Homer,
too. And so while the Germans had always been famous for their 'loyalty and weaponry', they would soon 'excel in ingenuity, erudition and
poetic inspiration and defeat all men of the world'. Brant's hymn of
German superiority culminated in a comparative observation covering
the whole history of Europe:

What was hidden to the learned Greeks and the skilful Italians was found by
the German genius (*ingenium Germanicum*): the new art. Tell me, cultivator of
Italy's soil, what do you have that equals such an invention? And you, France,
who proudly parade your front and neck, can you present a comparable work?
Say, do you still call the Germans barbarians, given that this is solely their
achievement?[103]

While German humanists praised the invention of print in the highest tones, they generally did not give much attention to its inventor.
Although Johannes Gutenberg was already famous at the time, only few
humanists actually called him by his name, let alone turned him into
a national hero. Instead, they portrayed the invention as a collective
achievement. This was a remarkably different treatment than that given
to well-known humanists, such as Erasmus or Johannes Reuchlin. It
still reflected the traditional distinction made between the liberal and
the mechanical arts. Humanists may have believed that ingenuity was
needed for some crafts, but they continued to regard them as subservi-
ent to higher occupations. This also explains why they heaped so much
praise on the invention of print. It was of great service to truly free
men – such as humanist scholars. By applauding it, they applauded
their own alleged greatness.

    Listing indigenous products and people in order to 'rebrand'
Germany as a civilised nation may have been an effective strategy, but
it was a defensive one as well. Some humanist nationalists combined
it with more aggressive measures, first of all by directly attacking the
foreigners who accused the Germans of barbarism. Naturally, this
approach was mostly targeted at Italian humanists. A typical argument
was to accuse them of misusing the term 'barbarian'. German humanists thereby capitalised on the term's ambiguity owing to its complex
history. Wimpfeling stressed its religious meaning, as it was introduced

[102] Celtis, *Libri odarum III*, 9.
[103] Brant, 'Ad dominum Johannem Bergmann de Olpe', in *Kleine Texte*, vol. I.2, no.
      228, 393.

by Roman Christians of Late Antiquity – and still used by some Italian humanists, such as Enea Silvio:

If, as Enea writes, Christianity has extinguished barbarism, and if we cultivate and love religion, then we are undeservedly and wrongfully dishonoured by the swearword 'barbarians'.[104]

Other German nationalists stuck to a secular understanding of barbarism but turned the tables by redefining its meaning. Irenicus reminded the Italians that Latin was originally considered a barbarian language, too, and that the Ancient Romans had been wrong when applying the term not just to the uneducated but also – out of frustration – to those resisting the Roman Empire. Anyway, he maintained, since the Empire had been transferred to the Germans, only a few people 'driven by envy and offended pride have been attributing the name "barbarians" to us'.[105]

A similar criticism was raised by Rhenanus against the French but presented with more sophistication. If 'barbarian' signified uneducated, he insisted, barbarism could not be an attribute of a nation because education had nothing to do with national identity. Thus it was 'intolerable' that the French treated the Germans as barbarians. 'Who is not born as a barbarian?' he asked, 'and who does not remain a barbarian, if he does not leave the state of ignorance through the study of the liberal arts?'[106]

While Rhenanus' argument amounted to an exclusion of the term 'barbarism' from nationalist discourse, Hutten, in the early Reformation, chose a contrary approach. He simply returned the compliment by painting the Italians and Romans as degenerate weaklings, falling back into barbarism:

If you consider good morals, the reputation of civility, the zeal for virtue, the constancy and integrity of the soul, this [i.e. the German] is a very cultivated nation (*cultissima est natio*), whereas the Romans are deformed by the most extreme barbarism. First, they are effete and corrupted by luxury; then, they are frivolous, of womanish inconstancy, rarely religious, fraudulent and malicious to an unrivalled degree (*quae vinci non possint*).[107]

Such aggressive rhetoric was typical of the early years of the Reformation, when Hutten wrote this anti-Roman polemic, but it was not at all uncommon during the decades before. Some German

[104] Wimpfeling, *Responsa et Replicae*, 130.
[105] Irenicus, *Germaniae exegesis II*, 30, fol. 38ʳ.
[106] Rhenanus, Letter to Jacobus Favre, in *Briefwechsel*, 41.
[107] Hutten, 'Die Anschawenden', in *Gespräch büchlin*, 164–5; idem, *Inspicientes*, 519.

humanists even attacked their Italian counterparts personally for their comments on the German nation. In 1498, Conrad Leonberg, a Cistercian monk and *homo trilinguis*, who corresponded with Reuchlin and Wimpfeling, wrote a letter to the little-known Jost Galtz von Ruffach, in which he declared himself, to say the least, displeased with the latter's admiration for Gian Antonio Campano. This Curial humanist was a red rag to German nationalists, because he was post-humously exposed as a hypocrite. He had visited Ratisbon in 1471 to deliver a speech against the Turks at the Imperial Diet, in which he planned to praise the Germans as a 'vivid and perennial fountain of the nobility' in all parts of Europe (*fontem nobilitatis vivum et perennem*).[108] While Campano was waiting in vain to address the Diet, he wrote let-ters to Italian correspondents, letting them know that the Germans showed the same devotion to drinking as the Italians to writing, and that Germany was 'all in all one single robber's cave, and among its nobility the bigger robber enjoys the greater fame'.[109] In no uncertain terms, Leonberg expressed his disgust that a German scholar dared to admire this enemy of his nation:

A weakling, a fag, a wanker, a cocksucker, an epileptic insults the Germans, antagonises the Germans, attacks the Germans! I praise his eloquence, his clean and sober style; I hate his slander, cannot stand, and cannot bear it. You, my Jost, whom Germany has nourished, are unworthy if you can bear this indifferently. I am not ashamed to be a German (*ego me Germanum esse non vereor*). You see how the Muses have now moved from Latium to Germany as they had moved from Greece to Latium – and still, Campano dares to boast that he has written that Ratisbon speech, which 'Italy reads and Germany does not catch'.[110]

Leonberg's vocabulary may not have satisfied the taste of refined Ciceronians, but his xenophobic aggression was shared by many high-ranking German humanists. Celtis suspected that many foreign histo-rians would be found, 'who hiss like vipers against our prowess' and disparage 'our glorious deeds with fabrications and fraudulent inven-tions'.[111] Trithemius even suspected Italian authors of having destroyed the *History of the German Wars* by Pliny the Elder, because they wanted the true glory of the ancient Germans to be forgotten.[112] And

---

[108] Campano, *Oratio in Conventu Ratisponensi*, 92.
[109] Quoted in Voigt, *Italienische Berichte*, 176–8; Krebs, *Negotiatio Germaniae*, 174–6.
[110] Quoted in Schlecht, *Zur Geschichte des erwachenden deutschen Bewusstseins*, 357–8.
[111] Celtis, *Oratio in gymnasio*, 45 (translation revised by Hirschi); idem, *De Italis histori-ographis* (Epigrams, II, 58).
[112] Trithemius, Dedication of the *Catalogus illustrium virorum* to Jacob Wimpfeling, 1491, in Wimpfeling, *Briefwechsel*, vol. I, 165.

Pirckheimer warned his learned countrymen not to trust any accounts by Italian and Roman historians at all:

Full of hatred, they have denigrated the victories and glorious deeds of our people; they have presented determined men as indecisive, persecutors as refugees and victors as defeated. We can observe that everybody tends to praise his own people more than a foreign one. Nevertheless, nothing should distinguish history more than the truth; if it is neglected, history becomes a fable and an old wife's tale.[113]

The reproach against foreign historians for distorting the German past was often accompanied by the criticism of previous German generations for neglecting to write the history of their people. Pirckheimer, in the same passage, lamented 'the sad fate of the German people' to have been granted no historians 'who preserve the memory of its especially glorious achievements in an appropriate manner'.[114] Bebel, in similar words, exclaimed that 'one is inclined to cry and bemoan the unjust condition of our ancestors, that there are many among the Germans who accomplish great deeds, but none who write them down'.[115]

Ascribing the absence of national histories in the past to mere negligence was, of course, a suitable means to explain away the non-existence of German nationalists in the ancient past, with whom the humanists could have identified. However, it proved an efficient way to demonstrate the importance and usefulness of one's own literary undertakings. Thanks to the humanists, the reputation of Germany had finally taken a turn for the better.

The criticism of German ancestors for failing to defend national honour indicates that the discourse of the civilised nation was often Janus-faced. After all, it was not without risk for German humanists to declare their nation fully civilised, because they would then have undermined their own educational mission. Therefore, many of them simultaneously portrayed Germany as a civilised nation *vis-à-vis* foreign calumniators and as a nation in desperate need of civilisation *vis-à-vis* German audiences. Italy was thus treated as both an enemy and an example.

In his lecture at the University of Ingolstadt, Celtis stirred up the audience by claiming that 'we are so pleased with our worthlessness and ugly barbarism' and that 'we are always ready to rebuke others with a vocabulary typical of schoolboys, but we do not smell our own stink'.[116] The remedy recommended to his countrymen was to take the Italians as an example:

---

[113] Pirckheimer, *Schweizerkrieg*, 32.
[114] Ibid.   [115] Bebel, *Oratio*, 97, 1.
[116] Celtis, *Oratio in gymnasio*, 59 (translation revised by Hirschi).

I will give you no other reason for the ever-flourishing condition of Italy than the fact that its people surpass us in no other blessing than the love and cultivation of letters. By this they overawe other nations as if by force of arms, and win their admiration for their ingenuity and industry.[117]

Becoming more civilised, according to Celtis, meant becoming more powerful, too. Thus Germany, after the *translatio imperii*, now finally had to accomplish the *translatio studii*. Naturally, he did not regard the French, but rather the Italians, as current possessors of universal knowledge. To emphasise what an effort was still needed to transform the Germans into cultivated beings, he did not shy away from portraying his countrymen as Campano had done: 'noble gentlemen, abandon and eliminate those acts of robbery, which, as they say, are considered acts of virtue amongst us!'[118]

Humanist nationalists expressed their frustration about Germany's lack of civilisation not only in public speeches, but also in correspondences with fellow scholars and even in private notes. Wimpfeling, in a letter to his pupil Thomas Wolf of 1503, conceded that he admired 'the aptitudes of the Italians, who, well educated from an early age, learn necessary and useful things'. As to his own nation, he concluded: 'If we would only imitate the Italians with first attempts, at least in our City of Strasbourg!'[119]

Eight years before, Wimpfeling had made an even more sobering diagnosis of the state of German culture in a gloss to a letter by his friend Dietrich Gresemund (1477–1512), who, staying in Padua, had admitted his envy of the Italians' *gloria litteraria*. Wimpfeling commented:

The fact that the Germans are despised and ridiculed by the Italians and that we are reproached with all kinds of vices is evident in that they call anyone whom they want to scold a 'German', and a father calls an infant or a boy who has done something wrong a 'German pig' … If they would only wrongly, not rightly blame us! Most of our fellow countrymen are brutes, pigs and churls, shallow people in pompous clothes, in womanish hats and shoes, in madness, improvidence, drunkenness, holding the sciences in contempt etc.[120]

The sense of collective inferiority expressed in this passage was not specifically German, though, as some historians have thought. Compared to the reaction by the early French humanists to Petrarch's polemical writings (as discussed above), it was just an explicit admission of the same jealous admiration which Clamanges and Montreuil implicitly

---

[117] Ibid., 53 (translation revised by Hirschi).
[118] Ibid., 45 (translation revised by Hirschi).
[119] Wimpfeling, Letter to Thomas Wolf, 1503, in *Briefwechsel*, vol. I, 423.
[120] Ibid., vol. 1, 240.

conceded by their refutation of Petrarch through the imitation of Petrarch.

Besides, deploring the barbarism of fellow countrymen was also a welcome means to celebrate one's own exclusivity and to underline the urgency of one's self-imposed educational mission. As the organisational backbone for their civilising enterprise, German humanists founded the so-called 'sodalities' (*sodalitates*). The idea of establishing a learned society that represented, cultivated and spread the new humanist education was suggested by Celtis. After he came back from a two-year trip to Italy in 1489, he soon spoke of a plan to found a 'Platonic Academy' in Germany, thereby hoping to push forward the *translatio studii*.[121] A few years later he began to put his idea into practice.

Contrary to the Platonic academies in Florence and Rome, Celtis envisaged a society with a national 'holding' and several regional 'representations'. This concept of a *Sodalitas litteraria per Germaniam* was an early expression of the later popular wish to constitute learned societies representing an entire nation. However, it was all much more impressive on paper than in reality. The 'Literary Sodality for Germany' was only visible in Celtis' classification of letters sent to him by German correspondents. He stored them under the rubric: 'Scripts of letters and poems by the literary Sodality to Conrad Celtis'. This is how Emperor Maximilian had the honour of becoming a member, too.[122]

On a regional level, at least, things went a bit further. In humanist strongholds, such as Augsburg, Strasbourg and Worms, occasional sodality gatherings were organised, for instance to welcome a well-known humanist to the town. Normally, participants of these gatherings consisted of humanist scholars and their local patrons – learned patricians, clerics and noblemen. The bond between them was also celebrated in publications officially edited by the sodality and in letters sent to the sodality. How German humanists perceived themselves as sodalists is well expressed in a letter by Wimpfeling's nephew, the jurist Jacob Spiegel, to the sodality of the Alsatian town Sélestat. Spiegel hailed the sodalists with the words: 'Farewell and triumph, you glorious victors over barbarism!'[123]

When Spiegel wrote his letter in 1520, the sodalists had not much more time left to triumph. With scholarly priorities shifting and many humanist friendships strained by the early Reformation, the tentative

---

[121] Celtis, Letter to Sixtus Tucher, 1491, in *Briefwechsel*, 32.
[122] Klaniczay, 'Die Akademie', 4 / 13.
[123] Spiegel, Letter to the Sodality of Sélestat, 1520, in Wimpfeling, *Briefwechsel*, vol. II, 840.

sodality life soon came to an end – and so did the humanist ambition of civilising the entire German nation.

7.6   Germany – the authentic nation

In their attempts to present and preserve Germany as a unique nation faithful to its traditions and free of influence from abroad, German humanists were not acting in complete isolation. Rather, they amplified and radicalised two existing political discourses, which had both been established during the second half of the fifteenth century, one by the German clergy, and one by the Habsburg dynasty.

With the Curia re-established in Rome and the conciliarist movement vanquished after 1450, the Papal appetite for secular power and splendour gradually grew. To finance the expenditures of the Curia, Renaissance popes set up an elaborate system to collect dues and duties, which would become the model of the modern state. In Germany, it was the higher clergy – bishops, abbots and their legal staff – who first complained about the drain of money from the German nation to Rome because they were the first to feel the financial pressure exerted by the Curia. Their *Gravamina* were soon accompanied with more popular and more polemical treatises, now often written by members of the lower clergy. They combined the complaint against financial exploitation with broad accusations of decadence and irreligion in Rome. The German nation, according to these voices, not only had to end its financial bleeding caused by Papal greed, but also needed to protect itself against malign influence from the Italian-dominated Curia. By the end of the fifteenth century, leading German humanists had tuned into this xenophobic discourse, widened it to a refusal of all Latin (*welsch*) cultures and simultaneously prepared the ground for the Reformation's take-off as a national movement against the Italianised Papacy.

The House of Habsburg, on the other hand, contributed to the humanist concept of the 'authentic nation' by combining its traditional royal duty of disciplining public morals (*disciplina morum*) with a protectionist economic policy wrapped up in patriotic rhetoric. The disciplinary measures mostly concerned drinking, cursing and clothing. In 1495, the Diet of Worms issued legal sanctions against public drinking and profanity.[124] In 1497, an Imperial decree condemned opulent clothing (*Uberflüßigkait der Klaidung*), too.[125] In 1506, Maximilian addressed

---

[124] *Reichstagsakten Mittlere Reihe*, vol. V, no. 458, 575–7.
[125] Müller (ed.), *Des Heiligen Römischen Reichs, Teutscher Nation Reichstagstheatrum*, vol. II, 2, 116.

the German estates 'regarding the gold and silk, which are now regularly worn by all people, noblemen and commoners, in dresses and jewelleries'. Buying luxurious clothes, he said, was harmful to the nation: 'The German nation is damaged and impoverished', because 'considerable money and goods are wasted and removed from German lands to Latin lands (*Wellsche land*)'. These resources, the Emperor argued, would otherwise have been 'of more use to the personal and common good of Germans'.[126] Maximilian's underlying motivation was to promote the German textile industry and thereby tie up financial capital within the Empire – which would then be accessible for taxation by the Habsburg treasury. This policy had already been introduced in France under Louis XI.[127] While Maximilian criticised the importation of foreign clothes for financial reasons, the German humanists took up the topic to deplore the moral corruption of Germans by foreign habits.

What brought a completely new dimension to the humanist concept of the 'authentic nation', though, was the construction of a historical narrative that described an original state of happy isolation. The most important historical source for this was the *Germania* by Tacitus. This work had been discovered in a German monastery in the mid-1450s and then directly brought to Italy, where it was first studied and politically instrumentalised by Enea Silvio Piccolomini in the winter months between 1457 and 1458, shortly before he was elected Pope. Enea Silvio used the text to counter the *Gravamina* by the then Chancellor of the Archbishop of Mainz, Martin Mayer (*c.* 1420–71), who had addressed his complaints about the Curia's financial exploitation of the German nation to him personally. In Enea Silvio's reply, Tacitus' ethnographic sketch appeared as a description of barbarian brutes, punished with paganism and poverty.[128] The humanist Cardinal used the text to argue for a profound difference between ancient and contemporary Germany and to credit the Curia for having civilised and enriched its inhabitants. According to him, blaming the Church for impoverishing the German nation amounted to biting the hand that fed it. Tacitus' claim that the *Germani* were indigenous people of pure blood was not mentioned at all.

When German humanists started to comment on Tacitus' *Germania* about forty years later, they declared Enea Silvio's depiction of the ancient Germans a malicious distortion and offered a starkly contrasting reading of the text. Now, the old Germans appeared as unspoilt and

---

[126] Janssen (ed.), *Frankfurts Reichscorrespondenz*, 737.
[127] Schmidt, 'Bien public', 196–8.
[128] Piccolomini, *Germania*.

unbeaten warriors, leading a simple and virtuous life, needing no written laws, thanks to their good morals, rejecting foreign habits, goods and blood, defending their collective property and singularity, loving freedom and practising chastity.

By establishing this nationalist interpretation of the *Germania*, German humanists actually misread Tacitus' text in a similar way to Enea Silvio. They tried to extract a clear message and an unambiguous value judgement from an ethnographic description that refused to draw an explicit conclusion, exercised restraint in moral verdicts and offered ambivalent or even contradicting assessments of both German and Roman culture. However, the nationalist misinterpretation proved so powerful that even modern scholars continued to regard Tacitus' writing as a one-sided account that presented the *Germani* as models of manliness, virtue and independence to a degenerate and enslaved Roman public.[129]

The main reason why this little ethnographic essay fascinated German humanists (and later generations of German nationalists) so much was that, apart from a few sections,[130] it portrayed the *Germani* as the exact opposite of the *Romani*, without defining the opposition, as could be expected from a Roman author, as hierarchical. This stylistic device of polarisation was attributed to all aspects of life. The wet, cold and hostile climate of Germany was contrasted with the mild weather of the Mediterranean (Chapter 2/5), the absence of money and jewels with Roman capitalism and pageantries (Chapter 5). German log cabins, dugouts and scattered settlements were opposed to the urbanised stone architecture of the Romans (Chapter 16), German nakedness and functional clothing to Roman fashion and delicate fabrics. The Germans painted their faces to frighten their enemies, the Romans to impress their friends and countrymen (Chapter 38). The Germans picked a fight in a fit of violent temper and ended it in a bloodbath; the Romans used violence where law and reason demanded it. German women were chaste maidens, faithful wives and stalwart warriors in contrast to the refined and sensual ladies of the Roman upper class (Chapter 8 / 18–19). Finally, the Germans were an indigenous people 'free from intermixture with foreigners, either as settlers or casual visitants', whereas the Romans were immigrants to Italy, heavily influenced by Greek culture and rulers over an Empire with a mobile and multiethnic population (Chapter 2).

---

[129] For the history of this misinterpretation see Timpe, 'Die Absicht', 109–10; Lund, 'Zur Gesamtinterpretation der Germania', 1860.
[130] See Hirschi, *Wettkampf der Nationen*, 324.

How ambiguous most of these oppositions were, can be exemplified by a central motif for German nationalists: the *libertas Germanorum*. German 'liberty', in contrast to Roman autocracy, was alternately associated with military power (Chapter 37), a foreign threat to Rome (Chapter 33), permanent belligerence (Chapter 14), indiscipline and inefficiency (Chapter 11), self-endangering recklessness (Chapter 24), barbarian irrationality and genuine sincerity (Chapter 22). The *Germani*, as depicted by Tacitus, were by no means noble savages, raised by nature to freedom, simplicity and integrity. They rather corresponded to the stoic character type of *homo iracundus*, described as choleric, superstitious, aggressive, impatient, inconstant and tiring fast.[131]

Stoic thinking may also be the clue to the value judgements hidden in Tacitus' *Germania*. By describing German and Roman cultures as polar opposites, the Roman author probably criticised both to equal degrees. What he implicitly evoked as an ideal society was, instead, a middle ground, distanced from all extremes, governed by manliness *and* reason, upholding liberty *and* order.

So, although German humanists widely quoted and commented on Tacitus' *Germania*, they drew a very different picture of their alleged ancient ancestors. Ambiguity was replaced with clarity, and negative connotations with positive affirmations. To give just a few examples: the motif of indigenousness and pure blood was combined with the idea of original nobility and contrasted with the Roman 'filth of peoples collected from everywhere' (*passim collecta populi colluvies*).[132] Meanwhile, the motif of lawlessness was turned into proof of Germans' natural goodness: 'Our justness', Bebel argued, 'is thus inherent to our genius by the grace of nature (*naturae bonitate*), not formed by laws, and even if I did admit that we once were raw and wild (*rudes et barbaros*), the ignorance of vice has helped us more than the knowledge of virtue has helped other nations.'[133]

Ultimately, the motif of German liberty was freed from any associations with chaos and self-destruction and reduced to the idea of an outward freedom. In this sense, it mainly served to stress the ancient Germans' complete rejection of foreign influences and their strong intention to dominate other nations. Aventinus referred to an early King of the Germans: 'King Herman wanted the Germans to be the freest people in the whole world that overruns all other nations and is not overrun by anybody.'[134]

---

[131] Lund, 'Zur Gesamtinterpretation der Germania', 1879–81.
[132] Bebel, *Oratio*, 101, 2.
[133] Idem, Dedication of the Proverbia Germanica to Gregor Lamparter, in *Opuscula nova*, fol. Aii[r].
[134] Aventinus, *Bayerische Chronik*, vol. I, 109.

Although Tacitus provided an excellent basis for the construction of an authentic nation, German humanists also relied on a range of other sources, both ancient and medieval, to sustain their historical narrative of a wilfully chosen and fiercely defended national isolation. Based on Pliny the Elder and other ancient ethnographers, who tried to harmonise the differing names used by Greeks and Romans for barbarian peoples, humanist nationalists identified all collective terms for northern forest barbarians with the Germans.[135] While contemporary Italian humanists still associated these names with martial destruction and cultural darkness, their German counterparts added them to the highlights of their early national history. Bebel compiled a long list of tribal names that allegedly belonged to the Germans, including the 'Franks, Burgundians, Goths, Vandals, Gepids, Rugii, Heruli, Turcilingi, Lombards, Normans, Picts, Quadi, Scots, Angles, Swabians and Saxons' – and, not forgetting, the Huns.[136] Aventinus went one step further by offering an etymological explanation for such a variety of collective terms:

The names *Scythae, Cimbri, Getae, Daci, Dani* are not proper names of a people, but common warrior names, as in our times the Swiss[!] and the Landsknecht. We are called Scythae because the ancient Germans were good at shooting with the bow, Gothi because of our goodness (*güte*) and virtue, Cimbri because of our belligerent (*kriegparn*), manly courage.[137]

By turning tribal names into warrior titles, Aventinus created a united German front against the Roman Empire. Thereby almost all Roman defeats on the European continent could become German victories, as was the case in Aventinus' *Bavarian Chronicle*.

Aventinus was not the first to congratulate his national ancestors for having repeatedly damaged and finally destroyed the Roman Empire. Johannes Cochlaeus (1479–1552), a German humanist with rather weak nationalist inclinations who later defended the Roman Church against Luther's Reformation, had already pronounced in 1512, that 'all those peoples, who have so often defeated and eventually annihilated the former world power, Rome, and the whole of Italy, were Germans'.[138] Cochlaeus expressed the same anti-Roman national pride as another moderate nationalist, Rhenanus, when he cited the 'triumphs of the Goths, the Vandals and the Franks' in Italy and Rome as examples of German glory.[139]

---

[135] Pliny the Elder, *Natural History (Historia naturalis)* IV, 25.
[136] Bebel, *De laude 19*, 130.
[137] Aventinus, *Chronica*, 399.
[138] Cochlaeus, *Brevis descriptio*, 56.
[139] See the quotation at the head of this chapter.

Cochlaeus and Rhenanus can be considered moderate nationalists because they did not join other German humanists in demanding and celebrating a broad national resistance against foreign influences. Aventinus and Hutten, for instance, systematically looked for proof of such resistance in the works of ancient and medieval writers. Both referred to Florus' account of the famous massacre of Varus' legions by Germanic warriors in AD 9, claiming that his description of particular cruelties committed against jurists documented an early German refusal of Roman law and Roman lawyers.[140] While the Roman historian had specified the barbarian atrocities to evoke a sense of horror in his 'civilised' readership, the German humanists proudly recited the same atrocities to document their ancestors' consequential treatment of foreign invaders.

Hutten – who, incidentally, had twice travelled to Italy to study the law – drew a direct line between the ancient and the recent past by saying that 'these little doctors [of laws]' had still been 'unknown' in Germany in his grandfather's days. 'It is such a short while ago', he added, 'that they have intruded with their red hats to devastate, as they please, the whole of Germany like a thunderstorm'.[141] He thus urged his countrymen to chase them away once more and to re-establish the good old home-grown *summum jus Germanorum*.[142] With such rhetoric, Hutten and other humanists paid their tribute to popular xenophobia, which had already been targeting experts of Roman law for quite some time. A leaflet published in German verse in 1493, for instance, had called on German princes to expel the 'bloodsuckers' (*Blutsauger*), who 'brought foreign laws into our country', once and for all.[143]

It was tricky enough to denounce the members of a learned profession as foreign invaders, especially when prestigious German humanists, such as Reuchlin, Brant and Peutinger, had come from their midst. Things became even more awkward when Aventinus celebrated the ancient Germans as staunch enemies of the book. He therefore referred to an episode that allegedly took place in the Athens of late Antiquity. Aventinus did not mention his source, but the original account of this episode must have been a fragment by the East Roman historian Petrus Patricius (*c.* 500–65). It reported an incident during the pillage of Athens by 'the Scythians' in AD 269. When the looting warriors

---

[140] L. Annaeus Florus, *Epitome of Roman History* (*Epitoma de Tito Livio*) II, 30, 36–8; Hutten, *Praedones*, 198; Aventinus, *Bayerische Chronik*, vol. I, 605.

[141] Hutten, *Praedones*, 192.

[142] Idem, Letter to Crotus Rubeanus, 1518, in *Epistolae*, 179–81; Ridé, *L'image du Germain*, vol. I, 459.

[143] Quoted in Janssen, *Geschichte*, vol. I, 590–1.

'collected all the books to burn them', one of them interfered by saying that they should let the Romans read because then 'they would not care for war'.[144] Petrus Patricius added: 'He said so out of ignorance: had he been aware of the virtues of the Athenians and Romans, how renowned they were both in word and war, he would not have said so.'[145]

In Aventinus' *Bavarian Chronicle* the story appeared in a remarkably different light and with an opposite moral. The 'Scythians' were replaced with 'Goths, Bavarians and other Germans', and their actions in Athens were described as follows:

After they had conquered Athens, the most famous Imperial city in Greece with the most distinguished high school (*hohe schuel*) of the whole world, they amassed a large number of books on the market, piled them up and wanted to have them burned. At this point, a soldier stood up and dissuaded them from it, saying: 'leave the books to those fools, the Greeks; while they are occupied with them, they all become unfit for war and womanish creatures who cannot defend themselves; it is better and more convenient for us if they are equipped with books and pens than with harness and weapons.'[146]

There was no condemnation, but only silent approval of this statement. Accordingly, Aventinus maintained that the term 'crude Germans' (*grobe Teutsche*) had not only been used by the ancient Greeks and Romans, but also by the ancient Germans – as a proud self-designation. His Germans were not barbarians, but primitivists; not ignorant, but wise; not uncivilised by nature, but by will. They defended their national culture because it was both morally and militarily superior to those of Greece and Rome.

Aventinus exemplified this argument with another episode set in Ancient Greece, this time adapted from the biography of Alexander the Great by the Roman historian Quintus Curtius Rufus from the first century AD.[147] A short section of an address by a Scythian ambassador to Alexander was modified and amplified in the following declaration by a German warrior:

With us crude Germans, it is not the custom to take an oath and to seal a deed in order to declare our fidelity to someone; we just believe and trust each other, and everyone treats each other as they like it; believing and trusting is our highest worship; doing good, giving faithful advice and helping each other is our religion, with which we honour God. You clever Greeks, though, are so wary and wise that you do not trust either each other or other humans; you want to have deeds under seal, you have to swear a scholarly oath to God and

---

[144] Boissevain (ed.), *Casii Dionis historiae*, vol. III, 745.
[145] For a translation and interpretation of Patricius' short fragment, see Millar, *Government*, vol. II, 265 / 292.
[146] Aventinus, *Bayerische Chronik*, vol. I, 956.
[147] Quintus Curtius Rufus, *Historiae Alexandri Magni Macedonis VII*, 26–9.

all his saints. You are indeed a fine and foolish people to count on someone fearing and following the Gods, when he may disrespect them or even doubt their existence.[148]

Alexander the Great was vilified in the same speech as a 'murderer and robber' driven by 'greed and avarice'. Such attributions differed markedly from the pictures drawn of the Macedonian King in ancient and medieval writings. Aventinus may have partly used Alexander and the Greeks as surrogates for the Pope and the Italians. There was a certain Lutheran touch to his account of the ancient Germans exercising brotherly love and the ancient Greeks invoking the saints. Indeed, Aventinus wrote his *Bavarian Chronicle* in the 1520s and early 1530s. In 1529, he was imprisoned for a short time by the Bavarian authorities 'because of the gospel' (*ob evangelium*). But if he actually sympathised with the Protestant faith, it was less for theological reasons than for the nationalist conviction that Luther's belief was a creation and expression of German culture.

Apart from the heroic history of the staunch manliness and militarism of the Germans, Aventinus outlined a second, less glorious, story about the flagging virility of a neighbouring nation – the fate of France. At the time when King Herman trained his German countrymen in military techniques, a King named 'Bard' designed a different scheme of education on the other side of the Rhine:

He invented the art of singing, endowed a big choir, focused on feasts and holidays, taught people to dance, sing, hop and court; ... It was a disgusting thing: west of the Rhine one learned to dance and sing, which serves for jesting, shame and amusement, east of the Rhine one learned to make war, hit and stab, which belongs to seriousness.[149]

This is one of the earliest examples of a widespread commonplace in early modern national discourses – not only in Germany, but also in England and elsewhere. It traced the incrementally refined and increasingly French-speaking culture at European courts back to the 'degenerate' condition of the French nation and denounced the European hegemony of French language, literature and lifestyle as a danger to the virility and integrity of one's own nation.

Aventinus projected this process, which had barely started during his lifetime, into the past, when reporting on the cultural self-defence of the German humanists' greatest national hero, Charlemagne. Once again, a figure hailed as a paramount ruler in medieval historiography was thereby significantly transformed, though this time not in

---

[148] Aventinus, *Bayerische Chronik*, vol. I, 359–60.
[149] Ibid., 118.

a disparaging way.[150] As I outlined in Chapter Four, the first medieval Emperor in the West had long been used to justify the German possession of the Empire. He was therefore identified as a German-speaking man, born and buried in the German lands. The key source for this was the *Life of Charlemagne* (*Vita Caroli Magni*) by Einhard, a scholar at the Frankish court and client of Charlemagne. Einhard not only described his master's death in Aachen, but also recounted that the Emperor had given the months and winds new names 'in his own tongue'.[151] Luckily for German authors of later generations, Einhard enumerated these names – they clearly had a Germanic sound. In the same paragraph, Einhard presented Charlemagne as the author of an unfinished grammar of his language, which was probably stretching the truth, but still wonderful stuff for German humanists, such as Trithemius, who were eager to treat the King of the Franks as one of their own.

Aventinus painted Charlemagne as a humanist *avant la lettre*, too, but he added a contrasting portrait of the Emperor as a nationalist primitivist. For this, he combined accounts by Einhard and Notker of Saint-Gall (*c.* 840–912), who had authored a collection of anecdotes about the Emperor entitled *De Carolo Magno*. Aventinus' starting point was a description of Charlemagne's appearance. After emphasising that the Emperor's facial features had been 'of the German kind' (*nach der Teutschen art*), he described his style of clothing:

As to dresses and shoes he always abided by the German way in use at the time: he wore a shirt, jacket or coat not much costlier than those of a commoner ... For dresses of foreign nations and different kinds, he had, even if they were costly, nothing but contempt.[152]

Aventinus followed Einhard quite closely in this passage;[153] he just replaced 'Frankish' (*Francicus*) with 'German' and occasionally added 'in the German way' (*auf teutsche monier*) to clarify that Charlemagne had always meant to make a nationalist statement with his clothing.

In a similar way, he then mixed and modified two anecdotes by Notker about Charlemagne disciplining his men for wearing jewellery and luxurious clothing. One anecdote was about his courtiers buying fine Venetian dresses and then being forced to go hunting with the Emperor to become aware of the limited functionality of their purchases. The other anecdote was about his soldiers being dressed up with 'silk or gold

[150] For early images of Charlemagne in the Carolingian Age see McKitterick, *Charlemagne*, 1–56.
[151] Einhard, *Life of Charlemagne* (*Vita Caroli Magni*), 29.
[152] Aventinus, *Bayerische Chronik*, vol. II, 152–3.
[153] Einhard, *Life of Charlemagne* (*Vita Caroli Magni*), 23.

or silver' and then rebuked by him for handing over their 'worldly goods to the enemy' in the case of their death in battle.[154] Both anecdotes had a religious undertone, admonishing 'other-worldly' values. This was replaced by Aventinus' nationalist call for cultural isolation:

The Germans and the Franks, after having been at war in company with the Italians (*Walhen*) and the French, adopted their short tailored little coats and skirts. When Emperor Charlemagne saw this, he became angry and screamed: 'Oh, you Germans and free Franks, you are so imprudent and inconstant! It is not a good sign that you are adopting the dresses of those whom you vanquished and fought and whose masters you are: if you take their clothes, they will take your hearts. What is the point of these Latin (*wälsche*) clothes and cuts? They do not cover your body, leave it half naked, are neither good for cold nor heat, for rain nor wind; and when someone has to do their business in the field (to put it politely), it does not cover them and their legs freeze.' Charlemagne then sent out a messenger so that these French clothes were neither bought nor sold in Germany.[155]

Charlemagne here appeared as a forerunner of Emperor Maximilian's *disciplina morum*, though blessed with more nationalist fervour. To him, the question of foreign clothes was not just an issue of financial loss and functional folly, but of national identity and personal character. Changing clothes was not merely an external procedure. It directly affected the personality, leading to a 'change of heart'.

Aventinus' concept of an authentic nation may have been exceptional in terms of breadth and depth, but not in terms of ideology and methodology. His – and other humanists' – national history of a hard-won cultural isolation was by no means invented from scratch. It was established by philologically refined *bricolage*. Aventinus collected a huge amount of ancient and medieval source material, extracted what was suitable, added what was missing, and reassembled the rewritten pieces to form a new narrative. The result was less than consistent, but much more credible than any pure invention of a national past.

Entrenching the 'authentic nation' in an ancient past served to strengthen its profile in the present. Ancient reports about the Germanic disdain for merchants, for instance, directly led to the rhetorical expulsion of contemporary merchants from the German nation. To repudiate unwelcome foreign commodities and customs, humanists helped themselves to the language of plague and disease, using it not only in a metaphorical, but also in a literal sense. Hutten commented on the importation of commercial goods from abroad:

---

[154] Notker, *De Carolo Magno*, 167.
[155] Aventinus, *Bayerische Chronik*, vol. II, 153–4.

It is, indeed, incredible that things which are not from here are of any good to the people born here. If they were, nature would have made sure that they grew here. This is why people want these products not for their benefit, but for their pleasure, and you merchants put them into circulation not to serve the body, but to entertain it. And so it is no wonder that our health is at risk and that we tend to catch all kinds of sicknesses. Besides, you have imported silk and infinite kinds of foreign clothes, through which Germany's original strength is weakened and the best morals are corrupted, as womanish pomposity and disgraceful effeminacy have permeated throughout human life ... It is against nature, I say, to bring here what is not from here.[156]

Hutten's ideal of a self-subsistent and thus healthy nation was not limited to commodities. Ideas and habits developed abroad were deemed just as dangerous, and so the humanist knight denounced clerics and lawyers as 'un-German' Germans, too.

Hutten launched his literary attacks against the alleged internal enemies of the German nation in the early years of the Reformation. Many of his arguments, though, had already been in use before. Celtis, in his *Amores* of 1502, indulged in primitivist day-dreams about the egalitarian happiness of a self-sufficient nation and even expressed his fear that the spread of 'Italian excesses' could lead to the importation of another Italian disease: homosexuality.[157] Wimpfeling, a secular priest and devout son of the Catholic Church, repeatedly portrayed German mendicants as foreign parasites depriving the Germans of their religious righteousness and moral integrity.[158]

'Integrity' (*integritas*) was indeed a key term in Wimpfeling's vocabulary of national authenticity. He expanded its meaning to a Christian-German hyper-virtue comprising 'maturity' (*maturitas*), 'constancy' (*constantia*), 'veracity' (*veritas*), 'sincerity' (*sinceritas*) and 'simplicity' (*simplicitas*).[159] Traditionally, the prime candidates to incorporate all vices opposed to integrity would have been women. Although Wimpfeling did not spare them, he added a new representative of the hyper-vice: the foreigner (*alienigena*). Consequently, the Alsatian humanist warned young Germans against going abroad to study because they could return mentally and physically contaminated, deprived of their *Germanica integritas*.[160]

Of particular worry to him were theologians going to Rome. Under the strong influence of the Eternal City, one could easily become an

[156] Hutten, *Praedones*, 172.
[157] Celtis, *Quattor libri amorum*, II, 9 / IV, 4.
[158] Wimpfeling, *Agatharchia*, fol. 8ᵛ.
[159] Wimpfeling, *De integritate*, 26; Herding, Vorwort, in Wimpfeling, *Adolescentia*, 133.
[160] Ibid.

'Italianised German' (*Germanus Italicatus*) and thus a threat to every German staying at home. Wimpfeling recited a German saying, which had already been quoted by the so-called 'Upper Rhine Revolutionary' a few years before:[161] 'Beware of a bold redhead (*roten kalen*) and an Italianised German (*dutschen vualen*)!' This proverb treated the alienated compatriot as a contradiction in terms, whereas another dictum, which appeared in Luther's *Table Talks*, branded him as a heretic: 'An Italianised German is a living devil (*ein lebendiger Teufel*).' Luther, who also believed that the Italian air was bad for German bodies, gave the Italian illness caught by Germans a name, too: 'Epicureanism' (*Epicurismum*).[162]

By the time of the Reformation, the feared figure of the *Germanus Italicatus* or *Semigallus* already had some foreign counterparts. At the beginning of the sixteenth century, the French poet and dramatist Pierre Gringoire (1475–1539) proclaimed there was 'nothing worse' than an 'Italianised Frenchman'.[163] And in 1553, the English diplomat Thomas Wilson (1524–81) published a treatise entitled *The Arte of Rhetorique*, in which he ridiculed the 'Angleschi Italiani', who spoke an un-English tongue 'pouder[ed] like women's faces'.[164]

Anyone who had travelled abroad and been receptive to foreign cultural influences could qualify as a contaminated and contaminating countryman. German humanists particularly attacked the triad of clerics, merchants and lawyers – and not, as Peter Burke has suggested, courtiers imitating Italian aristocratic culture.[165]

It is important to identify correctly which social groups were most repeatedly stigmatised in these terms. After all, they had more in common with Renaissance humanists than probably any other group. They belonged to the most mobile and well-educated section of society, and they frequently entertained social relations with foreigners because their occupations transcended national borders. In this sense, it was only logical that humanists could also insult each other as nationally impure creatures. Hutten set the example by giving Erasmus the unfriendly recommendation to 're-emigrate to your Gallo-Germans', to which the cosmopolitan humanist aptly commented: 'He is expelling me from Germany.'[166]

---

[161] Franke (ed.), *Das Buch der hundert Kapitel*, fol. 14ª. For the Upper Rhine Revolutionary, see Chapter 6.2 of this book.
[162] Luther, *Tischreden*, fol. 605ʳ / 607.
[163] Quoted in Burke, *The Fortunes*, 113.
[164] Quoted in Shrank, *Writing the Nation*, 191.
[165] Burke, *The Fortunes*, 113–14.
[166] Hutten, *Expostulatio*, 239; Erasmus answer quoted in Huizinga, *Erasmus*, 43.

The social proximity or even personal familiarity between calumnia-tors and calumniated can be seen as a further sign of the fundamen-tal contradiction that underlies the concept of an 'authentic nation'. The people capable of creating and cherishing such a concept generally have a profile that qualifies them as ideal enemies, not citizens of their purist community dream. In order to feel and formulate a collective need for authenticity, one has to be estranged and educated. From this perspective, humanist nationalists were expressing a deep uneasiness about their own social positions and cultural identities when slandering lawyers, clerics and merchants as foul compatriots. Therefore, the dis-course of national authenticity should be seen, to a large degree, as an inward aggression turned outward.

8   A German Emperor for the German people

> Above all, if one cannot have a German prince elector or prince, any king has to be a German by ancestry and origin, so that the honour of our nation is preserved and the common man is satisfied.
>
> Albrecht of Brandenburg, Archbishop of Mainz, *Notes*, 1519

> We are German by blood and disposition, by birth and tongue.
>
> Charles I, King of Spain, *Letter to the Prince Elector of Saxony*, 1519

To modern observers, the political system of pre-modern Europe may easily appear to be the exact opposite of a nationalist order. Monarchs primarily pursued dynastic ambitions, not nationalist agendas. They married their children and grandchildren off to families of foreign rulers, and, as a result, regularly ruled – on perfectly legal grounds – over peoples with whom they shared neither culture nor language. Indeed, dynastic politics was at odds with nationalism in many respects, not least because it was based on hereditary rights established in the early medieval period, when the concept of the nation was not envisaged.

However, the late medieval and early modern period offers ample evidence, too, that dynastic politics both shaped nationalist culture and was shaped by it in return. Emperor Maximilian's impact on humanist nationalism in Germany was no exception in this regard. Many kings portrayed themselves as paragons of patriotic statesmanship and as defenders of national honour while cultivating their family ties and fostering their territorial claims all over Europe.

Such behaviour certainly looks contradictory now but, more importantly for us, it was often a cause for conflict at that time. Many newly crowned monarchs who inherited territory they did not grow up in faced a sceptical or even hostile public on their arrival. Nationalist reservations could play a big part in such reactions. After all, a king coming from abroad risked violating the basic principle of national freedom, which was that the ruler and the ruled had to belong to the same nation.

To encourage acceptance, a foreign-born-and-bred king could either demonstrate his willingness to assimilate quickly to the native culture or assert that he had already been raised in it abroad due to his blood ties to the local dynasty. Charles of Habsburg (1500–58), the main protagonist of this chapter, used both tactics on different occasions – with mixed results. After growing up in a predominantly French-speaking court in the Burgundian Low Countries, he became King of Spain in 1516. When he entered his new realm the following year, the Spanish aristocracy greeted him with open hostility. It only quietened down when Charles formally accepted the demands of the Spanish Cortes to learn Castilian as quickly as possible, not to confer any royal offices to foreigners and to appoint only native Spaniards as ambassadors of Spain.[1] The agreement shows that the nationalist reservations within the Spanish aristocracy had much to do with aspirations for dignities and sinecures.

The young King and his entourage quickly learned their lesson – and overcompensated. When launching his next campaign for the Imperial crown in 1518, Charles presented himself as a true German. After his successful election, he had the opposite experience of that in Spain. He was welcomed as a national hero in Germany, but only a few years later, when it became apparent that he was not as German as he had pretended to be, and that his huge power base abroad compromised the German princes' ambitions within the Empire, he was denounced as a foreign destroyer of German liberty.

Elective monarchies, such as the Empire, are especially rewarding when analysing the impact of nationalist beliefs on pre-modern politics because their election rules were generally more flexible and adaptable to changing circumstances than succession laws in hereditary monarchies. We have only to analyse an election where kings and princes of foreign territories acted as serious contenders to find out how important the nationality of a candidate to the throne was considered to be and how much this affected the electoral procedure. The Imperial election of 1519 is a perfect example of this.

The death of Emperor Maximilian in 1519 and the subsequent process leading to the coronation of his grandson, Charles, transformed the national discourse in Germany just as much as the early Reformation. Both events were interlinked in many ways, but as their causes and effects were mostly independent from each other, I propose to analyse them separately.

---

[1] Pietschmann, 'Zum Problem', 62–70; Ochoa, 'Die Diplomatie', 187.

8.1   The introduction of nationality as an election criterion

The discussions of the significance of nationality to qualify as Emperor had an interesting prehistory with a decisive turn in the fifteenth century. Before we take a closer look at it, I wish to say a few words about the general situation at the outset of the election campaign.

When the German prince electors were choosing Maximilian's successor, their leading criteria could hardly have been more contradictory: the importance of electing an Emperor of German origin was stressed like never before, but there was no German prince with enough power, authority and money to compete with the three foreign candidates – the Kings of Spain, France and England. As a result, Charles I, Francis I and Henry VIII found themselves in a position to persuade the electorate that they were more German than their royal rivals.

The King of England was certainly the most handicapped and the King of Spain the least by the terms of this competition. Yet, the intense canvassing of the French and the Spanish King indicates that the race for the 'most German' foreign King was only decided shortly before the election. It cannot even be ruled out that it was the Habsburg treasury (or rather the loans granted to the Habsburgs by the Fugger family) which tipped the balance in the end.

At least a small part of the huge bribes paid by Charles was given directly to the legal counsellors of the prince electors. Among them were the people leading the discussion about nationality as an election criterion, to whom we can now turn.

A few months before the election, Duke Frederick of Saxony, Luther's protector and one of the most respected prince electors, asked scholars at his own university in Wittenberg and counsellors to his cousin George of Saxony to give advice 'as to how the election of a Roman King shall proceed according to the law and if someone not belonging to the German nation shall be eligible'.[2]

The seven legal experts who submitted their reports all agreed that the Roman Emperor had to be German. While confirming Charles of Spain to meet this condition (he was Maximilian's grandson after all), they refused (with good reasons, but dubious motives) to accept Francis' claim to descend from Charlemagne. With this, most referees indicated a clear preference for the Habsburg candidate; only one came to the conclusion that a German prince in general – and the elector of Saxony in particular – would be the best choice.[3]

---

[2] Quoted in Klippel, *Die Aufnahme*, 102.
[3] *Reichstagsakten*, Jüngere Reihe, vol. I, 621–9.

How did the legal counsellors justify their argument on a candidate's nationality? The main piece of evidence was a document issued by Pope Innocent III in 1202 and later entitled *Decretale Venerabilem*. Its original purpose had been to corroborate the Pope's claim to have the right to intervene in the election of a Roman King when he deemed a candidate unacceptable. The reason why the document became important, however, was that, in order to sustain the Pope's claim, it gave a brief history of how the Empire had been established. The crucial sentence was that the Apostolic See had 'transferred the Roman Empire in the person of Charlemagne from the Greeks to the Germans' (*Romanum Imperium in personam magnifici Caroli a Graecis transtulit in Germanos*).[4] Based on this short wording, the legal experts in 1519 made their case. They could feel comfortable about its validity because they were not the first to bring it forward.

Nonetheless, their conclusion was, to say the least, not intended by the curial author of the *Decretale Venerabilem*. His point had been that the *translatio imperii ad Germanos* was reflected in the suffrage of the German prince electors – and not in the nationality of the Emperor. We can say this with certainty because the *Decretale* also clarified who was ineligible for the throne (and could thus be refused by the Pope). The list of exclusion criteria contained 'excommunicated', 'tyrants', 'idiots', 'heretics' and 'pagans' – but not foreigners![5] In order to add the criterion of nationality, as the legal experts of 1519 did, one had to engage in some very selective reading of the document.

Probably the first scholar who explicitly did so was the Italian canonist Nicolò de' Tudeschi, called Panormitanus (1386–1445). He had been an active supporter of the conciliarist movement at the Council of Basle (1431–49). Based on Panormitanus' re-interpretation of the *Decretale Venerabilem*, Peter of Andlau (1420–80), Professor of Law at the University of Basle, argued in 1460 that the transfer of the Roman Empire to 'the renowned German nation' was to be understood as 'active and passive' (*active et passive*). In other words, both the electors and the elected had to be Germans. Andlau made this comment in a *Booklet on the Caesarean Monarchy* (*Libellus de Caesarea monarchia*), which he dedicated to Emperor Frederick III.[6] So almost from the start, the fully 'Germanised' re-reading of the *Decretale Venerabilem* was linked to the Habsburg dynasty.

A few decades later, humanist nationalists regularly referred to the *Decretale* in order to prove that Charlemagne was German, not

[4] *Decretalium Collectiones*, 79–82, here 80.   [5] Ibid.
[6] Peter of Andlau, *Libellus II*, title 3, 186–7.

French, and that, consequently, French kings were ineligible for the Imperial throne.[7] By 1519, the phrase 'transferred in the person of Charlemagne ... to the Germans' had been taken completely out of its original context. And so it had become possible to make a convincing case that the nationality of the Emperor was the crucial element in the German possession of the Empire.

The expert reports by the legal counsellors were immediately used to weaken the candidacy of Francis I. George of Saxony, who labelled the French 'hereditary enemies of the German tongue' (*erbfint Deutzen gzunges*), sent letters to other German princes, in which he tried to dissuade them from supporting the King of France.[8] The Landgrave of Hesse, for instance, was admonished to 'be and remain a good German' by furthering what had to be preserved 'for the honour of the German nation'. George added that 'the Frenchman is so little to be trusted' and that it would be shameful 'to give away the Empire, which our forefathers and the German nation have attained with hard, honest, manly and virtuous deeds'.[9]

Due to this nationalist rhetoric, the criterion of 'Germanness' gained such importance in the course of the campaign that even the Habsburg camp felt constrained to readjust its propaganda. In March 1518, Charles had still counted on traditional dynastic loyalty when supposing that due to his 'affinity and proximity of lineage' he would be able 'to pay a cheaper price' for the Empire than the King of France.[10] In the end, he not only paid more than his rival, but he also stressed his nationality more than his lineage. In the final weeks before the election, the King of Spain became, at least on paper, more German than ever before. In a letter to Frederick of Saxony, he called himself 'German by blood and disposition, by birth and tongue'.[11] And in a 'campaign advertisement' sent to all prince electors, he boasted of being 'a German born and educated, who is also able and adept at speaking and writing in the German language'.[12]

This was, to put it mildly, an exaggeration. At most, young Charles had some passive knowledge of German. His polyglot entourage at the Royal Court of Spain capitalised on the fact that he was still a widely unknown figure in the Empire and that he was residing so far away that the German princes could hardly verify his claims. To push the

---

[7] See for instance Nauclerus, *Memorabilium ... commentarii*, vol. II, fol. 625; Wimpfeling, *Germania*, 24–5.

[8] *Reichstagsakten*, Jüngere Reihe, vol. I, 705–6.

[9] Ibid., 750.   [10] Ibid., 73.   [11] Ibid., 747.

[12] Werbungen Karls I. und Franz' I. bei den Kurfürsten, June 1519, in Kohler (ed.), *Quellen zur Geschichte Karls V.*, 47.

campaign for the Imperial throne, a few Germans among Charles' functional elite played a crucial role. They would compose letters and advertisements in the German language, which Charles would then copy to give proof of his own German writing skills before they were dispatched to Germany.[13]

Contrary to Charles, Francis I could not benefit from the fortunate circumstance of being a dark horse. Nevertheless, he tried to 'Germanise' himself as much as possible and he equally tried to 'de-Germanise' his Habsburg rival. The French envoys to Germany were instructed to tell the prince electors that the territories of the Spanish King were too far away from the Empire and that the Spanish and the Germans could not stand each other, whereas the French and the Germans had always been on cordial terms.[14] The Duke of Brunswick, one of Francis' most important German allies, added that the French King dressed like a German.[15]

Francis himself tried to give a historical dimension to the special relationship between the two nations in his official campaign letter. He declared that 'the Germans and the French have had a common state in former times and have both taken their origins from each other'. Furthermore, he maintained that the French kings 'have embellished the German nation with churches, monasteries and common and special buildings and enhanced it with various treasures'.[16]

It was a risky strategy to canvass for the votes of prince electors by portraying Charlemagne's reign as a German-French joint venture. This was a version of history which, for obvious reasons, neither German humanists nor most legal counsellors to German princes wanted to hear. What made things even worse for the King of France was an endorsement from the wrong quarter. Pope Leo X, by 1519 one of the most unpopular figures in Germany, recommended Francis to the prince electors, and his nuncio even dared to assert that 'the French belong to you' (*Franci ex vestris sunt*).[17]

In the French camp, a few people seemed to have realised that the higher the criterion of nationality was rated, the lower the King's chances of being elected would be. Antoine Duprat (1463–1535), the Chancellor of France and an eminent legal scholar, directly criticised the expert advice given by the seven counsellors to the Dukes of Saxony. He argued that neither the *Decretale Venerabilem* of 1202 nor the *Golden Bull* of 1356 said that only Germans were eligible to be Roman King

---

[13] Laubach, 'Wahlpropaganda', 226.
[14] *Reichstagsakten*, Jüngere Reihe, vol. I, 155.
[15] Ibid., 283.   [16] Ibid., 51.   [17] Ibid., 759.

and Emperor. And he added that the Pope had reserved the right to take the Empire away from the Germans, if they neglected their duties towards Christianity. According to Duprat, he had every reason to do so.[18] The Chancellor of France may have brought forward a legally superior argument to the one by his German counterparts, but tactically he played a loser's game, as his case amounted to an assault on the electors themselves.

How crucial was the criterion of nationality in the end? We do not know for sure, first of all because Charles of Spain was both paying the highest bribes and claiming to be the most German. What we can say with certainty, however, is that nationality was one of the critical factors in the decision-making process.

Some contemporaries even regarded it as the most crucial of all. One of them was the Protestant historian Johannes Sleidanus (1506–56), author of the seminal *Commentaries on the Situation of Religion and State in the Reign of Emperor Charles V (De statu religionis et rei publicae Carolo Quinto Caesare commentarii)*, which was first published in 1555. Following the model of ancient historians, Sleidanus restaged the final showdown before the election with the real historical actors delivering fictitious orations.

The author chose the prince elector of Mainz to make the last stump speech for Charles and the prince elector of Trier to do the same for Francis. In both speeches Sleidanus summarised the most important points made by the two camps, and in both speeches, he started with nationality. The Archbishop of Mainz argued that 'our laws' prohibited the election of foreigners (*exteros*), which is why Francis had to be ruled out 'without any doubt' (*nulli dubium*); among all the Germans, he continued, Charles was to be seen as the best candidate. The Archbishop of Trier, in contrast, contended that both Kings were foreigners ('we must not, by the bias of an elaborate interpretation, take Charles for a German'), but that Francis was to be preferred because 'the French are related to us by origin and have almost the same laws and customs'.

Eventually, it was the Duke of Saxony who, according to Sleidanus' dramatic staging, clinched the competition. He declared the King of France ineligible by law and pointed out that the Emperor had to be both German and powerful. Charles, the Duke concluded, was the only candidate to satisfy these two conditions – he was powerful because of his vast territorial possessions and German because of 'his domicile in Germany' (*Germania domicilium habere*).[19]

---

[18] Ibid., 623; Laubach, 'Wahlpropaganda', 220–2.
[19] Sleidanus, *De Statu ... Commentarii*, I, fol. 17–22; idem, *Wahrhafftige Beschreibung*, I, XXII–XXIX.

8.2   The impact of popular xenophobia

Aside from the introduction of nationality as an election criterion, there was yet another new dimension to the Imperial election of 1519. This was the amalgamation of scholarly nationalism and popular xenophobia. The urban population in Germany had already been exceptionally agitated before Maximilian's death. During the early years of the Reformation, German cities were inundated with broadsheets and leaflets, containing polemical texts and inflammatory illustrations. At the same time, preachers raised their tirades against the Roman Curia to a new level of aggression. This intensified the urban culture of fear, which already had a long history within city walls.[20] Thus, at the time of the Imperial election, German cities were an ideal hotbed for xenophobia.

But how could popular fear of foreigners have an impact on such an exclusive business as the Imperial election? The answer is simple: the election was to a large degree an urban event. Both the voting and crowning took place in the Imperial city of Frankfurt. Weeks before the election, the candidates had their campaign headquarters set up, if not in Frankfurt, then in a nearby city such as Mainz or Koblenz. And although the royal envoys in charge of these headquarters may have tried to keep their distance from the local population, they could not avoid being affected by the mood of the public.

A graphic account of this uncomfortable situation was given by the English diplomat Richard Pace (1482–1536), who had been sent to Germany by King Henry VIII with the thankless task of championing his hopeless candidacy. In June 1519, Pace reported back to England that the whole population was behind the King of Castile and ready to fight the King of France. According to Pace, the French envoy, who stayed in Koblenz, did not dare to come to Frankfurt for fear of assaults by the local populace. He himself, Pace added, had almost been thrown out of Frankfurt because he had been mistaken for a Frenchman. In his next report, written just one day later, the English diplomat noted that during the previous night the Papal nuncio had to escape from the city in disguise after coming out in favour of the King of France. 'He was right to do so', Pace commented, 'because his life was in danger here.' And on 24 June, just four days before the final vote, he reported that the German counts marched on a castle near Frankfurt, ready to declare war on the French if Francis were to be elected. Meanwhile, the prince electors were staying down in the city 'in great distress and fear of the people'.[21]

---

[20] Graf, 'Der adel dem purger tregt hass', 197–8.
[21] *Reichstagsakten*, Jüngere Reihe, vol. I, 411–21.

The envoy of King Henry VIII may have, as some historians have suggested, overstated his account to underscore the pointlessness of his own diplomatic mission. However, several other sources confirm that the exceptional political activity by the urban populace was a matter of concern to all parties involved.[22] The Archduchess Margaret of Austria (1480–1530), who was both aunt of and mentor to Charles, expressed her delight at the German people's 'dislike for the French' and called for further measures 'to incite them even more against them' (*pour encoires plus les anymer contre eulx*).[23] Indeed, the Habsburg propaganda targeted the public more than any other with textual and visual material, which strengthened the long-cultivated image of the House of Habsburg as the true German Imperial dynasty.[24]

To the prince electors, though, the willingness of the populace to intervene in their own privileged duties looked more like a threat than a blessing. With one exception: the Archbishop of Mainz, Albrecht of Brandenburg, cleverly exploited the fear of his fellow electors to make the choice of Charles seem inevitable. When he justified his own vote for the Spanish King, he more than once referred to the danger emanating from the 'common man' (*gemeine Mann*).

Albrecht argued that, on the one hand, a candidate to the throne needed to be rich enough to bear the biggest part of the financial burden coming with the honour of the Imperial office; otherwise, he would have to impose oppressive taxes on the 'common man', which could only lead to a rebellion (*buntschuch*). On the other hand, the candidate had 'to be a German by ancestry and origin, so that the honour of our nation is preserved and the common man is satisfied'.[25] How the honour of the nation and the satisfaction of the common man were related to each other is hard to say from this quotation. Still, it is significant enough for us to see that they could actually be related as early as the beginning of the sixteenth century.

After Charles I of Spain had been elected Emperor Charles V, the Basle-born 'common man' Pamphilus Gengenbach (*c.* 1480–1525), a printer and popular writer, composed a poem of praise to the prince electors:

All of you, prince electors, merit all honours as you have elected the one whom all Germany has desired. This is Charles of Austria … God himself has done it, and mass murder would have happened (*es wär groß mord geschehen*), had he not accomplished it.[26]

[22] Ibid., 495; Laubach, *Wahlpropaganda*, 229–31.
[23] *Reichstagsakten*, Jüngere Reihe, vol. I, 318.
[24] Wohlfeil, 'Grafische Bildnisse', 28–34 / 47.
[25] *Reichstagsakten*, Jüngere Reihe, vol. I, 843–4.
[26] Liliencron (ed.), *Die historischen Volkslieder*, vol. III, 234.

The counter-factual reasoning by our popular poet is to be taken in the same way as that of today's historians – with a pinch of salt. What it tells us, though, is that the view on the Imperial election did not necessarily differ a lot between the top and the bottom of the social hierarchy. To both princes and populace, it apparently appeared pivotal to put a German man on the Imperial throne.

8.3   From German hero to Spanish invader – the transformation of Emperor Charles V

The honeymoon of young Emperor Charles did not last for long. His popularity in Germany had probably reached its peak before he even entered the country for his coronation in 1520. As long as he was not seen and heard, it was far easier to place great expectations on him. Ulrich von Hutten, for instance, imagined the Emperor to be the 'restorer of German freedom' (*widerbringer der teütschen freyheit*); Martin Luther seriously hoped to make 'the German Emperor' the leader of his Church reform, and others believed that *nomen est omen* and expected Charles to become the new Charlemagne[27] (see Figure 11).

After Charles' arrival, the enthusiasm quickly cooled. The Emperor-elect could not disguise the fact that his cultural Germanness had been hugely exaggerated, and he did not want to hide his desire to remain a staunch defender of the Roman Church. After the Diet of Worms in 1521, where he issued the famous ban on Martin Luther, Charles left Germany again, having stayed for less than a year. During that busy period, he had only acquired a little knowledge of German politics and hardly established a political network within the Empire. The nationalist rhetoric used to orchestrate his election and coronation was just as rapidly abandoned as it had been introduced.

In the following eight years, Charles governed his huge territory from within Spain. He consolidated his power over the Spanish peninsula and concentrated his military ambitions on defeating the King of France in Italy. For both purposes, Germany was fairly insignificant and so it became a geographical and political periphery of his Empire. Charles only travelled to Germany for a second time in 1530 after a longer sojourn in Italy, where he was crowned Emperor by the Pope. His brother Ferdinand, the Archduke of Austria, had to press him hard to make the journey over the Alps and to convoke a Diet in Augsburg.[28]

---

[27] Hutten, 'Vadiscus', in *Gespräch büchlin*, 85; Luther, 'An den christlichen Adel deutscher Nation', in *WA*, vol. vi, 465.
[28] Kohler, *Karl V.*, 202–8.

Figure 11 This double portrait of Charlemagne and Emperor
Charles V was published as the frontispiece for the 1521 Cologne
edition of Einhard's *Life and Deeds of Charlemagne*. It is indicative
of the huge expectations placed upon Charles V shortly after
his election to the Imperial throne. Charlemagne, who was
the greatest national hero of German humanists, is depicted
in a modest functional dress, as it was described as typically
'Frankish' in Einhard's early medieval biography and re-labelled
typically 'German' by humanist nationalists such as Aventinus
(see Chapter 7.6). Charles V, wearing contemporary clothes
similar to his grandfather Maximilian I, represents the New
Charlemagne, who would restore the national honour brought
to Germany by the founder of the Empire. As dedicatee of
Charlemagne's biography, he was invited by the editors to learn
directly from the life of his great predecessor.

The Emperor's low estimation of Germany's importance was widely shared by his closest political advisors. Charles already had a brains trust made up of functional elites from Burgundy and Spain before the election of 1519, and he hardly changed it afterwards. The driving force behind Charles' Imperial politics was his High Chancellor, Mercurino Gattinara (1465–1530), a Piedmont-born jurist, who had already been in the service of the Duchy of Burgundy for ten years, when he was given the powerful office in 1518. For Gattinara, the self-promotion of Charles as an 'original German' (*original Allemand*) was only a means to the end of a Universal Monarchy (*Monarchia Universalis*).[29] As in Antiquity, the political centre of this new Empire had to be Italy, not Germany.[30] It would, according to Gattinara's estimation, bring peace to Christianity and war to the Turks.

The political ideology of Gattinara could not have been more alien to the ideals of humanist nationalists. In many ways, it harked back to the political thinking of thirteenth- and fourteenth-century Italy. Gattinara was most influenced by Italian political thinkers of the so-called Ghibelline tradition, supporters of the emperors against the popes. To legitimise his political goals publicly, he even tried to bring into print Dante's widely forgotten *De Monarchia*, which had been written in the early fourteenth century.

From this perspective, the rapid waning of Charles' image as a German national hero looks self-inflicted. For Charles, the merits of the Imperial crown had little to do with the German lands, and so he permitted himself to neglect the traditional realm of his newly acquired Empire and to give up his self-promotion as a German. With hindsight, his political strategy appears to be a mistake of colossal proportions, as it facilitated the spread of the Reformation, sowed the seeds of his own demise within the Empire and finally led to his resignation from all his offices in 1556.

However, this is only one side of the story. The other side is a bit more complicated, but also more telling about the tricky relationship between dynastic and national politics at the beginning of the early modern period. To understand its development, we once again have to return to the pre-election negotiations and take a second look at the prince electors.

The canvassing for the Imperial crown started more than one year before the election and it was the old Emperor Maximilian who

---

[29] *Reichstagsakten*, Jüngere Reihe, vol. I, 526.
[30] See for instance Gattinara's Memorandums of 1521 and 1527, in Kohler (ed.), *Quellen zur Geschichte Karls V.*, 84 / 133.

had initiated the formal talks. To secure the throne for his grandson, Maximilian issued a decree at the Diet of Augsburg in 1518, in which he made far-reaching concessions in the name of Charles. The Habsburg candidate committed himself to appoint 'only men of the proper German nation by ancestry and birth' to a newly projected Imperial government (*Reichsregiment*) and to establish this government 'in the middle of the German nation'. He further agreed to have his 'personal residence for the majority of the time in the German lands' and he even accepted having all speeches and writings, plus all external and internal documents composed by himself, his governors or regents written in 'no other than the German language'.[31]

This decree had quite an impact, because after the election of Charles, the prince electors set up an election contract (*Wahlkapitulation*), in which they incorporated the concessions made by Maximilian. Not satisfied with this, they dictated a few additional terms. The Emperor, the contract states, had no permission to hold a Diet 'outside the Empire of the German nation'; furthermore, he was not allowed to form 'alliances and unions with foreign nations', unless he had the prince electors' consent, and he could bring 'foreign troops' to Germany only if the estates of the Empire gave their official approval.[32]

The negotiations leading to the election contract indicate that even those prince electors who promoted Charles did not believe their own words about his indubitable affinity to the German nation. Albrecht, the Archbishop of Mainz, had been one of the key negotiators involved in the making of Maximilian's decree of 1518. His strategy was to treat Charles as a Spaniard when bargaining the terms of his election, and to portray him as a German when justifying his decision to support him. Tactically, this may have been a clever approach because it helped him and the German princes to secure or even strengthen their positions as regional powers within the Empire. Structurally, though, it increased rather than alleviated the tensions between dynastic and national politics.

In terms of national politics, the purpose underlying the election contract was legally to separate the two crowns on Charles' head as clearly as possible and to give the Imperial crown precedence over the Spanish. Thereby, the prince electors wanted to ensure that German politics remained unaffected by the Emperor-elect's Spanish power-base and personnel.

[31] Weicker, *Die Stellung der Kurfürsten*, 112.
[32] *Reichstagsakten*, Jüngere Reihe, vol. I, 868–70.

However, what looked like a neat solution on paper could only lead to a mess in practice, because it neglected the rules of dynastic politics. Royal government was still mainly run by a mobile, multifunctional court and based on the identification of family matters with state business. So, even if Charles had been willing to put in place a nationally distinct administrative apparatus in Germany, it would have hardly changed his political practice. His court would have still been dominated by functional elites and noble families from Burgundy and Spain, and his aim would have still been to connect and not to separate his different dominions.

As a consequence, the Emperor, from early on, did not comply with several concessions made in the election contract, and in return the German princes soon started to fear for their powers and privileges. This situation brought about another transformation of the national discourse, which completely reversed its former political implications under the reign of Frederick III and Maximilian I. German princes now gradually turned into defenders of 'German liberty' (*teutsche Libertät*) against the Emperor! Thus, they took over as political protectors and representatives of the German nation. In public propaganda and official correspondence, the rhetoric of national freedom now served the pursuit of princely interests. It proved even more useful under the growing religious polarisation caused by the Reformation, because it offered a diplomatic formula to build a bridge between rulers of different faiths. If one united to defend German liberty, the message went, religious dissent had no relevance.

The first big occasion to test the new rhetoric arose in the late 1520s, when Charles' plan became public to have his brother, Ferdinand, elected Roman King as soon as he himself was crowned Emperor by the Pope. The princely counter-campaign was orchestrated by Leonhard von Eck (1480–1550), privy counsellor to the Dukes of Bavaria. Eck pushed the candidacy of his own master, Duke William IV, and after gaining the Pope's support, he even addressed the King of France to raise the pressure on the Habsburgs. Francis I received a Bavarian memorandum, which warned him that the House of Habsburg wanted to 'occupy the Empire by hereditary law and remove the liberty and freedom of Germany'. Eck even speculated that Charles could take away the Empire to 'the enemy of Germany' – Spain.[33]

For the King of France, it was indeed an attractive opportunity to fight the Emperor on his own turf in the name of German liberty, not

---

[33] *Reichstagsakten*, Jüngere Reihe, vol. VII / 2, 1127.

least because it allowed Francis to align with Protestant princes, too. In the following decades, such 'unholy' coalitions happened time and time again. For Francis' German allies, however, it was a game with high stakes. Forging pacts with a foreign power against their own overlord could easily damage the credibility of their national discourse within the Empire. In 1531, most prince electors did not follow the German opponents of the Habsburgs and swiftly made Ferdinand the new Roman King.

The mutation of Charles from German hero to Spanish invader was only completed when he declared war on the political arm of German Protestantism, the so-called Schmalkalden League, in 1546. The leaders of the League tried to escape their encirclement by a frantic populist propaganda, in which they attacked Charles alternately as a puppet of the Pope and as an agent of a Spanish conquest attempt. For the latter reproach, they found welcome targets in the Spanish troops commanded by Spanish noblemen, who played a significant part in the Emperor's international army. A rhymed pamphlet written before the outbreak of the war first exhorted Charles not to subject Germany to the House of Austria and then continued:

> If we cannot persuade you and if it cannot change, then let's go, devout Germans, and hit out with joy; stab the Spanish swine and dogs as if they were frogs, and teach them well what it means to anger the Germans![34]

On the battlefield a few months later, things rather went the other way. In April 1547, the prince elector of Saxony and leader of the Schmalkalden League, John Frederick I (1503–54), suffered a crushing defeat at Mühlberg. He was captured by Spanish and Hungarian soldiers, who brought him to Fernando Álvarez de Toledo (1507–82), the Duke of Alba, before he was confronted by the Emperor, who immediately incarcerated him.

At the end of the Schmalkaldic War, the German princes' Spanish nightmare seemed to have come true. The Emperor's foreign army controlled large areas of Germany between the Alps and the North Sea, and some of the most senior rulers of the country were treated like criminals. Charles' overweening power, ostentatiously demonstrated at the Diet of Augsburg in 1548, quickly brought the remaining German princes of both Protestant and Catholic faith together. And while the Emperor still basked in the success of his German expedition, they prepared his final fall, counting on the help of the young King of France, Henri II, who was given the title 'vindicator of

---

[34] Liliencron (ed.), *Die historischen Volkslieder*, vol. IV, 333.

German freedom and the captive princes' (*vindex libertatis Germaniae et captivorum principum*).[35]

When the Franco-German coalition attacked in 1552, Charles could barely escape. After a desperate attempt to fight off Henri's invasion into the French-speaking territories of the Empire, he retreated to Brussels, where he later resigned. Although the House of Habsburg quickly recovered in Germany after Charles' disappearance into a Spanish monastery, its emperor never again occupied the undisputed position as prime protector of the German nation which Maximilian had held. This was partly to do with the Habsburgs' extraordinary family history and partly due to the enormous ramifications of the Reformation, which we will now discuss in the last chapter of this book.

---

[35] Pariset (ed.), 'La France', 264.

9   Nation and denomination

It is over with Germans ... Germany has been what it has been. The vast, utmost wickedness is everyday getting riper for slaughter ... I want to prophesy to Germany – not from the stars, but from theology and the Word of God – God's wrath, since it is impossible that Germany can go unpunished. It must suffer a great rout.

Martin Luther, *Table Talks*, quote from 1539

Mother Rome: O Germany, I tell you, if you keep and listen to Luther and his godless bunch for longer, nobody will endanger you as much as yourself. I, however, will then, out of motherly goodness, not be ready to ignore your misery, when seeing (God may forestall it!) that your members kill, burn and ravage each other in strife, that they wreck each other's bodies, goods and honours.

Johannes Cochlaeus, *A Pious Exhortation of Rome to Germany*, 1525

In 1517, when a little-known Augustinian monk with a doctorate in theology and a solid classical education entered the stage of church reform, the majority of German humanists immediately greeted him as one of their own. Quite a few, and probably the noisiest ones, even put their nationalist hopes on his broad shoulders. They expected him to restore the honour and freedom of the German nation by ending the alleged exploitation of Germany by the Roman Church and by purifying the German clergy from moral depravity and material excess. In Ulrich von Hutten's widespread dialogues, *Vadiscus or the Roman Trinity* (*Vadiscus sive trias Romana*) and *The Onlookers* (*Inspicientes*), both published in April 1520, Martin Luther's cause appeared as a nationalist enterprise for the liberation of Germany.

The initial support by humanists for the Wittenberg professor proved crucial in turning a local protest into a national reform movement. However, no humanist had asked for a theological revolution. When this was later delivered from the pen of the same monk, many of Luther's earliest proponents reacted with bewilderment and their love affair with the Reformation came to an abrupt end (see Figure 12). Most exponents of the older generation of German humanists, who had

Germanum Alcidem tollentem monstra Luthern'
Hostem non horres impia Roma tuum?
Ni ducis nasum respicem suspenderis unco
Germane n, & lasset pendula crista caput!
[...] ficut qui male sophistas,
[...]

Ecce cadit male sana cohors, cui cerberus ipse
Cedit, & is fauces ferilis hydra nouas.
Quin iguur fortem agnosces dominam[?] pa mb,
Tecedisi uclut confueet ista manus?
Errorem [...] fan Geruns, [...],
[...]

Figure 12 The depiction of Luther as 'German Hercules' in this
early Reformation woodcut by Hans Holbein the Younger differs
greatly from his contemporary portraits as a pious monk or a
learned prophet. Hercules represents the ideal of the active man,
which, in the Renaissance period, was attractive to both rulers and
humanists (see Figure 10). Holbein used the mythological figure for
a virtuosic display of allusions addressed to humanistically educated
connoisseurs. Luther is presented as an ally of the mostly young
anti-Roman German humanists, who hailed him as the liberator of
the German nation from Papal rule. At the same time, however, he is
depicted as a brute, who acts in scholarly disputes like his barbarian
ancestors in military battle. Holbein's woodcut may thus reflect a
growing anxiety among German humanists of the older generation
about Luther's rough language and uncompromising attitude.

started their literary career under Maximilian's reign, either quietly retreated from the new theological battlefield or marched with loud protests into the Catholic camp. Eventually, Luther's most tenacious opponents within Germany came from similar circles as his initial supporters. Catholic polemicists such as Johannes Cochlaeus (1479–1552), Johannes Eck (1486–1543) and Thomas Murner (1475–1537) were all humanist theologians.

Contrary to them, the younger generation of German humanists, headed by Luther's most brilliant disciple, Philipp Melanchthon (1497–1560), joined the Reformation movement in great numbers and tried to put their language skills, their classical knowledge and their rhetorical abilities at the service of Luther's theology.

As a result of this rapid change, Renaissance humanism in Germany was massively transformed during the first few decades of the Reformation. It lost much of its relative autonomy and appeal as a recipe for making great men. At the same time, it gained institutional authority through its introduction into school curricula, broadened its social base and became, in the form of biblical philology, an ancillary science to confessional theology.

Humanist nationalism was particularly affected by the Reformation and the subsequent confessional divide. Over a period of a few years, it split up into several, largely incompatible discourses. Apart from the princely discourse discussed in the previous chapter, we can distinguish between a Protestant, a Catholic and a non-confessional national discourse. All of them were, in one way or another, building on humanist nationalism, but they were using very different elements of it in order to construct contrasting or even antagonistic models of the German nation. In this process, only the non-confessional discourse could partly preserve the relative autonomy of the pre-Reformation concept of the nation.[1] The price of this preservation was, at least in the medium term, near political irrelevance. In the long term, however, the non-confessional discourse proved effective, as many of its motifs were adopted by nationalist thinkers of the Enlightenment and by modern nationalists, too.

In this chapter, I will discuss the impact of the German Reformation on humanist nationalism. As Luther was the central figure of this story, I will particularly focus on his writings. One purpose of my reflections

---

[1] I deliberately use the attribute 'non-confessional' to point out that this national discourse could express either indifference or irenic interest in confessional matters. My impression is that the former was more widespread than the latter and that the political and cultural impact of 'irenicist' national discourses was rather small before the second half of the seventeenth century. For a differing assessment see Schmidt, *Irenic Patriotism*.

is to explain why the political power and cultural appeal of nationalism still remained limited during the early modern period. Another purpose is to outline the relationship between nationalism and religious fundamentalism. This relationship is, as recent history shows, not easy to define, but a closer look at the history of early modern Europe may help to understand it better. After all, it was a period rife with religious fundamentalism, and at the same time, it was by no means void of nationalist ideas. A third and final purpose is to give some evidence for the continuing impact of humanist nationalism on early modern scholarship and its renewed relevance in the period of the Enlightenment.

9.1   Martin Luther's German nation

The misunderstanding by many German humanists that Luther would help to complete the renewal of Germany, which they themselves had started, was not entirely self-induced. In fact, Luther nourished these illusions considerably during the early years of the Reformation. He set himself the task of reforming the German nation, not Christianity as a whole – despite his claim that his religious doctrine had universal validity. He combined anticlerical with anti-Italian polemics. He used a rhetoric of liberation, which carried little precise meaning for quite a while. And he fashioned himself as a humanist by signing his letters to Erasmus and other scholars with *Eleutherius*, 'the Liberated'. This Greek pseudonym is also the reason why the German Reformer is not known to posterity by his original family name: in 1517, he changed it from Luder to Luther.

But even in the early 1520s, after Luther had clarified that he had something very different in mind from the aspirations of humanist nationalists, he continued to identify his sphere of action with the German nation. This is all the more striking because from early on, the resistance against the Reformation from within Germany clearly indicated that Luther's movement would only be joined by a segment of the German population. As a consequence, the Reformation was soon organised on the level of German territories and Luther became the protégé of a German prince. Still, he went on to maintain unwaveringly that he pursued 'only the happiness and salvation of the whole of Germany' (*alleyn des gantzen Deutschen lands glück und heyl*).[2]

Luther's choice of the German people as his main addressee had no theological foundation in the sense that he treated the Germans as a people chosen by God. It was, however, theologically motivated insofar

---

[2] Luther, *An die Ratherren aller Städte deutsches Lands*, in *WA*, vol. xv, 53.

as he regarded the teaching and reading of the Gospel in the vernacular as an indispensable practice for true believers. Luther said of himself that he could best hear and find God 'in the German tongue'.[3] If this was true for him, who had mastered Hebrew and Greek, it had to apply even more so to his less educated countrymen. Therefore, when Luther addressed his 'dear Germans' in the German vernacular, he did not so much express a nationalist attitude as the religious conviction that the Lord addressed all his creatures in their own mother tongue.

After his appeal *To the Christian Nobility of the German Nation* (*An den christlichen Adel deutscher Nation*) of 1520, in which he called on the Emperor and the German aristocracy to dismantle the Papal power structures within the German lands, Luther rarely attached a political agenda to his national discourse. In most of his writings, he preferred the words 'German lands' and 'Germany' to the more politicised 'German nation'. Based on his doctrine of the two swords, the German Reformer acted as prophet of God's invisible kingdom, while ostentatiously keeping his distance from the business of earthly politics. He would only comment on political matters when feeling cornered by enemies or pressurised by allies.

The writings produced on these occasions, though, give clear indications about his 'political theology'. According to Luther, every political authority, Catholic or Protestant, was ruling on God's behalf to keep order till the end of time. With this, Luther rejected all attempts to turn Germany into a Protestant nation by force. At the same time, he refused any ruler the right to act as the protector of the Christian faith. This argument was particularly directed against the Emperor – 'this poor mortal maggot bag' – who was not even allowed to wage war against the Turks in the name of Christ.[4] No human, Luther believed, could claim to know and represent God's will.

Luther's political theology could hardly have been more at odds with the basic ideas of humanist nationalism. Indeed, the German Reformer seemed to take particular pleasure in dismantling the commonplaces which humanist nationalists had established or occupied. It started with his completely new theory of the *translatio imperii*, which he formulated in his appeal to the German nobility in 1520. Luther declared the *translatio imperii* unlawful because the Pope could not have transferred what he had not possessed. The original Roman Empire, he claimed, had long been destroyed at that time. The Pope had given the Germans

---

[3] Idem, *Vorrede zu der vollständigen Ausgabe der 'deutschen Theologie'*, in *WA*, vol. I, 378–9.
[4] Brecht, *Luther und die Türken*, 12.

a 'different Roman Empire', and 'thereby we became servants of the Pope'. In other words, the *translatio imperii* had been God's way of punishing the Germans:

No one can think it a great thing to have an Empire given to him, especially if he is a Christian; so, we Germans can neither be puffed up because a new Roman Empire is bestowed on us; for in His eyes it is a trifling gift which He often gives to the most unworthy.[5]

With this interpretation, Luther dismissed any attempts to read the *translatio imperii* as proof of the extraordinary merits accumulated by the German nation. The Germans had done nothing to earn it and could not pride themselves on having it. In Luther's eyes, the humanist nationalists' take on history was deeply mistaken because nations, just like individuals, could not acquire honour by their own volition. They were only objects of divine play: 'For God the Lord it is a small thing to toss empires and principalities to and fro.'[6]

In later years, Luther loved to pick up rhetorical devices and whole topoi of humanist nationalism, particularly in his informal *Table Talks* – and then give them a deadly twist. He would, for instance, begin with a sentence in Latin: 'Germany has always been the best nation' (*Germania semper fuit optima natio*), and then continue in German: 'it will, though, go the same way as Troy, and one will say: Germania fuit, it is over.'[7]

One of his favourite practices was to replace nationalist commonplaces by his own truism 'the better the land, the worse the people' – a law which he derived from God's principle not to give all the advantages to the same people.[8] He would commence his talk in the tone of a classical *laudator patriae*: 'Germany is a very good land. It has enough of everything one needs to preserve life plentifully. It has various fruits, grains, wine, crops, salt, mines etc.' Instead of putting this description into a flattering contrast with other countries, as the humanists did, he would draw an unflattering comparison with the Germans: 'It is only lacking in that we do not esteem it and use it appropriately ... Indeed, we abuse it most shamefully, much worse than swine.'[9]

Luther not only ridiculed the humanist pride in German achievements of the past, he also rejected their optimism about Germany's great deeds in the future. According to his apocalyptic outlook, things could only get worse, and the future promised to be short and bad, as

---

[5] Luther, *An den christlichen Adel deutscher Nation*, in *WA*, vol. VI, 463.
[6] Ibid.   [7] Quoted in Ridé, *L'image du Germain*, vol. II, 710.
[8] Luther, *Tischreden*, fol. 603ᵛ.   [9] Ibid., fol. 601ᵛ.

the world was 'ripe for the slaughterhouse' (*reiff zur Schlachtbanck*).[10] From such a mindset, no nationalist thought was able to emerge.

Luther's anthropological pessimism was also expressed in his national stereotyping. Here, he followed in the footsteps of medieval authors such as Jacques de Vitry (1160/70–1240), who had enumerated regional stereotypes in order to present human sin in all its variations.[11] The German Reformer thus stressed the negatives when speaking about national characters. The French were, according to him, masters of deceit: 'they write differently than they speak and speak differently than they think'.[12] The Scots had the lead in haughtiness: they were 'the most arrogant, proud and presumptuous'.[13] The Spanish were the champions of cruelty: they were 'a very violent, tyrannical and ferocious people'.[14] All, though, were topped by the Italians, who combined a whole series of evils: they were 'the most insidious and treacherous', so 'no one trusts each other'; they were 'subtle, sly murderers', killing 'secretly with poison'; and they practised 'chastity as in Sodom', holding matrimony in contempt.[15]

Luther's depiction of his own countrymen may have been more colourful, but hardly less disdainful. He declared himself unsurprised that God had decided to punish the Germans with the Turks, because 'our German people are a terrible people, indeed, nearly half devil, half human'.[16] On the contrary, he was astonished that 'we Germans, who are much worse than the Jews ... are nevertheless not as much chased away and finished off'.[17]

To give a concise picture of the Germans, the Reformer often described them as swine. The creature symbolised the national sins of gluttony and inebriety: 'If I know my dear Germans well, these complete pigs', he speculated in his *War Sermon against the Turks* of 1529, 'then they shall, in their usual manner, sit down and buoyantly and safely booze'.[18] 'The German swine', he revealed on another occasion, 'drinks so much that it forgets its mother tongue'.[19]

Accusing the Germans of unquenchable thirst was not new in itself. Italian authors had long referred to Teutonic drunkenness as a sign of their northern neighbours' barbarism, and even German humanists

---

[10] Ibid., fol. 603ʳ.
[11] Jacques de Vitry, *Historia*, 92; another example from the thirteenth century is Alexander of Roes, *Memoriale*, 34.
[12] Luther, *Tischreden*, fol. 603ᵛ.   [13] Ibid., fol. 607ᵛ.
[14] Ibid., fol. 610ʳ.   [15] Ibid., fol. 606ᵛ-607ʳ.
[16] Luther, *Vom kriege widder die Türcken*, in *WA*, vol. xxx / 2, 107.
[17] Idem, *Ein Sendbrief von dem harten Büchlein wider die Bauern*, in *WA*, vol. xviii, 396.
[18] Idem, *Eine heerpredigt widder den Türcken*, in *WA*, vol. xxx / 2, 160.
[19] Idem, *WA*, vol. xlix, 758.

had found it hard to deny the charge. What was new, however, was Luther's scathing rhetoric of sinfulness. To highlight his countrymen's alleged drinking problem, he even brought an extra devil into play:

Every country, though, needs to have their proper devil – Italy (*Welschland*) hers, France hers. Our German devil will be a good wineskin and must be called Booze (*Sauff*) and has to be so thirsty and parched that any quantity of wine and beer, howsoever big, cannot quench his thirst. And (I fear) such eternal thirst will remain Germany's plague till Judgement Day.[20]

Given his sobering assessment of the German national character, Luther was not interested in blaming the people of 'surrounding countries' for calling the Germans 'beasts and mad animals' (*bestien und tolle thyier*).[21] They were, he thought, not so far from the truth:

There is no nation more despised than the Germans. The Italians call us beasts; the French and English deride us and so do all other countries. Who knows what God wants to do and will do with the Germans, but we truly deserve a good beating before God.[22]

The Germans were held in special contempt, but they were not the only ones to be despised. Luther believed that relations between different nations were generally unfriendly, dominated by human baseness of varying sorts: 'One country hates the other, as Italians, Spaniards, Hungarians and Germans.'[23] If a cultural exchange between nations took place, it generally happened in the form of a spreading and multiplication of sins: 'The Germans learn how to steal from the Spaniards, while the Spaniards learn to gorge and booze from the Germans.'[24]

So, did Luther have anything at all positive to say about the German nation? Yes, he did – but yet again, his comments were a dig at the German humanists of Maximilian's time. Germans, the Reformer maintained, were simple speakers of plain truth:

No virtue has made us Germans more famous and (as I think) more elevated and better preserved so far than that we have been taken for loyal, truthful, constant folks, who have stuck to yes, yes, no, no, as many histories and books testify.[25]

Such a statement was still in line with the opinions held by the more primitivist of humanists, but the main purpose of Luther's praise

[20] Idem, *Auslegung des 101. Psalms*, in *WA*, vol. LI, 257.
[21] Idem, *WA*, vol. XV, 36.
[22] Idem, *Tischreden*, fol. 603ᵛ.
[23] Idem, *Vermahnung an die Pfarrherrn wider den Wucher zu predigen*, in *WA*, vol. LI, 411.
[24] Idem, *Tischreden*, fol. 603ᵛ.
[25] Idem, *Auslegung des 101. Psalms*, in *WA*, vol. LI, 259.

was contrary to theirs. He linked the simpleness and frankness of the German character with the straightforwardness and clarity of the German language. 'To speak German' (*deutsch reden*) was identical with 'to speak clearly' (*deutlich reden*).[26] This was no language for quibbles and for lies, the Reformer alleged. For those who preferred to wrap the truth in lies, other languages were more helpful – Latin, for instance. In a table talk of 1538, Luther recognised many similarities between German and Greek, but not between German and Latin. According to him, the Latin language was not only 'meagre and thin' (*gering und dünne*), but also 'unregulated'![27]

Luther's presentation of the German language as a raw instrument for plain speech served a key function in his self-promotion. It represented the qualities which he claimed for himself in contrast to the humanist masters of elegant Latin. Although a careful and gifted literary stylist himself, Luther liked to pretend that, as a writer and preacher, he did not care about rhetorics and style at all. His was a typical rhetoric of anti-rhetoric, a form of virtuoso speech that disguised and denied its virtuosity in order to appear as genuine and spontaneous expression.

Luther must have learned this technique less from the Bible than from ancient Greek and Roman authors, either pre-Ciceronians or anti-Ciceronians. The rhetoric of anti-rhetoric followed the populist logic that a loss of elegance amounted to a gain of truthfulness – and the other way round. In his famous treatise *On the Bondage of the Will* (*De servo arbitrio*) of 1525, in which he attacked Erasmus for defending the capacity of Christians to influence their salvation, he likened the relation between content and style in the humanist text to 'garden rubbish or dung in gold or silver dishes'.[28]

As to himself, Luther wanted to appear the exact opposite of Erasmus. In 1537, after his most-hated humanist opponent had died, he described him with the simplistic formula 'words without things' (*verba sine re*), and then reversed the two nouns to express what he himself allegedly stood for: 'things without words' (*res sine verbis*). His truth was detached from language. This was indeed the shortest possible way to define his self-image *vis-à-vis* the humanists of the age of Maximilian. For one thing, it helped him to obscure the humanist influence on his scholarship. For another, it assisted in hiding a remarkable insecurity about his own standing among humanist theologians. And finally, it helped him to build a long-lasting legacy as the true-bred German scholar – crude,

[26] Hess, *Deutsch-lateinische Narrenzunft*, 39–40.
[27] Luther, *Tischreden*, fol. 606ʳ.
[28] Luther, *De servo arbitrio*, in *WA*, vol. XVIII, 601.

blunt and thorough – exposing the humanist nationalists as dubious countrymen.

If we consider Luther's national discourse as a whole, we find one remarkable similarity with his great humanist opponent. Luther, maybe even more than Erasmus, simultaneously absorbed and deconstructed national discourses. He absorbed them in various ways: he took the separation of humans into nations for granted, juggling with national stereotypes as if they were natural attributes of people; he only addressed himself to the German people, despite claiming universal validity for his theology and being rejected in many parts of the German lands; and he showed strong emotional attachment to Germany and its inhabitants – if he branded them as swine, it was because he considered himself their spiritual swineherd.

At the same time, Luther, more than anybody else, deliberately shook the foundations of nationalism, only recently constructed by the German humanists. He derided the defence of national honour and freedom as a vain effort driven by delusions about human nature. He dismissed the nationalist optimism about the revival of a great German past in the near future, prophesying a rapid decline to the end of the world. And he delegitimised the scholarly role of the learned politician, adopted by humanist nationalists to appear as independent political authorities, by denying scholars any right to a share of political power.

Luther's reaction to German humanists can be interpreted as a first encounter between religious fundamentalism and nationalism. Many historians are still reluctant to call Luther a religious fundamentalist, be it for fear of anachronistic judgements or for admiration of the great Reformer. Such precaution, I believe, is either unnecessary or mistaken. Describing Luther as a religious fundamentalist is both obvious and helpful – obvious, because he matches the criteria used today to label religious fundamentalists, and helpful, because it clarifies his deep alienation from pre-Reformation culture and scholarship, particularly from Renaissance humanism.

Luther can be distinguished as a religious fundamentalist in several respects: he was much more biblically literalist and much less compromising about his understanding of the Scripture than earlier humanist philologists and theologians; he radicalised the old bipolar world-view characterised by opposites such as the Lord and the Devil, salvation and damnation, heaven and earth; he fashioned himself as a prophet and justified his political interventions with religious imperatives; and he was ready to defend his religious convictions regardless of the costs involved. 'If they remove the Gospel from the German lands',

he proclaimed, 'then the land shall be removed with it'.[29] Such a statement definitely sounds fundamentalist to modern ears, and it probably
also did to many of Luther's older contemporaries, not least the sur-
viving humanists of Celtis' generation. However, to their grief, it did
not turn Luther into an extremist, but religious fundamentalism into
mainstream culture. And it made themselves outsiders.

At the beginning of the early modern period, Luther's radically bipolar mindset proved to have more popular appeal than the multipolarity of nationalism. Perhaps this was partly because it denied the rising
complexity of political culture flat out, instead of acknowledging it to a
certain degree, as most humanist nationalists were ready to. Anyway,
Luther's radicalised bipolar thinking was soon adopted by friends and
foes alike. In this sense, the process of confessionalisation – that is,
the forming of culturally uniform Christian denominations radically opposed to each other – turned out to be a long-term barrier to
nationalism's advancement into a dominant cultural and political position. Only when the political, economic and human cost of religious
fundamentalism was becoming apparent and confessional confrontations were losing their inexorability could nationalism become truly
powerful and popular.

However, Luther's writings also demonstrate that the legacy of
humanist nationalism could not simply be disposed of during the early
Reformation. It was already too deeply anchored in European culture. The concept of the nation, although profoundly transformed and
deprived of its autonomous value by confessionalisation, endured – and
even broadened – its social outreach, thanks to the new populism of
religious propaganda. Not least because of this growing outreach, confessionalisation would eventually prove, as we will see in the conclusion of this book, a catalyst for the empowerment of nationalism in
modernity.

9.2   The authentic nation of Protestants vs. the civilised nation of Catholics

Starting with Hutten, Luther's early humanist supporters adopted the
national myth of ancient Germany for the Protestant cause. The victories of Germanic barbarians against the Romans were reinterpreted
as antecedents to the present liberation of Germany from the Papal
yoke. Simultaneously, the Reformation was portrayed as a restoration
of the free German nation of ancient times. Thus, the discourse of the

---

[29] Idem, WA, vol. XXXI / 2, 303.

authentic nation soon had a strong Lutheran whiff to it. Arminius, for instance, the chief of the Cherusci, who had directed the massacre of the Roman legions in AD 9 and received the title of 'liberator of Germany' (*liberator Germaniae*) from Tacitus, would only lead a glorious afterlife as a *Protestant* national hero.[30]

For German humanists of Catholic faith, this situation was uncomfortable as they found themselves attacked as accomplices of a foreign intruder. If they wanted to retain their role as defenders of the German nation, they had to come up with a counter-strategy. Only a few did. One of them was Johannes Cochlaeus, who was probably Luther's most dogged German opponent during his lifetime. He combined the demonisation of Luther and his disciples as heretics with his denunciation of them as barbarian destroyers of German civilisation and national honour.

In 1524, Cochlaeus published a pamphlet, first in German, then in Latin, entitled *A Pious Exhortation of Rome to Germany, her Daughter in Christ* (*Pia exhortatio Romae ad Germaniam suam in fide Christi filiam*).[31] Reviving Enea Silvio Piccolomini's portrait of the Roman Church as the civilising benefactor of the German nation (see Chapter 7.6), he argued that Germany would suffer a relapse into barbarism should Luther's new doctrine succeed. As proof of his prediction, he gave an unflattering description of the Reformation's Saxon hub, Wittenberg. Visitors to the 'miserable, poor, filthy little town' would find 'nothing else than Lutheran – that is filthy – houses, unclean alleys, all paths and streets full of shit, a barbarian people (*barbarisch volck*) only engaged in beery brawls and rapacious merchants'.[32]

Speaking with the voice of Mother Rome, Cochlaeus concluded that Germany's inner degeneration had to be stopped by any means, if necessary through outside intervention. Half-threatening, half-reassuring, Rome told her daughter, Germany, that she would 'not be ready to ignore' her misery when seeing that her 'members kill, burn and ravage each other in strife, that they wreck each other's bodies, goods and honours'.[33]

By combining the images of barbarism and national self-mutilation through civil war, Cochlaeus created a language that made him look

---

[30] Tacitus, *Annales II*, 88; for Arminius as a distinctly Protestant hero see Münkler e.a., *Nationenbildung*, 305.

[31] For a short discussion of the pamphlet, see Samuel-Scheyder, *Johannes Cochlaeus*, 452–6.

[32] Cochlaeus, *Ein Christliche vermanung*, in Laube (ed.), *Flugschriften gegen die Reformation*, 629; the Latin text in Samuel-Scheyder, *Johannes Cochlaeus*, 684.

[33] Cochlaeus, *Ein Christliche vermanung*, in Laube (ed.), *Flugschriften gegen die Reformation*, 631.

prophetic after the brutal end of the Peasants' War in 1525. From the Catholic perspective, the peasants had been victims of Luther all along their way from sedition to slaughter. They appeared to have been lured into upheaval by the Reformer's vague promise of freedom, only later to be massacred at his command.

To Cochlaeus, the Peasants' War came as a confirmation 'that we Germans shall, from now on, rightly be considered by other nations as crazy and mad'.[34] He described the events as a German civil war, sparked off by 'the truculent and reckless monk' in Wittenberg. Because of Luther, 'our common fatherland, which until now has enjoyed such great honours ... has to fall into God's wrath and punishment, ... so that Germans congregate against Germans, one brother fights against the other, one friend against the other, one city against the other'. Germany's worst enemy came from within the nation: 'Which Turk or which powerful nation', Cochlaeus asked rhetorically, 'could have caused as much harm to Germany with all their forces as we have now done in a quarter of a year by ourselves?'[35]

A few other Catholic humanists, among them Hieronymus Emser and Thomas Murner, used a similar vocabulary of national decline and disaster in their writings.[36] However, it was not enough to turn the tables – at least rhetorically – on the Lutherans and to win back the role of defenders of the German nation. From early on, the Catholic national discourse fell, in terms of both size and scope, far behind its Protestant counterpart.

Ironically for Cochlaeus, official Rome did not care about this symbolic battle very much. During the first decades of the Reformation, the Curia gave its German humanist supporters little propagandistic support. Instead of promoting themselves as protectors of the German nation, the Pope and his closest advisors preferred to take the traditional route of publicly denouncing and legally pursuing Luther as a heretic.

However, the main reason for Catholicism's chronic failure to dominate the national discourse in Germany had not much to do with unhelpful Curial strategies. Starting with Cochlaeus, most Catholic scholars who were pitting the honour of the nation against their Protestant countrymen inevitably undermined their own language by

---

[34] Idem, 'Antwort auf Luthers Schrift *Wider die räuberischen und mörderischen Rotten der Bauern*', in Laube and Seiffert (eds.), *Flugschriften der Bauernkriegszeit*, 384.

[35] Ibid., 408–9.

[36] See, for instance, Emser, 'Wie Luther in seinen Büchern zum Aufruhr getrieben hat', in Laube and Seiffert (eds.), *Flugschriften der Bauernkriegszeit*, 358; Murner, 'An den großmächtigsten und durchlauchtigsten Adel deutscher Nation', in Laube (ed.), *Flugschriften gegen die Reformation*, 173–5.

simultaneously demanding obedience to Rome. They appealed to the honour of the nation, while denying its members full freedom. This was a fundamental contradiction, which could never be resolved. It facilitated the stigmatisation of Catholic countrymen as foreign-controlled citizens, a fate which early modern Catholics faced not only in Germany, but also in other confessionally divided countries, such as Britain, the Netherlands and Switzerland.

9.3 The continuity of a non-confessional national discourse

Although the Reformation opened up a deep rift in the humanist community, with many friendships being broken and correspondences coming to a halt, humanist studies did continue in the shadow of religious strife – and there was even the survival of a national discourse without confessional overtones. However, those humanists who carried on this discourse had to argue cautiously to avoid becoming embroiled in the confessional conflict. They therefore favoured forms of scholarship which helped to conceal their own convictions. One of the most advanced techniques of dissimulation was philological commentary, be it for editions of classical authors or of earlier humanist nationalists. In the role of philological commentators, a few humanists managed to compensate for the reduced margin of their national discourse with a higher level of intellectual complexity.

In Germany, one of them was Beatus Rhenanus. His philological endeavours brought about, among other achievements, a first edition of the *Roman History* by Velleius Paterculus (*c.* 19 BC–AD 38), new editions of the extant works by Pliny and Tacitus and the most complete collection of Erasmus' writings, published soon after his death. Another product of his comparative textual criticism was his *Three Books on German History* (*Rerum Germanicarum libri tres*) of 1531, which roughly covered the first millennium AD.

While it was still the goal of Rhenanus' historiography to document and increase the honour of the German nation, his means to achieve it became much more sophisticated. His close analysis of ancient sources prevented him from declaring any skirmish won by northern barbarians as a German triumph.[37] His familiarity with Tacitus enabled him to understand the complex meaning of the term 'German liberty' and to grasp the discontinuity of the political constitution which it described.[38]

[37] Rhenanus, *Res Germaniae*, I, 79.
[38] Ibid. I, 7 / II, 96–8.

His knowledge of early medieval history caused him to reject the image of Germany as a country free of foreign conquerors and of the Germans as a nation untainted by foreign blood.[39] And his critical assessment of the Franks helped him to give up the theory of the *translatio imperii*, to question the status of Charlemagne as a German hero and to date the beginning of a 'German kingdom under the name of the Roman Empire' almost two centuries later with the reign of Otto I.[40] In other words, although Rhenanus only intended to reconstruct the nationalist account of German history, he actually deconstructed it to a considerable degree, guided by his philological mastery.

The Alsatian philologist was also one of the first to re-edit nationalist treatises by earlier generations of German humanists. In 1532, just one year after his own *German History* had gone into print, Rhenanus published a second edition of Wimpfeling's *Epitome Rerum Germanicarum*, which had first been published in 1505. Compared to his treatment of ancient literature, he showed less respect for this contemporary text. He substantially revised Wimpfeling's own edition, in both style and content, clearly treating it as an incomplete work. In later editions of the *Epitome* – there were at least three in the second half of the sixteenth and one in the seventeenth century – it was this reworked version by Rhenanus which prevailed.

The history of later editions of humanist works is a good indicator for the continuity of a non-confessional national discourse during the early modern period. Although some of the nationalist texts written before the Reformation could also be used for confessional purposes, the most remarkable editing project was largely driven by a non-confessional agenda. In the early 1570s, the jurist Simon Schard (1535–73), an assessor at the Imperial Chamber Court (*Reichskammergericht*), prepared a four-volume collection of works on German history from the ancient to the recent past. The pre-Reformation humanists made up the core of the historical literature on the ancient and medieval period. Schard incorporated treatises, speeches and dialogues by – among others – Celtis, Wimpfeling, Peutinger, Pirckheimer, Trithemius, Bebel and Gebwiler. When Schard died in 1573, the collection was already in print. It appeared in 1574 in Basle. A second edition followed twenty years later and a third edition almost a hundred years later, in 1673. By then, the collection had become well-known under the title *Writers on German History (Scriptores Rerum Germanicarum)*.

Thanks to this and other publishing projects, the humanist nationalists of pre-Reformation Germany remained easily accessible throughout the

---

[39] Ibid. I, 20 / 78.   [40] Ibid. II, 90–6.

early modern period. They also remained widely read by German men of letters. When Johann Christoph Gottsched (1700–66), the dominant force of German literature during the early Enlightenment, spoke and wrote about the German nation, he echoed many of the commonplaces the Renaissance humanists had introduced into the national discourse. In his *Praise of Germany* (*Lob Germaniens*), written in rhymed verse, Gottsched addressed the German nation as the personified 'Queen of the World' (*Germanien, Du Königin der Welt*), celebrated the triumphs of the ancient Germans against the Romans, portrayed Charlemagne as the German restorer of the Roman Empire, presented the bombard and the printing press as German inventions and called on contemporary German poets to compete with foreign writers.[41]

So, although German 'patriots' writing in Latin were increasingly regarded as a contradiction in terms during the eighteenth century, many ideas developed by Renaissance humanists still exerted a considerable influence on contemporary thinkers. Even Johann Gottfried Herder, who generally believed that the national spirit could only be shaped and expressed by the national language, was inclined to make an exception for the Latin works by Ulrich von Hutten. The humanist knight, Herder maintained, had written in 'German Latin' (*Deutschlatein*) – Latin words animated with the German spirit.[42]

Partly due to such ideological twists, the legacy of humanist nationalism was again transformed and then transmitted to the modern nationalists of the nineteenth and twentieth centuries.

---

[41] Gottsched, *Lob Germaniens*; for an analysis of Gottsched's national discourse see Fulda, *Die Erschaffung der Nation*.
[42] Herder, *Hutten*, 482 / 494–5.

10   Conclusion

> After having demonstrated the utility of men of letters in relation to
> the laws & customs, let us say a word about the external advantages
> the state takes from them. This advantage, which is so envied among
> individuals, is no less envied among nations.
>
> Jean-Jacques Garnier, *The Man of Letters*, 1764

> In an enlightened century, in a century in which each citizen can
> speak to the entire nation by means of print, those who have the talent
> for instructing men and the gift of moving them – men of letters, in a
> word – are, among the dispersed public, what the orators of Rome and
> Athens were in the midsts of the public assembly.
>
> Guillaume-Chrétien de Lamoignon de Malesherbes,
> *Speech Given in a Public Session of the French Academy*, 1775

This book closes in a period of history where most other studies on
the origins of nationalism do not even begin. In the eyes of the leading
'modernist' theoreticians of nationalism, the Reformation era may look
like the Île de la Cité observed from the Eiffel Tower: very distant and
very irrelevant. But just as the Île de la Cité is of greater significance to
the making of Paris than the Eiffel Tower, I would argue that the distant
periods covered in this book are more central to the making of nations
and nationalism than the more conspicuous history of modernity.

Instead of repeating the main points of this book in the conclusion,
I prefer to present some general reflections on the significance of early
modern history – that is, roughly speaking, the period from the German
Reformation to the French Revolution – for the emergence of modern
nationalism. In recent years, a number of historians have identified the
Hebrew Bible as 'the chief inspiration of nationalism' and the English
Protestants of the early modern period as the first to be inspired.[1] They
argue that the example of the 'chosen people' in the Old Testament,
widely propagated through cheaply printed vernacular bibles and prayer
books, created a homogeneous religious-cum-national identity, which,

---

[1] To name just a few: Aberbach, *Jewish Cultural Nationalism*, 18; Greenfeld, *Nationalism*,
14; Hastings, *The Construction*, 58–9.

212

based on its radical exclusion of Catholics, became the foundation of modern nationalism. I agree that the Bible was an important resource for the construction of national myths – before and after the Reformation, both in and out of England – and that the period of confessionalisation played a crucial role in the transformation from pre-modern to modern nationalism.[2] However, I also believe that by relating the origins of nationalism to the Hebrew Bible and by treating nationalism as a modernised form of religious 'identity', the baby is thrown out with the bath water. This book has tried to demonstrate that it is vital to distinguish nationalism from religion as clearly as possible in order to understand its cultural and political significance in both the past and the present. How the relation between nationalism and religion during the confessional age can be described in a more nuanced way will be the subject of the first part of this conclusion.

10.1   Nationalism and confessional fundamentalism

In the previous chapter, I described the sixteenth and seventeenth centuries as a time largely dominated by religious fundamentalism. My argument was that after Renaissance humanists had introduced the concept of autonomous nations engaged in a multipolar competition between equals, the Reformation quickly re-established a bipolar and unequal system, which separated believers from infidels, the saved from the damned. The term 'fundamentalism' refers to the radicalism with which the confessional cultures tried to justify and enforce their own understanding of the Christian religion. Both Protestantism and Catholicism created fixed doctrines, which hardly permitted internal deviation and external agreement. Furthermore, they aggressively reduced the space of cultural spheres untouched by religiosity.

Does this description suggest that we have to understand the confessional age as a long 'regressive' phase, which inhibited a rapid transformation of humanist nationalism into modern nationalism? Not quite. Despite the deep conceptual contrasts between religious fundamentalism and nationalism, there are good reasons to assume that the two phenomena were closely linked and mutually influential in European history – and that they still are in some places of the world, such as India and Pakistan, Iran and Saudi Arabia, Israel and the United States.

---

[2] On this, see Chapters 4.5, 4.6 and 6.2 of this book plus my observations in Hirschi, 'Nationalmythen', 1099–101.

Almost from the start of the Reformation, nationalist arguments served confessional agendas and vice versa. Protestant fundamentalists in Britain, Holland, Germany and Switzerland stigmatised Catholic countrymen as enemies of the nation, while Catholic fundamentalists in France eventually did the same the other way around. Such attempts to align national and denominational boundaries brought about a plurality of self-declared 'Protestant nations' such as England, Sweden and Denmark and 'Catholic nations' such as France and Spain.

The process of confessionalisation also facilitated the depiction of the nation as a sacred community. This notion seems to have been particularly attractive to members of Protestant communities who did not share Lutheranism's clear separation of worldly politics and godly order – such as Scottish and Dutch Calvinists or English Puritans and Anglicans. Due to their political theology, these Protestants could easily portray their own nation as 'the people of Israel', 'the Elect Nation' or the 'Garden of Eden', in juxtaposition to foreign nations appearing as 'Babylon', 'Antichrist' or another biblical evil.

Confessionalisation thus enabled the re-establishment of bipolar oppositions between certain European states. Political propaganda, which constructed such a sacralised bipolarity, proved particularly functional in times of war against a foreign power (ideally of different denomination), as it focused both religious and nationalist aggression on one single opponent. The national discourses in England and Spain during the Anglo-Spanish War (1585–1604) are probably the best example of such a process.

So did confessionalisation temporarily eliminate the multipolarity of nationalism? I do not think so. On the one hand, the sacralisation of the nation was itself a multipolar process creating not one, but several New Israels, which were copying and sometimes even combating each other. Especially interesting in this regard is the multiplication of 'God's own countries' in the British Empire, reaching from New England in the seventeenth century to New Zealand in the nineteenth century – and each time challenging the British motherland's own claim to stand as the true Protestant nation.

On the other hand, the dynamics of European politics hardly allowed for stable and long-term bipolar oppositions. Even during the pinnacle of confessional fundamentalism in the first half of the seventeenth century, political confrontations remained influenced by other factors, too. Probably the most important was the continuing attempts of several European states to achieve imperial dominance, followed by a multipolar rebalancing of powers. Due to colonial expansion during the early modern period, this mechanism was no longer limited to Europe.

It soon became even more dominant in European colonies overseas, partly because they were less affected by confessionalisation.

The colonialism of the early modern period can thus be seen as the first of two steps in the globalisation of nations and nationalism. While the first step led to global competition between European nations, the second step, starting with the independence movements in Latin America around 1800, brought about a multipolarity of nations all over the world. The ideological flexibility of nationalism allowed, in most colonies, for an integration of local traditions into its European framework. Nevertheless, by adopting a nationalist discourse, the colonised inevitably had to play the colonisers at their own game. Therefore, even after being liberated from European rule, the newly minted nations from America to Africa to Asia remained strongly influenced by European political culture.

The religious fundamentalism of the confessional age was not only intertwined with contemporary nationalism, but also contributed to the success of modern nationalism. Protestants and Catholics transformed and intensified mass communication through the publication of broadsheets, leaflets and small-sized books, produced in large editions and distributed through institutionalised channels. They revolutionised the visual representations of the confessional community with tools as diverse as woodcuts, spectacles and parades. And they set up an educational system capable of indoctrinating young souls with the core principles of the confessional belief.

With this, confessionalism provided much of the propaganda media, symbolic tools and pedagogical methods which were later used by modern nationalists to turn the elite discourse of their pre-modern predecessors into a mass movement. As modernity became an age of populism like no other before, nationalism could become one of its most powerful political forces. In sum, while pre-Reformation history is crucial in understanding the origins of nationalism, the confessional age is important (but by no means sufficient) in comprehending the impact and shape of modern nationalism.

10.2   The modern legacy of the ancient learned politician

One of the main purposes of this book was to demonstrate how much the formation of nationalism owed to the complex legacy of Greek – and especially of Roman – Antiquity. This was a legacy in many ways at odds with Christian orthodoxy and resistant to sacralisation. During the confessional age, it was thus of limited use to religious fundamentalists, while serving the interests of moderates and sceptics. However,

Figure 13 This seventeenth-century portrait of Cicero by Jan
Witdoeck is claimed to be a copy 'of the ancient marble [bust]' (see
Figure 5), which is not quite accurate. It is a copy of a drawing by
Peter Paul Rubens in whose workshop Witdoeck was employed.
Considering that the ancient marble bust was also modelled on
an earlier statue, this engraving is actually a copy of a copy of a
copy. The successive transformations involved in this process may
explain why Witdoeck's Cicero bears little resemblance to the
ancient marble bust.

it gained renewed momentum as soon as confessional fundamentalism lost its grip on European political culture in the second half of the
seventeenth century.

A key component of the Roman legacy was the role of the learned
politician, constructed and represented above all by Cicero (see Figure
13). In Chapter Seven, I traced the transformation of this role during the
Renaissance and analysed its significance for humanist nationalism. In
the following paragraphs, I would like to outline how the same role was
again taken up and transformed in the period of the Enlightenment –
and how it related to a modernised concept of the nation.

In February 1775, the *Académie Française* held a public session in Paris. The highlight of the event was the inaugural address by a newly elected member of this exclusive club, who, until then, had hardly made his reputation among men of letters with scholarly or literary works, but rather with official interventions in the book market. It was Guillaume-Chrétien de Lamoignon de Malesherbes (1721–94), the former *Directeur de la Librairie*, who, between 1750 and 1763, had used his responsibility for state censorship and licensing to protect the editors of and contributors to the *Encyclopédie*.

In his address, Malesherbes attempted to describe – as a *citoyen* – the place of learning in the different realms of the state. After a few introductory remarks, he observed that the public of his time was 'driven by an eager curiosity about things which were once most indifferent to them'. In its midst, Malesherbes saw a new tribunal emerge, independent of all powers and respected by all powers. This tribunal had no limits of judicial power; it was 'a sovereign judge over all judges of the world'. Its personnel was composed of men, 'who have a talent for instructing men and a gift for moving them – in a word, the men of letters'. They were, according to Malesherbes, 'amid the public dispersed, what the orators of Rome and Athens were in the middle of the public assembled'.[3]

However, contrary to the majority of Renaissance humanists, Malesherbes was well aware of the different circumstances under which enlightened thinkers played the political role of Demosthenes and Cicero. He used this awareness to foster the new enlightened myth of the scholar as a supreme politician and power holder. While the learned politicians of Antiquity, so he explained, spoke to a physically present public, contemporary men of letters, thanks to the printing press, wrote to an abstract body of citizens – *la nation entière*. This technical advantage, according to Malesherbes, made enlightened thinkers much more influential than their intellectual forebears, although they did not enjoy the political rights of Roman citizens. They compensated for this disadvantage with broader public outreach and higher political standing.

Malesherbes was neither bold nor original when he likened the enlightened men of letters to ancient orators. Eight years before his inaugural address, another new member of the Academy, Antoine-Léonard Thomas, had already given a speech entitled *The Man of Letters Considered as a Citizen*, in which he compared the *homme de lettres citoyen* to Demosthenes.[4] For most enlightened thinkers, the embodiment of

---

[3] Malesherbes, *Du rang que tiennent les lettres*, 151.
[4] Thomas, *Discours*, 204–5.

Figure 14 *Montesquieu (1689–1755) as a Roman-style man of letters*; medal engraving by Jacques Antoine Dassier, 1753.

the learned politician remained Cicero. Montesquieu, as a young man, compared Cicero to other ancient authors and concluded that he was the man, 'who had the greatest personal merit, and whom I most want to resemble'.[5] By saying this, Montesquieu referred to both Cicero the politician and Cicero the philosopher (see Figure 14). Such an appraisal of the Roman *orator doctus* was by no means limited to France. The eighteenth century was rife with Ciceromania, and it would be easy to quote similar words of admiration by British and German authors.[6]

---

[5] Montesquieu, *Discours sur Cicéron*, 93.
[6] See, for instance, Henry St John Bolingbroke's (1678–1751) famous *Letters on the Spirit of Patriotism*, written in 1736 and published in 1749, where Cicero is praised as the greatest philosopher-cum-politician and, together with Demosthenes, held up as a role model to every man 'who presumes to meddle in the affairs of a government, of a free government I mean'; Bolingbroke, *Letters*, 49 (and 43).

Malesherbes and others used the ancient model of the learned politician to provide authority to contemporary men of letters as the leaders of an allegedly self-empowered nation, newly in charge of judging and instructing government. Furthermore, they portrayed men of letters as the pride of their own nation and as the envy of other nations. According to the Parisian professor of Hebrew, Jean-Jacques Garnier (1729–1805), author of a little-known, but remarkable treatise on *The Man of Letters* (*L'homme de lettres*), this symbolic value was not the least of 'the external advantages the state takes from them'.[7]

Enlightened thinkers thus assumed the double role of *internal* representatives of the nation (in the sense of advocates of the public *vis-à-vis* the power holders) and of *external* representatives of the nation (in the sense of exponents of national honour *vis-à-vis* other nations). In the latter role, they followed in the footsteps of humanist nationalists, but in the former, they took a new road, which would eventually lead to modern nationalism. By distancing themselves from the ruling classes and standing as an independent counter-power to the government, public scholars could now lead the nation against the state. And so enlightened men of letters, with the transformation of Cicero's learned politician, composed the prelude to the French Revolution.

10.3   Coda

This last episode of the French Enlightenment highlights once more how intimately the history of nationalism has been intertwined with the history of European scholarship. Nationalism, far from serving as intellectual weaponry for the philosophically poor, as leading 'modernist' theoreticians have argued (see Chapter 2.1), was created and cherished by major and minor political thinkers who lived in Western European countries between the fifteenth and the twentieth centuries. Its history gives ample evidence of both the enormous impact and the stupendous self-delusions of European scholars eager to act on the political stage.

With its competitive energy, nationalism boosted the singular dynamics of European history. It contributed much to the destructiveness and probably not less to the richness of European political culture. These two legacies of nationalism can hardly be separated from each other, and it thus seems pointless to distinguish between good and bad forms of nationalism.

---

[7] Garnier, *L'homme de lettres*, 165.

However, there is every reason to assume that nationalism, at least in the near future, will endure, despite all attempts by politicians and scholars to herald the start of a post-national period. The multipolarity of nations is too deeply embedded in Western political culture to be removed from it within a few decades. And this is the situation we have to deal with, whether we like it or not.

Bibliography of works cited

PRIMARY SOURCES

Alexander von Roes, *Memoriale*, in *Schriften*, ed. and trans. by Herbert Grundmann and Hermann Heimpel, Weimar 1949.

Aristotle, *Nicomachean Ethics*, trans. by Terence Irwin, Indianapolis 1999.

Augustine, *The City of God against the Pagans (De Civitate Dei adversus paganos)*, trans. by R. W. Dyson, Cambridge 1998.

Aventinus, Johannes, *Bayerische Chronik*, in *Johannes Turmair's sämmtliche Werke*, Munich 1883, vols. IV–V.

Chronica von ursprung, herkomen und taten der uralten Teutschen, in *Johannes Turmair's sämmtliche Werke*, Munich 1881, vol. I, 299–372.

Baldus de Ubaldis, *In primam digesti veteris partem commentaria*, Venice 1572.

Bebel, Heinrich, *Apologia pro defensione imperatorum contra Leonhardum Iustinianum*, in *Schardius Redivivus sive Rerum Germanicarum Scriptores varii*, ed. by Simon Schard, Gießen 1673, vol. I, 109–15.

De laude, antiquitate, imperio, victoriis rebusque gestis Veterum Germanorum, in *Schardius Redivivus sive Rerum Germanicarum Scriptores varii*, ed. by Simon Schard, Gießen 1673, 117–34.

Opuscula nova, Strasbourg 1514.

Oratio ad Augustissimum atque Sacratissimum Romanorum Regem Maximilianum, in *Schardius Redivivus sive Rerum Germanicarum Scriptores varii*, ed. by Simon Schard, Gießen 1673, 95–104.

Boissevain, Ursul Philip (ed.), *Casii Dionis historiarum Romanorum quae supersunt*, vol. III, Berlin 1901.

Bolingbroke, Henry St John, *Letters on the Spirit of Patriotism: on the Idea of a Patriot King: and on the State of Parties at the Accession of King George the First* (1736), London 1775.

Brant, Sebastian, *Kleine Texte*, ed. by Thomas Wilhelmi, Stuttgart and Bad Cannstatt 1998, 2 vols.

Bruni, Leonardo, *Vita Ciceronis*, in *Opere letterarie e politiche*, ed. by Paolo Viti, Turin 1996, 411–99.

Campano, Gian Antonio, *De Pii II, Pont. Max. Commentariis historicis, orationibus, et scriptis aliis*, in *Epistolae et poemata*, Leipzig 1707, 1–13.

Oratio in Conventu Ratisponensi ad exhortandos principes Germanorum contra Turcos: Et de laudibus eorum, in *Omnia Campani Opera*, Venice 1502, fol. 90–5.

Oratio in Funere Pii II, in *Opera omnia*, Rome 1495.

Pii II pontificis maximi vita (c. 1470), in Giulio C. Zimolo (ed.), *Le vite di Pio II di Giovanni Antonio Campano e Bartolomeo Platina*, Bologna 1964, 7–87.

Celtis, Conrad, *Briefwechsel*, ed. by Hans Rupprich, Munich 1934.

Fünf Bücher Epigramme, ed. by Karl Hartfelder, Hildesheim 1963.

Libri odarum quattuor; Liber epodon; Carmen saeculare, ed. by Felicitas Pindter, Leipzig 1937.

Norimberga, trans. into German by Gerhard Fink, Nuremberg 2000.

Oratio in Gymnasio in Ingelstadio publice recitata, Latin and English, in *Selections from Conrad Celtis 1459–1508*, ed. by Leonard Forster, Cambridge 1948, 36–65.

Cicero, Marcus Tullius, *Dream of Scipio (Somnium Scipionis)*, in *On the Commonwealth: and, On the Laws*, trans. by James E. G. Zetzel, Cambridge 1999, 95–102.

On Duties (De officiis), trans. by Miriam T. Griffin and Eileen M. Atkins, Cambridge 1991.

On Invention (De inventione), in *The Fourteen Orations Against Marcus Antonius, the Treatise on Rhetorical Invention, the Orator, Topics, on Rhetorical Partitions, Etc*, trans. by Charles Duke Yonge, London 1879.

On the Commonwealth (De re publica), in *On the Commonwealth: and, On the Laws*, trans. by James E. G. Zetzel, Cambridge 1999, 1–102.

On the Ideal Orator (De oratore), trans. by James M. May and Jakob Wisse, Oxford 2001.

On the Laws (De legibus), in *On the Commonwealth: and, On the Laws*, trans. by James E. G. Zetzel, Cambridge 1999, 105–75.

Orations against Catiline I–IV *(In Catilinam)*, in *Political Speeches*, trans. by Dominic H. Berry, Oxford 2006, 134–203.

Philippics (Philippicae), in *The Fourteen Orations Against Marcus Antonius, the Treatise on Rhetorical Invention, the Orator, Topics, on Rhetorical Partitions, Etc*, trans. by Charles Duke Yonge, London 1879.

Cochlaeus, Johannes, *Brevis descriptio Germaniae (1512): Mit der Deutschlandkarte des Erhard Etzlaub von 1512*, ed. and trans. by Karl Langosch, Darmstadt 1960.

Corpus Iuris Civilis, Iustiniani Digesta, ed. by Theodor Mommsen, Berlin 1868–70, 3 vols.

Decretalium Collectiones, in *Corpus Iuris Canonici*, ed. by Emil Ludwig Richter, Leipzig 1879–81, vol. II.

Deutsche Reichstagsakten, Jüngere Reihe: Deutsche Reichstagsakten unter Kaiser Karl V., Göttingen and Munich, 1893–, 20 vols.

Deutsche Reichstagsakten, Mittlere Reihe: Deutsche Reichstagsakten unter Maximilian I., Göttingen and Munich 1973–, 8 vols.

Einhard, *Life of Charlemagne (Vita Caroli Magni)*, in idem, Notker of Saint-Gall, *Two Lives of Charlemagne*, trans. by Lewis Thorpe, London 1969, 49–92.

Erasmus, Desiderius, *A Complaint of Peace Spurned and Rejected by the Whole World*, in *Collected Works*, trans. by Betty Radice, Toronto 1986, vol. XXVII, 289–322.

Opus Epistolarum, ed. by Percy Stafford and Helen Mary Allen, Oxford 1906–65, 12 vols.

Praise of Folly (Laus stultitiae), and, Letter to Maarten Van Dorp, 1515, trans. by Betty Radice, London 1993.

The Ciceronian (Ciceronianus): A Dialogue on the Ideal Latin Style, trans. by Betty N. Knott, in *Collected Works of Erasmus: Literary and Educational Writings*, Toronto 1986, vol. XXVIII, 323–448.

Fabri, Felix, *Evagatorium in Terrae Sanctae, Arabiae et Aegypti peregrinationem*, ed. by Conrad Dieter Hassler, Stuttgart 1843–9, 3 vols.

Fichte, Johann Gottlieb, *Reden an die deutsche Nation*, Leipzig 1824.

Florus, L. Annaeus, *Epitome of Roman History (Epitoma de Tito Livio)*, trans. by Edward Seymour Forster, Cambridge, MA, 1984.

Franke, Annelore (ed.), *Das Buch der hundert Kapitel und der vierzig Statuten des sog. Oberrheinischen Revolutionärs*, Berlin (East) 1967.

Garnier, Jean-Jacques, *L'homme de lettres*, Paris 1764.

Gebwiler, Hieronymus, *Libertas Germaniae, qua Germanos Gallis, neminem vero Gallum a Christiano natali, Germanis imperasse*, in *Schardius Redivivus sive Rerum Germanicarum Scriptores varii*, ed. by Simon Schard, Gießen 1673, 219–26.

Geoffrey of Monmouth, *The History of the Kings of Britain*, Latin and English, ed. by Michael D. Reeve, trans. by Neil Wright, Woodbridge 2007.

Gobelinus Person, *Cosmidromius*, ed. by Max Jansen, Münster 1900.

Gottsched, Johann Christoph, *Lob Germaniens*, in *Ausgewählte Werke: Gedichte und Gedichtübertragungen*, Berlin (East) 1968, vol. I, 12–17.

Harsdörffer, Georg Philipp, *Lobrede Des Geschmackes*, Nürnberg 1651.

Schutzschrift für die Teütsche Spracharbeit (1644), in *Frauenzimmer Gesprächsspiele*, part I, ed. by Irmgard Böttcher, Tübingen 1968, 339–96.

Herder, Johann Gottfried, *Briefe zur Beförderung der Humanität: Beilage* (1795), in *Sämmtliche Werke*, ed. by Bernhard Suphan, Berlin 1881, vol. XVII.

Hutten, in *Sämmtliche Werke*, ed. by Bernhard Suphan, Berlin 1893, vol. IX, 476–97.

Idee zum ersten patriotischen Institut für den Allgemeingeist Deutschlands (1787), in *Sämmtliche Werke*, ed. by Bernhard Suphan, Berlin 1887, vol. XVI, 600–16.

Hesdin, Jean de, *Magistri Iohannis de Hisdinio contra Franciscum Petrarcham Epistola*, ed. by Enrico Cocchia in *Atti della Reale Accademia di Archeologia, Lettere e Belle Arti*, 7 (1920), 112–39.

Horace, *The Complete Odes and Epodes*, trans. by David West, Oxford 1997.

Humboldt, Wilhelm von, *Gesammelte Schriften*, ed. by Albert Leitzmann, Bruno Gebhardt and Wilhelm Richter, Berlin 1903–36, 17 vols.

Hutten, Ulrich von, *Cum Erasmo Roterodamo, Presbytero, Teologo expostulatio*, in *Schriften*, ed. by Eduard Böcking, Leipzig 1859, vol. II, 180–248.

Epistolae, ed. by Eduard Böcking, vol. I (1506–20), Leipzig 1859.

Gespräch büchlin, in *Deutsche Schriften*, ed. by Heinz Mettke, Leipzig 1972–4, vol. I, 1–188.

Inspicientes, in *Opera quae extant omnia*, ed. by Joseph Herman Münch, Schaffhausen 1823, vol. III, 511–40.

Praedones, in *Opera quae extant omnia*, ed. by Joseph Herman Münch, Schaffhausen 1823, vol. IV, 157–230.

Irenicus, Franciscus, *Germaniae exegeseos volumina duodecim*, Hagenau 1518.

Iustiniani Imperatoris institutionum libri quattuor, ed. by J. B. Moyle, Oxford 1923.

Jacques de Vitry, *Historia Occidentalis*, ed. by John Frederick Hinnebusch, Freiburg i. Ü. 1972.

Janssen, Johannes (ed.), *Frankfurts Reichscorrespondenz von 1376–1519*, Freiburg i. Br. 1866, vol. 2.

Johann Eberlin von Günzburg, *Ein zamengelesen bouchlin von der Teutschen Nation gelegenheit, Sitten vnd gebrauche, durch Cornelium Tacitum vnd etliche andere verzeichnet* (1526), ed. by Achim Masser, Innsbruck 1986.

Kohler, Alfred (ed.), *Quellen zur Geschichte Karls V.*, Darmstadt 1990.

Lamoignon de Malesherbes, Guillaume-Chrétien de, *Du rang que tiennent les lettres entre les différens ordres de l'état: Discours prononcé dans la séance publique du 16 février 1775*, in *Œuvres inédites*, Paris 1808, 149–67.

Langkabel, Hermann (ed.), *Die Staatsbriefe Coluccio Salutatis: Untersuchungen zum Frühhumanismus in der Florentiner Staatskanzlei und Auswahledition*, Wien 1981.

Laube, Adolf (ed.), *Flugschriften gegen die Reformation (1518–1524)*, Berlin 1997.

Laube, Adolf, and Hans Werner Seiffert (ed.), *Flugschriften der Bauernkriegszeit*, Berlin 1978.

Leibniz, Gottfried Wilhelm, *Ermahnung an die Teutsche ihren Verstand und Sprache besser zu üben*, ed. by Carl Ludwig Grotefend, Hanover 1846.

Lex Salica: The Ten Texts with the Glosses, and the Lex Emendata, ed. by John Murray, London 1880.

Liliencron, Rochus von (ed.), *Die historischen Volkslieder der Deutschen vom 13. bis 16. Jahrhundert*, Leipzig 1865–9, 5 vols.

Lucian of Samosata, *Life of Demonax*, in *The Works of Lucian of Samosata*, trans. by Henry Watson Fowler and Francis George Fowler, Oxford 1905, vol. III, 5–12.

Lupold of Bebenburg, *Ritmaticum querulosum et lamentosum dictamen de modernis cursibus et defectibus regni ac imperii Romani*, in *Politische Schriften des Lupold von Bebenburg*, ed. by Jürgen Miethke and Christoph Flüeler, Hanover 2004, 507–24.

Tractatus de iuribus regni et imperii Romanorum, in *Politische Schriften des Lupold von Bebenburg*, ed. by Jürgen Miethke and Christoph Flüeler, Hanover 2004, 233–409.

Luther, Martin, *D. Martin Luthers Werke* [*WA*]: *Kritische Gesammtausgabe*, Weimar 1883–
Tischreden oder Colloqvia, Eisleben 1566.

Mesnardière, Jules de la, *La Poëtique* (1640), Geneva 1972.

Montesquieu, Charles de Secondat de, *Discours sur Cicéron*, in *Œuvres complètes*, Paris 1949, vol. I, 93–8.

Müller, Johann Joachim (ed.), *Des Heiligen Römischen Reichs, Teutscher Nation Reichstagstheatrum (1440–1500)*, Jena 1713–19, 2 vols.

Nauclerus, Johannes, *Memorabilium omnis aetatis et omnium gentium chronici commentarii*, 2 vols., Tübingen 1516.

Notker of Saint-Gall, *De Carolo Magno*, in idem, Einhard, *Two Lives of Charlemagne*, trans. by Lewis Thorpe, London 1969, 93–172.

Pariset, Jean-Daniel (ed.), 'La France et les princes allemands: Documents et commentaires (1545–1557)', *Francia*, 10 (1982), 229–301.

Peter of Andlau, *Libellus de Cesarea Monarchia: Kaiser und Reich*, ed. and trans. by Rainer A. Müller, Frankfurt a. M. and Leipzig 1998.

Petrarch, Francesco, *Book without a Name (Liber sine nomine)*, trans. by Norman P. Zacour, Toronto 1973.

Epistolae de rebus familiaribus et variae, ed. by Giuseppe Fracassetti, Florence 1859–83, 3 vols.

Invectives, trans. by David Marsh, Harvard 2003.

Letters of Old Age (Epistolae rerum senilium), trans. by Aldo S. Bernardo, Saul Levin and Reta A. Bernardo, New York 2005, 2 vols.

Rerum vulgarium fragmenta, ed. by Giuseppe Savoca, Florence 2008.

Piccolomini, Enea Silvio, *Briefwechsel*, ed. by Rudolf Wolkan, Vienna 1909–18, 3 vols.

Germania, ed. by Adolf Schmidt, Cologne and Graz 1962.

Pentalogus, ed. by Christoph Schingnitz, Hanover 2009.

Pirckheimer, Wilibald, *Schweizerkrieg*, trans. by Karl Rück, Munich 1895.

Pliny, *Natural History (Historia naturalis)*, trans. by H. Rackman and W. H. S. Jones, 10 vols., Cambridge, MA, 1938–83.

Rhenanus, Beatus, *Briefwechsel*, ed. by Adalbert Horawitz and Karl Hartfelder, Leipzig 1886.

Rerum Germanicarum libri tres, Basle 1531.

Sallust, *The Conspiracy of Catiline (Bellum Catilinae)*, in *The Jugurthine War/ The Conspiracy of Catiline*, trans. by Stanley Alexander Handford, London 1963, 151–233.

The Jugurthine War (Bellum Iugurthinum), in *The Jugurthine War/The Conspiracy of Catiline*, trans. by Stanley Alexander Handford, London 1963, 15–150.

Salutati, Coluccio, *Epistolario*, ed. by Francesco Novati, Rome 1891–1911, 4 vols.

Scaliger, Julius Caesar, *Poetices Libri Septem* (1561), Stuttgart 1964.

Schottelius, Justus Georg, *Ausführliche Arbeit Von der Teutschen Hauptsprache*, Braunschweig 1663.

Sleidanus, Johannes, *De statu religionis et rei publicae Carolo Quinto Caesare commentarii*, Strasbourg 1555.

Warhafftige Beschreibung geistlicher und weltlicher Historien, Basle 1557.

Stieler, Kaspar, *Der Teutschen Sprache Stammbaum und Fortwachs*, Nuremberg 1691.

Tacitus, *The Annals (Annales)*, trans. by J. C. Yardley, Oxford and New York 2008.

Thomas, Antoine-Léonard, *Discours prononcé dans l'Académie Française (De l'homme de lettres considéré comme citoyen)*, in *Œuvres complètes*, Paris 1825, vol. IV, 191–216.

Vitruvius, *Ten Books on Architecture*, trans. by Morris Hicky Morgan, Cambridge, MA, 1914.

Von der Hardt, Heinrich, *Magnum oecumenicum Constantiense concilium*, Frankfurt a. M. and Leipzig 1696–1700, 6 vols.

Von der Vogelweide, Walther, *Spruchlyrik*, in *Werke*, Stuttgart 1994, vol. I.

Weinrich, Lorenz (ed.), *Quellen zur Reichsreform im Spätmittelalter*, Darmstadt 2001.

Wiesflecker-Friedhuber, Inge (ed.), *Quellen zur Geschichte Maximilians I. und seiner Zeit*, Darmstadt 1996.

Wilkins, Ernest H. (ed.), 'Petrarch's Coronation Oration', *Publications of the Modern Language Association*, 68 (1953), 1241–50.

Wimpfeling, Jacob, *Adolescentia*, in *Jacobi Wimpfelingi opera selecta*, ed. by Otto Herding, Munich 1965, vol. I.

Agatharchia id est bonus principatus vel epitoma contitionum boni principis, Strasbourg 1498.

Briefwechsel, in *Jacobi Wimpfelingi opera selecta*, ed. by Otto Herding and Dieter Mertens, Munich 1990, vol. III.

De integritate libellus, Strasbourg 1505.

Epitoma Germanicarum Rerum, in *Schardius Redivivus sive Rerum Germanicarum Scriptores varii*, ed. by Simon Schard, Gießen 1673, 170–199.

Germania, in Notker Hammerstein (ed.), *Staatslehre der frühen Neuzeit*, Frankfurt a. M. 1995, 9–95.

Responsa et Replicae ad Eneam Silvium, in Enea Silvio Piccolomini, *Germania*, ed. by Adolf Schmidt, Cologne and Graz 1962, 125–46.

Zesen, Philipp von, *Rosen-mând*, Hamburg 1651.

SECONDARY SOURCES

Aberbach, David, *Jewish Cultural Nationalism: Origins and Influences*, New York 2008.

Allmand, Christopher, *The Hundred Years War: England and France at War 1300–1450*, Cambridge 1988.

Anderson, Benedict, *Imagined Communities: Reflections on the Origin and Spread of Nationalism* (1983), London and New York 1991.

Anderson, Matthew Smith, *The Rise of Modern Diplomacy, 1450–1919*, London 1993.

Asher, Robert E., *National Myths in Renaissance France: Francus, Samothes and the Druids*, Edinburgh 1993.

Beaune, Colette, *The Birth of an Ideology: Myths and Symbols of Nation in Late Medieval France*, trans. by Fredric L. Cheyette, Berkeley 1991.

Bell, David A., *The Cult of the Nation in France: Inventing Nationalism, 1680–1800*, Cambridge, MA, 2001.

Blanning, Tim, *The Romantic Revolution*, London 2010.

Böhm, Helmut, 'Gallica Gloria': Untersuchungen zum kulturellen Nationalgefühl in der älteren französischen Neuzeit, Freiburg i. B. 1977.

Bourdieu, Pierre, *Outline of a Theory of Practice*, Cambridge 1977.

Boureau, Alain, 'The Letter-Writing Norm, a Mediaeval Invention', in idem, Roger Chartier and Cécile Dauphin (eds.), *Correspondence: Models of Letter-Writing from the Middle Ages to the Nineteenth Century*, Cambridge 1997, 24–58.

Brecht, Martin, 'Luther und die Türken,' in Bodo Guthmüller and Wilhelm Kühlmann (eds.), *Europa und die Türken in der Renaissance*, Tübingen 2000, 9–27.

Burke, Peter, *The Fortunes of the Courtier: The European Reception of Castiglione's 'Cortegiano'*, Philadelphia 1995.

Camargo, Martin, 'Ars dictaminis, ars dictandi', in Gert Ueding (ed.), *Historisches Wörterbuch der Rhetorik*, Tübingen 1992–, vol. I, 1040–6.

Cecchetti, Dario, *Petrarca, Pietramala e Clamanges: Storia di una 'querelle' inventata*, Paris 1982.

Contamine, Philippe, 'Mourir pour la patrie', in Pierre Nora (ed.), *Les lieux de mémoire*, Paris 1986, vol. II: *La Nation*, 11–43.

Daub, Susanne, *Leonardo Brunis Rede auf Nanni Strozzi: Einleitung, Edition und Kommentar*, Stuttgart 1996.

Deutsch, Karl W., *Nationalism and Social Communication: an Inquiry into the Foundations of Nationality*, Cambridge, MA, 1953.

Enenkel, Karl A. E., *Die Erfindung des Menschen: Die Autobiographik des frühneuzeitlichen Humanismus von Petrarca bis Lipsius*, Berlin and New York 2008.

Englund, Steven, 'The Ghost of Nation Past' (review of *Les Lieux de mémoire*, ed. by Pierre Nora, vol. I: *La République*, vol. II: *La Nation*), *The Journal of Modern History*, 64 (1992), 299–320.

Erdmann, Karl Dietrich, *Die Ökumene der Historiker: Geschichte der Internationalen Historikerkongresse und des Comité International des Sciences Historiques*, Göttingen 1987.

Fantham, Elaine, 'The Contexts and Occasions of Roman Public Rhetoric', in William J. Dominik (ed.), *Roman Eloquence: Rhetoric in Society and Literature*, London and New York 1997, 111–28.

The Roman World of Cicero's 'De Oratore', Oxford 2004.

Finsen, Hans Carl, *Die Rhetorik der Nation: Redestrategien im nationalen Diskurs*, Tübingen 2001.

Flood, John L., 'Nationalistic Currents in Early German Typography', *The Library*, 15 (1993), 125–41.

Foot, Sarah, 'The Historiography of the Anglo-Saxon "Nation-State"', in Len Scales and Oliver Zimmer (eds.), *Power and the Nation in European History*, Cambridge 2005, 125–42.

Fournier, Marcel, *Les statuts et privilèges des universités françaises depuis leur fondation jusqu'en 1789*, Paris 1890–4, 4 vols.

Fulda Daniel, 'Die Erschaffung der Nation als Literaturgesellschaft: Zu einer meist übergangenen Leistung des Publizisten Gottsched', in *Denkströme: Journal der Sächsischen Akademie der Wissenschaften* 4 (2010), 12–29.

Furr, Grover, 'France vs. Italy: French Literary Nationalism in "Petrarch's Last Controversy" and a Humanist Dispute of c. 1395', *Proceedings of the Patristic, Medieval and Renaissance Conference*, 4 (1979), 115–25.

Gellner, Ernest, *Nations and Nationalism*, Oxford 1983.

Thought and Change, London 1964.

Goodblatt, David, *Elements of Ancient Jewish Nationalism*, Cambridge 2006.

Graf, Klaus, '"Der adel dem purger tregt hass": Feindbilder und Konflikte zwischen städtischem Bürgertum und landsässigem Adel im späten Mittelalter', in Werner Rösener (ed.), *Adelige und bürgerliche Erinnerungskulturen des Spätmittelalter und der Frühen Neuzeit*, Göttingen 2000, 191–204.

Grafton, Anthony, 'Invention of Traditions and Traditions of Invention in Renaissance Europe: The Strange Case of Annius of Viterbo', in idem and Anne Blair (eds.), *The Transmission of Culture in Early Modern Europe*, Philadelphia 1990, 8–38.

What was History? The Art of History in Early Modern Europe, Cambridge 2007.

Graus, František, *Die Nationenbildung der Westslawen im Mittelalter*, Sigmaringen 1980.

Greenfeld, Liah, *Nationalism: Five Roads to Modernity*, Cambridge, MA, 1992.

Hankins, James (ed.), *Renaissance Civic Humanism: Reappraisals and Reflections*, Cambridge 2000.

Harth, Helene, 'Überlegungen zur Öffentlichkeit des humanistischen Briefs am Beispiel der Poggio-Korrespondenz', in Heinz-Dieter Heimann (ed.), *Kommunikationspraxis und Korrespondenzwesen im Mittelalter und in der Renaissance*, Paderborn, Munich, Vienna and Zurich 1998, 127–37.

Hastings, Adrian, *The Construction of Nationhood: Ethnicity, Religion and Nationalism*, Cambridge 1997.

Hayes, Carlton J. H., *Essays on Nationalism*, New York 1928.

Helmrath, Johannes, 'Der europäische Humanismus und die Funktionen der Rhetorik', in Thomas Maissen and Gerrit Walther (eds.), *Funktionen des Humanismus: Studien zum Nutzen des Neuen in der humanistischen Kultur*, Göttingen 2006, 18–48.

'Rhetorik und "Akademisierung" auf den deutschen Reichstagen im 15. und 16. Jahrhundert', in Heinz Duchhardt and Gerd Melville (eds.), *Im Spannungsfeld von Recht und Ritual: Soziale Kommunikation in Mittelalter und Früher Neuzeit*, Cologne, Weimar and Vienna 1997, 423–46.

Herde, Peter, 'Politik und Rhetorik in Florenz am Vorabend der Renaissance: Die ideologische Rechtfertigung der Florentiner Außenpolitik durch Coluccio Salutati', *Archiv für Kulturgeschichte*, 47 (1965), 141–220.

Hess, Günter, *Deutsch-lateinische Narrenzunft: Studien zum Verhältnis von Volkssprache und Latinität in der satirischen Literatur des 16. Jahrhunderts*, Munich 1971.

Hirschi, Caspar, 'Boden der Christenheit und Quelle der Männlichkeit: Humanistische Konstruktionen Europas am Beispiel von Enea Silvio Piccolomini und Sebastian Münster', in Jürgen Elvert and Jürgen Nielsen-Sikora (eds.), *Leitbild Europa? Europabilder und Ihre Wirkungen in der Neuzeit*, Stuttgart 2009, 46–66.

'Das humanistische Nationskonstrukt vor dem Hintergrund modernistischer Nationalismustheorien', *Historisches Jahrbuch*, 122 (2002), 355–96.

'Eine Kommunikationssituation zum Schweigen', in Klaus Bergdolt, Joachim Knape, Anton Schindling and Gerrit Walther (eds.), *Sebastian Brant und die Kommunikationskultur um 1500*, Wiesbaden 2010, 219–52.

'Germanenmythos', in Friedrich Jaeger (ed.), *Enzyklopädie der Neuzeit*, Stuttgart 2008, vol. IV, 551–5.

'Höflinge der Bürgerschaft – Bürger des Hofes: Zur Beziehung von Humanismus und städtischer Gesellschaft', in Gernot Michael Müller (ed.), *Humanismus und Renaissance in Augsburg*, Tübingen 2010, 31–60.

'Konzepte von Fortschritt und Niedergang im Humanismus am Beispiel der "translatio imperii" und der "translatio studii"', in Christoph Strosetzki and Sebastian Neumeister (eds.), *Die Idee von Fortschritt und Zerfall im Europa der frühen Neuzeit*, Heidelberg 2008, 37–55.

'Mittelalterrezeption', in Friedrich Jaeger (ed.), *Enzyklopädie der Neuzeit*, Stuttgart 2008, vol. VIII, 610–17.

'Nationalgeschichte', in Friedrich Jaeger (ed.), *Enzyklopädie der Neuzeit*, Stuttgart 2008, vol. VIII, 1084–7.

'Nationalmythen', in Friedrich Jaeger (ed.), *Enzyklopädie der Neuzeit*, Stuttgart 2008, vol. VIII, 1097–107.

'Vorwärts in eine neue Vergangenheit: Funktionen des humanistischen Nationalismus in Deutschland', in Thomas Maissen and Gerrit Walther (eds.), *Funktionen des Humanismus: Studien zum Nutzen des Neuen in der humanistischen Kultur*, Göttingen 2006, 362–95.

Wettkampf der Nationen: Konstruktionen einer deutschen Ehrgemeinschaft an der Wende vom Mittelalter zur Neuzeit, Göttingen 2005.

Hobsbawm, Eric, *Nations and Nationalism: Programme, Myth, Reality*, Cambridge 1990.

Hobsbawm, Eric and Terence O. Ranger (eds.), *The Invention of Tradition*, Cambridge 1983.

Huizinga, Johan, 'Erasmus über Vaterland und Nation', in *Gedenkschrift zum 400. Todestage des Erasmus von Rotterdam*, Basel 1936, 34–49.

Janssen, Johannes, *Geschichte des deutschen Volkes*, Freiburg i. Br. 1913, vol. I.

Jaumann, Herbert, '"Respublica literaria" als politische Metapher: Die Bedeutung der "Res Publica" in Europa vom Humanismus zum 18. Jahrhundert', in Marc Fumaroli (ed.), *Les premiers siècles de la République européenne des Lettres*, Paris 2005, 73–88.

Joachimsen, Paul, 'Der Humanismus und die Entwicklung des deutschen Geistes', *Deutsche Vierteljahresschrift für Literaturwissenschaft und Geistesgeschichte*, 8 (1930), 419–80.

Kantorowicz, Ernst H., '"Pro patria mori" in Medieval Thought', *American Historical Review*, 56 (1951), 472–92.

The King's Two Bodies: A Study in Medieval Political Theology (1957), Princeton 1997.

'The Sovereignty of the Artist: A Note on Legal Maxims and Renaissance Theories of Art', in *Selected Studies*, New York 1965, 352–65.

Kibre, Pearl, *The Nations in the Mediaeval Universities*, Cambridge, MA, 1948.

Klaniczay, Tibor, 'Die Akademie als die Organisation der intellektuellen Elite in der Renaissance', in idem and August Buck (eds.), *Sozialgeschichtliche Fragestellungen in der Renaissanceforschung*, Wiesbaden 1992, 1–15.

Klein, Josef, 'Politische Rede', in Gert Ueding (ed.), *Historisches Wörterbuch der Rhetorik*, Tübingen 1992–, vol. VI, 1465–1521.

Klippel, Rainer, *Die Aufnahme der Schriften Lupolds von Bebenburg im deutschen Humanismus*, Frankfurt a. M. 1954 (typescript).

Koch, Peter, 'Ars arengandi', in Gert Ueding (ed.), *Historisches Wörterbuch der Rhetorik*, Tübingen 1992–, vol. I, 1033–40.

Kohler, Alfred, *Karl V. 1500–1558: Eine Biographie*, Munich 1999.

Kohn, Hans, *The Idea of Nationalism: A Study in Its Origins and Background* (1944), New Brunswick 2005.

Koselleck, Reinhard, 'Zur historisch-politischen Semantik asymmetrischer Gegenbegriffe', in *Vergangene Zukunft: Zur Semantik geschichtlicher Zeiten*, Frankfurt a. M. 1979, 211–59.

Krebs, Christopher B., *Negotiatio Germaniae: Tacitus' Germania und Enea Silvio Piccolomini, Giannantonio Campano, Conrad Celtis und Heinrich Bebel*, Göttingen 2005.

Kristeller, Paul Oskar, *Renaissance Thought and the Arts: Collected Essays*, Princeton 1990.

Laubach, Ernst, 'Wahlpropaganda im Wahlkampf um die deutsche Königswürde 1519', in *Archiv für Kulturgeschichte*, 53 (1971), 207–48.

Lauterbach, Klaus H. (Hrsg.), *Der Oberrheinische Revolutionär (Buchli der hundert Capiteln mit XXXX Statuten)*, MGH, Scriptores 10, Staatsschriften des späteren Mittelalters 7, Stuttgart 2009.

Leersen, Joep, *National Thought in Europe: A Cultural History*, Amsterdam 2008.

Levin, Michael J., 'A New World Order: The Spanish Campaign for Precedence in Early Modern Europe', *Journal of Early Modern History*, 6 (2002), 233–64.

Lund, Allan A., 'Zur Gesamtinterpretation der Germania des Tacitus', in Wolfgang Haase (ed.), *Aufstieg und Niedergang de Römischen Welt*, Berlin and New York 1991, vol. xxx.3, 1858–1988.

Marchal, Guy P., '"Bellum justum contra judicium belli": Zur Interpretation von Jakob Wimpfelings antieidgenössischer Streitschrift *Soliloquium pro Pace Christianorum et pro Helvetiis ut resipiscant...*', in Nicolai Bernard and Quirinus Reichen (eds.), *Gesellschaft und Gesellschaften*, Bern 1982, 114–37.

Maurer, Michael, '"Nationalcharakter" in der frühen Neuzeit: Ein mentalitätsgeschichtlicher Versuch', in Reinhard Blomert, Helmut Kuzmics and Annette Treibel (eds.), *Transformationen des Wir-Gefühls: Studien zum nationalen Habitus*, Frankfurt a. M. 1993, 45–81.

McKitterick, Rosamond, *Charlemagne: The Formation of a European Identity*, Cambridge 2008.

McManamon, John M., *Funeral Oratory and the Cultural Ideals of Italian Humanism*, Chapel Hill and London 1989.

Mendels, Doron, *The Rise and Fall of Jewish Nationalism: Jewish and Christian Ethnicity in Ancient Palestine*, New York 1992.

Mertens, Dieter, 'Celtis ad Caesarem: Oden I, 1–2 und Epode I', in Ulrike Auhagen, Eckard Lefèvre and Eckart Schäfer (eds.), *Horaz und Celtis*, Tübingen 2000, 67–85.

'Die Rede als institutionalisierte Kommunikation im Zeitalter des Humanismus', in Heinz Duchhardt and Gerd Melville (eds.), *Im Spannungsfeld von Recht und Ritual: Soziale Kommunikation in Mittelalter und Früher Neuzeit*, Cologne, Weimar and Vienna 1997, 401–21.

'Jakob Wimpfeling: Pädagogischer Humanismus', in Paul Gerhard Schmidt (ed.), *Humanismus im deutschen Südwesten: Biographische Profile*, Sigmaringen 1993, 35–57.

'Maximilians gekrönte Dichter über Krieg und Frieden', in Franz Josef Worstbrock (ed.), *Krieg und Frieden im Horizont des Renaissancehumanismus*, Weinheim 1986, 105–23.

Reich und Elsass zur Zeit Maximilians I.: Untersuchungen zur Ideen- und Landesgeschichte im Südwesten des Reiches am Ausgang des Mittelalters, Freiburg i. Br. 1977 (typescript).

Miethke, Jürgen and Lorenz Weinrich (eds.), *Quellen zur Kirchenreform im Zeitalter der großen Konzilien des 15. Jahrhunderts: Part 1, Die Konzilien von Pisa (1409) und Konstanz (1414–1418)*, Darmstadt 1995.

Millar, Fergus, *Government, Society, and Culture in the Roman Empire*, Chapel Hill and London 2004.

Monfasani, John (ed.), *Kristeller Reconsidered: Essays on his Life and Scholarship*, New York 2006.

Morsel, Joseph, 'Die Erfindung des Adels: Zur Soziogenese des Adels am Ende des Mittelalters – das Beispiel Frankens', in Otto Gerhard Oexle and Werner Paravicini (eds.), *Nobilitas: Funktion und Repräsentation des Adels in Alteuropa*, Göttingen 1997, 312–75.

Morstein-Marx, Robert, *Mass Oratory and Political Power in the Late Roman Republic*, Cambridge 2004.

Muhlack, Ulrich, 'Die Germania im deutschen Nationalbewusstsein vor dem 19. Jahrhundert', in Herbert Jankuhn and Dieter Timpe (eds.), *Beiträge zum Verständnis der Germania des Tacitus*, Göttingen 1989, vol. I, 128–54.

Müller, Harald, *Habit und Habitus: Mönche und Humanisten im Dialog*, Tübingen 2006.

Münkler, Herfried, Hans Grünberger and Kathrin Mayer, *Nationenbildung: Die Nationalisierung Europas im Diskurs humanistischer Intellektueller: Italien und Deutschland*, Berlin 1998.

Murphy, James J., *Rhetoric in the Middle Ages: A History of Rhetorical Theory from Saint Augustine to the Renaissance*, Arizona 2001.

Newman, Jane O., 'Redemption in the Vernacular: The Language of Language Theory in Seventeenth-Century "Sprachgesellschaften"', *Monatshefte*, 79 (1987), 10–29.

O'Leary, Brendan, 'On the Nature of Nationalism: An Appraisal of Ernest Gellner's Writings on Nationalism', *British Journal of Political Science*, 27 (1997), 191–222.

Ochoa Brun, Miguel-Ángel, 'Die Diplomatie Karls V.,' in Alfred Kohler, Barbara Haider and Christine Ottner (eds.), *Karl V. 1500–1558: Neue Perspektiven seiner Herrschaft in Europa und Übersee*, Vienna 2002, 181–96.

Ochsenbein, Peter, '"Beten mit zertanen Armen": ein alteidgenössischer Brauch', *Schweizerisches Archiv für Volkskunde*, 75 (1979), 129–72.

Ouy, Gilbert, 'La plus ancienne œuvre retrouvée de Jean Gerson: Le brouillon inachevé d'un traité contre Juan de Monzon (1389–1390)', in *Romania*, 83 (1962), 433–92.

'Paris: L'un des principaux foyers de l'humanisme en Europe au début du XVe siècle', *Bulletin de la société de l'histoire de Paris*, 94–95 (1967–68), 71–98.

'Pétrarque et les premiers humanistes français', in Giuseppe Billanovich and Giuseppe Frasso (eds.), *Petrarca, Verona e l'Europa*, Padua 1997, 415–34.

Pietschmann, Horst, 'Zum Problem eines frühneuzeitlichen Nationalismus in Spanien: Der Widerstand Kastiliens gegen Karl V.,' in Otto Dann (ed.), *Nationalismus in vorindustrieller Zeit*, Munich 1986, 55–71.

Polenz, Peter von, *Deutsche Sprachgeschichte vom Spätmittelalter bis zur Gegenwart*, Berlin and New York 1991–99, 3 vols.

Post, Gaines, '"Blessed Lady Spain": Vincentius Hispanus and Spanish National Imperialism in the Thirteenth Century', *Speculum*, 29 (1954), 198–209.

'Two Notes on Nationalism in the Middle Ages', *Traditio*, 9 (1953), 281–320.

Ridé, Jacques, *L'image du Germain dans la pensée et la littérature allemandes de la redécouverte de Tacite à la fin du XVIe siècle*, Paris and Lille 1977, 3 vols.

Roberts, Michael, 'Rome Personified, Rome Epitomized: Representations of Rome in the Poetry of the Early Fifth Century', *American Journal of Philology* 122 (2001), 533–65.

Roelcke, Thorsten, 'Der Patriotismus der barocken Sprachgesellschaften', in Andreas Gardt (ed.), *Nation und Sprache: Die Diskussion ihres Verhältnisses in Geschichte und Gegenwart*, Berlin 2000, 139–68.

Roshwald, Aviel, *The Endurance of Nationalism: Ancient Roots and Modern Dilemmas*, Cambridge 2006.

Rüegg, Walter, 'Der Humanist als Diener Gottes und der Musen', in *Anstöße: Aufsätze und Vorträge zur dialogischen Lebensform*, Frankfurt a. M. 1973, 152–67.

'Die Funktion des Humanismus für die Bildung politischer Eliten', in Gerlinde Huber-Rebenich (ed.), *Humanismus in Erfurt*, Rudolstadt and Jena 2002, 13–32.

Saccaro, Alexander Peter, *Französischer Humanismus des 14. und 15. Jahrhunderts: Studien und Berichte*, Munich 1975.

Samuel-Scheyder, Monique, *Johannes Cochlaeus: Humaniste et adversaire de Luther*, Nancy 1993.

Scales, Len, 'Late Medieval Germany: An Under-Stated Nation?' in Len Scales and Oliver Zimmer (eds.), *Power and the Nation in European History*, Cambridge 2005, 166–91.

Schmidt, Alexander, 'Irenic Patriotism in Sixteenth and Seventeenth Century German Political Discourse', *Historical Journal* 53 (2010), 243–69.

Vaterlandsliebe und Religionskonflikt: Politische Diskurse im Alten Reich (1555–1648), Leiden 2008.

Schmidt, Hans-Joachim, '"Bien public" und "raison d'Etat": Wirtschaftslenkung und Staatsinterventionismus bei Ludwig XI. von Frankreich?' in Jan A. Aertsen and Martin Pickavé (eds.), *'Herbst des Mittelalters'? Fragen zur Bewertung des 14. und 15. Jahrhunderts*, Berlin and New York 2004, 187–205.

Kirche, Staat, Nation: Raumgliederung der Kirche im mittelalterlichen Europa, Weimar 1999.

Schneidmüller, Bernd, *Nomen Patriae: Die Entstehung Frankreichs in der politisch-geographischen Terminologie (10.-13. Jahrhundert)*, Sigmaringen 1987.

Schnell, Rüdiger, 'Deutsche Literatur und deutsches Nationsbewusstsein in Spätmittelalter und Früher Neuzeit', in Joachim Ehlers (ed.), *Ansätze und*

Diskontinuität deutscher Nationsbildung im Mittelalter, Sigmaringen 1989, 247–319.

Scholz, Peter, 'Der Senat und die Intellektualisierung der Politik: Einige Bemerkungen zur Krise der traditionellen Erziehung in der späten römischen Republik', in Carsten Kretschmann, Henning Pahl and Peter Scholz (eds.), *Wissen in der Krise: Institutionen des Wissens im gesellschaftlichen Wandel*, Berlin 2004, 17–27.

Schröcker, Alfred, *Die deutsche Nation: Beobachtungen zur politischen Propaganda des ausgehenden 15. Jahrhunderts*, Lübeck 1974.

Shrank, Cathy, *Writing the Nation in Reformation England 1530–1580*, Oxford and New York 2004.

Simone, Franco, *Il rinascimento Francese: studi e ricerche*, Turin 1961.

Skinner, Quentin, *The Foundations of Modern Political Thought*, Cambridge 1978.

Šmahel, František, 'Die nationale Frage im hussitischen Böhmen', in Hans Rothe (ed.), *Deutsche in den böhmischen Ländern*, Cologne, Weimar, Vienna 1992, 67–82.

Smith, Anthony D., *The Ethnic Origins of Nations*, Oxford and New York 1986.
'The Origins of Nations', *Ethnic and Racial Studies*, 12 (1989), 340–67.
The Cultural Foundations of Nations: Hierarchy, Covenant and Republic, Oxford 2008.

Smith, Jay. M., *Nobility Reimagined: The Patriotic Nation in Eighteenth-Century France*, Ithaca 2005.

Smith, Tom W., and Seokho Kim, 'National Pride in Cross-national and Temporal Perspective', *International Journal of Public Opinion Research*, 18 (2006), 127–36.

Stewart, Frank Henderson, *Honor*, Chicago and London 1994.

Stichweh, Rudolf, 'Universitätsmitglieder als Fremde in spätmittelalterlichen und frühmodernen europäischen Gesellschaften', in Marie-Theres Foegen (ed.), *Fremde der Gesellschaft*, Frankfurt a. M. 1991, 169–91.

Stukenbrock, Anja, *Sprachnationalismus: Sprachreflexion als Medium kollektiver Identitätsstiftung in Deutschland (1617–1945)*, Berlin 2000.

Tennant, Elaine C., *The Habsburg Chancery Language in Perspective*, Los Angeles and London 1985.

Thomas, Alfred, *Anne's Bohemia: Czech Literature and Society, 1310–1420*, Minneapolis 1998.

Thomas, Heinz, 'Die deutsche Nation und Martin Luther', in *Historisches Jahrbuch*, 105 (1985), 426–54.

Timpe, Dieter, 'Die Absicht der Germania des Tacitus', in Herbert Jankuhn and Dieter Timpe (eds.), *Beiträge zum Verständnis der Germania des Tacitus*, Göttingen 1989, vol. I, 106–27.

Tönnies, Ferdinand, *Community and Civil Society*, Cambridge 2001.

Van Acker, Lieven, 'Barbarus und seine Ableitungen im Mittellatein', *Archiv für Kulturgeschichte*, 47 (1965), 125–40.

Viroli, Maurizio, *For Love of Country: an Essay on Patriotism and Nationalism*, Oxford 1997.

Voigt, Klaus, *Italienische Berichte aus dem spätmittelalterlichen Deutschland: Von Francesco Petrarca zu Andrea de' Franceschi (1333–1492)*, Stuttgart 1973.

Weber, Max, *Economy and Society: an Outline of Interpretive Sociology*, Berkeley 1978.

Weicker, Bernhard, *Die Stellung der Kurfürsten zur Wahl Karls V. im Jahr 1519*, Berlin 1901.

Widmer, Berthe, *Enea Silvio Piccolomini in der sittlichen und politischen Entscheidung*, Basle 1963.

Wilkins, Ernest H., *Petrarch's Later Years*, Cambridge, MA, 1959.

'The Coronation of Petrarch', *Speculum*, 18 (1943), 155–97.

Witt, Ronald G., *Coluccio Salutati and his Public Letters*, Geneva 1976.

In the Footsteps of the Ancients: The Origins of Humanism from Lovato to Bruni, Leiden 2000.

Wittchow, Frank, 'Von Fabius Pictor zu Polydor Vergil: Zur Transformation narrativer Modelle der antiken römischen Geschichtsschreibung in der Humanistenhistorie', in Johannes Helmrath, Albert Schirrmeister and Stefan Schlelein (eds.), *Medien und Sprachen humanistischer Geschichtsschreibung*, Berlin and New York 2009, 47–75.

Wohlfeil, Rainer, 'Grafische Bildnisse Karls V. im Dienste von Darstellung und Propaganda', in Alfred Kohler, Barbara Haider and Christine Ottner (eds.), *Karl V. 1500–1558: Neue Perspektiven seiner Herrschaft in Europa und Übersee*, Vienna 2002, 21–56.

Worstbrock, Franz Josef, 'Konrad Celtis: Zur Konstitution des humanistischen Dichters in Deutschland', in Hartmut Boockmann, Ludger Grenzmann, Bernd Moeller and Martin Staehelin (eds.), *Literatur, Musik und Kunst im Übergang vom Mittelalter zur Neuzeit*, Göttingen 1995, 9–35.

Wrede, Martin, *Das Reich und seine Feinde: Politische Feindbilder in der reichspatriotischen Publizistik zwischen Westfälischem Frieden und Siebenjährigem Krieg*, Mainz 2004.

Zimmer, Oliver, *A Contested Nation: History, Memory and Nationalism in Switzerland*, Cambridge 2003.

Index

CPSIA information can be obtained
at www.ICGtesting.com
Printed in the USA
LVHW010845241219
641578LV00014B/278/P